John Paul Johnson
9-10-87
Shreveport, LA

Studies in
PAUL'S EPISTLES

Studies in
PAUL'S EPISTLES

by
Frederic L. Godet

KREGEL PUBLICATIONS
Grand Rapids, Michigan 49501

Studies in Paul's Epistles by Frederic L. Godet.
Copyright ©1984 by Kregel Publications, a
division of Kregel, Inc. All rights reserved.

Library of Congress Cataloging in Publication Data

Godet, Frederic Louis, 1812-1900.
   Studies in Paul's Epistles.

  Reprint. Originally published: Studies on the Epistles.
London: Hodder and Stoughton, 1889.
  "Translated by Annie Harwood Holmden"—Origi-
nal t.p.
  1. Bible. N.T. Epistles of Paul—Criticism, interpreta-
tion, etc.—Addresses, essays, lectures. I. Title.
BS2650.G63 1984   227'.06   84-7138
ISBN 0-8254-2723-1

Published in the United States of America

CONTENTS

6   **Contents**

PUBLISHER'S PREFACE

Frederic L. Godet is known for his firm defense of the orthodox Christian position. He withstood the growing theological liberalism in Protestant theology and schools of his day. He is remembered as one of the most influential Swiss Protestant Reformed scholars of his generation.

Of him, it was written, "Unquestionably, Frederic L. Godet is one of the first, if not the very first, of contemporary commentators on the Scriptures. His portraits and his descriptions are projected upon the canvas with the brilliancy of the fluorescent light as compared with the oil lamp of ordinary comprehension." Godet's writings belong to the select and limited class of books which touch the common things with a freshness, penetration, and harmony of view, which, in the highest degree of it, we call genius.

He took his undergraduate work at the University of Neuchatel and studied theology at Bonn and Berlin under Johann A. Neander. He was ordained to the Christian ministry in 1836 and served as Professor of Biblical Exegesis and Critical Theology. In 1873, he was one of the founders of the Evangelical Free Church of Neuchatel and Professor of New Testament Exegesis in the Free Evangelical Theological School. His extensive training in and use of the original languages (Hebrew and Greek) of the Scriptures became a reservoir of understanding and truth from which flowed, through his pen, the originality and beauty of his commentaries.

"There is no other book in which the results of modern criticism are so conveniently accessible and so admirably sifted," wrote the editor of the *Expositor* with regard to *Studies in Paul's Epistles*.

Here Godet offers a popular, consecutive account of the Pauline epistles, treating them as a whole, and summing up vividly and clearly their history and their teaching. In this volume, there is much that is fresh, original and suggestive, and the reader will receive much profit and great help in sermon preparation. Dr. Godet maintains a level of careful scholarship, critical sagacity and practical piety.

Without doubt, the mature and careful expressions on important doctrinal matters used by this highly respected orthodox exegete will have a great and lasting value for the student of the epistles of Paul.

STUDIES IN PAUL'S EPISTLES

1

EXCITEMENT AMONG THE EARLY CHRISTIANS OVER THE SECOND COMING

(1 and 2 Thessalonians)

THE Church of Thessalonica, founded by St. Paul, was established and developed into vigorous life in the course of three or four weeks. Such rapid growth is a fact unique in missionary annals, and the Apostle Paul himself recognises it as a proof of God's special intervention. "Knowing, brethren beloved of God, your election, how that our gospel came not unto you in word only, but also in power, and in the Holy Ghost, and in much assurance ; even as ye know what manner of men we showed ourselves toward you for your sake."[1] The Apostle had distinctly felt the power of God working amongst the Thessalonians through him, and their election had been revealed to his heart in the very fact of that powerful co-operation.

It was now at least fifteen years since St. Paul had been called both to the personal acceptance of the gospel and to the preaching of that gospel to others.

---

[1] 1 Thess. i. 4, 5.

He had thus been made an Apostle, and for three years had preached Christ at Damascus and in Arabia. In this comparative retirement his own spiritual life gained stedfastness, and strong in the faith he then went up to Jerusalem, re-entering for the first time the city which he had left as a zealous Pharisee and persecutor of Christ. His stay there was but short: in obedience to a Divine intimation and to the advice of the other apostles, he returned for a time to Tarsus, his native town. It has often been denied that the quotations from Greek poets which are to be found in St. Paul's writings are proofs of his having had a certain degree of Greek culture; and to support this denial it has been asserted that he was too young when brought to Jerusalem, and there educated, to have previously imbibed the elements of profane literature. But those who maintain this view forget this sojourn of St. Paul at Tarsus, when he must at least have been considerably over thirty, since before the age of thirty he would hardly have been sent on a mission to Damascus as delegate of the Sanhedrin. During the few years which he now spent with his relatives, waiting until God should call him to his work among the Gentiles, he had time to acquire a good knowledge of literature, and no doubt tried to do so, in order to be more fit for the work which lay before him. The literary resources of his native town, at that time a rival of Athens and Alexandria, would therefore, no doubt, be made use of by him as far as this was possible for a Jew. This period of waiting was, however, soon brought to a close by the coming of Barnabas to claim St. Paul's services for the recently founded Church at Antioch. This Church was the first Christian community composed for the greater part of converted pagans, and seems to have been destined to become the starting-point of the activity of St. Paul, as the Apostle of the Gentiles. The Divine call to begin a distinctly missionary work was not, therefore, long wanting in the midst of this flourishing Church, and about the year A.D. 45 Barnabas and Paul were ordained as missionary apostles by the laying on of hands, and sent on their first errand into the pagan world. Their travels in Cyprus and in the southern provinces of Asia Minor appear to have detained them some years. On their return the two missionaries had to go to Jerusalem in order to have an important question settled, namely, whether Christian communities formed of newly converted pagans were to be subjected to the law of Moses. The apostles and the mother Church having decided in favour of the liberty of pagan converts (Gal. ii. 1-10), Paul again left Antioch for a second missionary voyage, accompanied this time by Silas, a prophet of the Church at Jerusalem. They began by visiting together those Churches in Asia Minor to which St. Paul's first journey had given birth, taking with them Timothy, a young member of one of these Churches, and, without remaining long anywhere except in

Galatia (where an illness obliged St. Paul to stay some time), they arrived, constrained as it were by God Himself, at Troas, at the western extremity of Asia Minor. There they found a physician named Luke, probably already a believer, which fact can easily be accounted for if, according to an old tradition, he was really a native of Antioch. At the Divine summons, all four crossed the channel which divides Asia from Europe, and, arriving at Philippi, founded there the first European Church. This probably took place in the autumn of the year A.D. 52. St. Paul did not stay long at Philippi; he, together with Silas and Timothy, soon left this city, bearing in his body the marks of the Lord Jesus, and went on to Thessalonica, three days' journey to the west of Philippi, and capital of the second district of Macedonia. Instead of being, like Philippi, an entirely Roman town, peopled by veteran soldiers, Thessalonica was a rich and commercial Greek city, and situated, as it was, at the end of the gulf formed by the peninsula of Mount Athos, and possessing an excellent harbour, it might be regarded as the Trieste of that period. A flourishing colony of Jews was settled in the midst of this commercial Greek population, and, enjoying many more advantages than did their poorer and less numerous brethren who lived at Philippi, they had built for themselves a synagogue. Thither, according to the mode of action which he had adopted from the first, St. Paul at once went in order to begin his missionary work in Thessalonica. Not only were the Jews of the place to be found assembled there,—those Jews whom he considered as having a right to the first offer of the blessings of the gospel,[1]—but with them were many Gentiles who, disgusted with their ancient super- stitions, had found in the Jewish monotheism the purer religious atmosphere for which they longed. This interesting part of the population formed, as it were, a bridge providentially placed as a help to the Apostles in spanning the abyss which separated paganism from Judaism.

The success of the Apostle's preaching at Thessa- lonica was wonderful, especially among these proselytes, and among their still heathen fellow-citizens. Not only did some of the poorer classes accept the gospel, but many belonging to the wealthiest families of high rank were, by baptism, admitted into the Church, and not more than three sabbaths had elapsed before a numerous and flourishing Christian community was formed. Such success provoked violent irritation on the part of the Jewish population, who, bribing some men of the very lowest class, contrived to excite a tumult in the city. Having failed in their attempt to possess themselves of Paul's person, they dragged his host, a Jew named Jason, before the rulers, who obliged him to give security for the tranquillity of the town, since the Jews accused Paul of setting up another king

---

[1] Rom. i. 16—" To the Jew *first* and also to the Greek."

in opposition to Cæsar, because he had spoken of Christ's second coming; as though they themselves had not been anxiously awaiting the coming of the Messiah.

Being anxious to avoid bringing his Thessalonian friends into trouble, St. Paul left the city and its beloved Church after a stay of about four weeks; and going thence towards the south, stopped first at Berea, then at Athens, and finally fixed his abode for the time being at Corinth. He had left behind him his two companions, as they were to visit once more the young Churches at Philippi and Thessalonica and bring back an account of how they were prospering. We can easily imagine the anxiety and impatience with which St. Paul was awaiting their return at Corinth, and the joy with which he welcomed them and gathered from their lips all they had to tell of the stedfastness, activity, and perseverance of the Macedonian converts. We seem to hear, as it were, the joyful report of Silas and Timothy, and the Apostle's ejaculation of thanksgiving, when we read these words in the First Epistle to the Thessalonians, iii. 6-8: "Now, when Timothy came unto us from you and brought us glad tidings of your faith and love, we were comforted over you, brethren, in all our distress and affliction, through your faith; for *now we live*, if ye stand fast in the Lord." The long anxious waiting had been to him as a cessation of life, but on hearing the words, "All is well, our Thessalonians stand fast," he lived again in them.

It was then, no doubt, that Paul wrote his First Epistle
to the Thessalonians, A.D. 53, a few months after he had
left their city in the spring of the year.   Indications of
the precise period can be found in Acts xviii. 5 : "And
when Silas and Timothy came down from Macedonia,
Paul was constrained by the word, and testified to the
Jews that Jesus was the Christ;" that is to say, he
gained new strength for his apostolic duties.

Under these circumstances, what would St. Paul's
letter be most likely to contain ?   Surely an answer to
Timothy's report.   Why do not we say, and why does
the Apostle not say, "the report of Timothy *and of
Silas*"?   Doubtless because the latter had not returned,
as the former had done, from visiting the Thessalonians,
or, at any rate, not so recently.

The Epistle begins as though coming from the three
men who had together laid the foundations of the
Church at Thessalonica, for St. Paul always behaved
with the greatest tact and delicacy in regard to his
fellow-workers, never failing to let those who had
shared with him the labour and the peril share the
honour also.   This juxtaposition of the three names of
Paul, Silas or Silvanus, and Timothy, at the beginning
of the Epistle, is precisely what prevents our fixing any
other period than the one we have mentioned for the
writing of the letter, as, after this sojourn at Corinth,
these three men never happened to be together again,
Silas having left St. Paul in order to help St. Peter in
his missionary work (1 Peter v. 12).

The first three chapters are an outpouring of the Apostle's heart and of the hearts of his two fellow-workers towards this young Church so full of strength and courage, but exposed to so many kinds of persecution and suffering for the sake of the gospel. As usual, St. Paul begins by giving vent to the feelings of thankfulness which fill his heart to overflowing whenever he recals the wonderful results of his short stay at Thessalonica, in the rapid development of a Church in which abound faith, hope, and charity, those blessed fruits of the gospel (i. 3). This reminds him of the two facts which can alone explain so extraordinary a success : the marvellous power which possessed him while he was preaching the word to them (vv. 4, 5), and the joyful eagerness with which they accepted that preaching (v. 6).

Their election has thus become a fact to which he can bear experimental witness, and they are now a pattern to the other Churches, so that in this city of Corinth, where he is staying, he has no need to publish the Divine work wrought amongst them, for their opponents (the Jews) have themselves spread abroad the report from synagogue to synagogue even unto Achaia (vv. 7-10).[1]

But as St. Paul is well aware of the calumnies these very men have been circulating against him, he goes

---

[1] The pronoun *they themselves* is related to no substantive in the preceding verse but the readers were sure to understand who were meant.

on to remind the Thessalonians of what his own life
had been amongst them, and speaks freely of his
unselfish and loving conduct, of which they had been
witnesses (ii. 1-12). Then he joyfully describes how
their faithfulness, and especially their patience, have
answered to his devotedness, as their conversion had
before answered to his preaching (13-16). Therefore
his love for them has not failed since the day of his
departure from among them, in proof of which he tells
them that he had once or twice tried to visit them
again, but that, having been unable to do so, he had
sent Timothy unto them, although he himself had
thereby been left alone in Athens. Now, since
Timothy's return, new life has gladdened his spirit
at hearing the good report given of them, and he
beseeches God unceasingly that he may be permitted
to see them again (ii. 17-iii. to end). Truly, no father
could write more tenderly to his absent children!
After this outpouring, which is a thanksgiving from
beginning to end, the Apostle goes on to treat of those
matters which are the real object of the Epistle, and
which were certainly suggested to him by Timothy's
report. First come three exhortations, bearing on the
three special dangers to which the young community
might be exposed in the midst of a corrupt, commercial
Greek city : to purity of life (iv. 1-5), to honesty and
good faith (6-8), and to brotherly love (9-12). In the
last two or three verses, St. Paul alludes to a rather
uncommon sin, that of an idle life, in which a man,

instead of working for his livelihood, is content to wait for whatever help may come to him from others. This seems strange ; does it mean that even at this early period Christian charity was apt to be abused ? Perhaps ; yet this warning will doubtless be best understood if considered, by a natural association of ideas, as a transition introducing the next subject. In the chapters iv. 13-v. 11 St. Paul passes on from exhortation to teaching, and speaks of the second coming of Christ from two different points of view ; first, as it regards a special apprehension of the Thessalonians (iv. 13-18) ; secondly, in a more general view (v. 1-11) ; and if this portion be read together with the last verses of the preceding exhortation, it will appear likely that the carelessness with which many attended to the affairs of this life, was due to religious excitement created by their immediate ex-pectation of the Second Advent.

In chap. iv. 13-18 St. Paul answers the anxious thoughts which were saddening many of the Thes-salonian Christians, and of which Timothy had no doubt told him. At the second coming of the Lord, would those who were already dead be deprived of their share in the Church's joyful and triumphant union with her Head, of which this earth was to be the scene ? The Apostle says nothing to damp the ardour of their expectation, but he explains more precisely the way in which the event will take place, so as to dispel all anxiety in his readers' minds. Together with the

signal of the Lord's reappearance, those who have died
in the Lord, will, first of all, rise from their graves;
after that, those who belong to Christ and are still alive
on earth will be caught up to meet Him, and together
they shall remain with Him eternally. This answer
leaves many questions unsolved, and St. Paul evidently
does not mean to touch upon any other point than
the one which especially interested the Thessalonians.
This is consistent with his usual mode of treating every
subject; he never carries it further than the precise
need requires. In 1 Cor. xv. he goes into fuller detail,
announcing a transformation of the body which will
take place in the living members of Christ on earth,
at the same time as the resurrection of those already
dead. But this detail is there closely connected with
the subject treated in that chapter, namely, the resurrection of the body. It would seem as though he
meant that the contact of the glorified Saviour with
the earth will be but for an instant, and that, as the
consequence of this sudden apparition, His reunion
with the elect will be perfected in a sphere above this
visible world. The Apostle declares, at the same time,
that what he says here is not as coming from him, but
from the Lord. Does he mean to allude thereby, as
some have thought, to words which were uttered by
Jesus Christ on earth? If so, it could only be to the
verses in Matt. xxiv. 30, 31; but nothing is there said
of what St. Paul specially emphasises, the distinction
between two classes of believers—the dead who are

raised up, and the living who are *caught* up.   We think
therefore that St. Paul rather alludes to a special
revelation which has been vouchsafed to him, in the
same way as when he speaks of a special mystery
having been revealed to him (1 Cor. xv. 51 ; Rom. xi.
25).

After this, he enlarges the circle of his teaching
on the Lord's second coming, and speaks in the next
verses of Christ's advent in a more general acceptation.
He reminds his readers that he has already instructed
them upon this matter, and this time only urges
earnestly upon them the duty which must result from
this solemn expectation ; namely, that of living continually in the divine light of holiness, this being the
light which will illumine the earth at Christ's reappearance.   They need not then be afraid of the Great Day
taking them by surprise, as it will surprise the rest
of the world, plunged deep in carnal security.   Perhaps
St. Paul here alludes to the state of the world as
described by our Lord in Luke xvii. 26-37 ; compare
this with Matt. xxiv. 37-44.

The Apostle ends his twofold teaching by exhorting
his readers to watch over each other, to honour those
who are in authority over them, to keep alive in their
hearts the flame of spiritual life (joy, prayer, constant
thanksgiving), not to quench the manifestations of the
Holy Spirit in their assemblies, and finally to work out
their own perfect sanctification, body, soul, and spirit,
trusting the while in God's faithful help.

It will be seen that the Church's constant thought was of the Lord's re-appearance, which was believed to be very near at hand, and that this expectation even caused some of its members to stray out of the sober, austere path of their earthly duties. St. Paul alludes to these people both before and after his treatment of the subject (iv. 11, 12, and v. 14), for the term *disorderly*, in this last verse, precisely designates people of this sort (compare 2 Thess. iii. 6, 11). It even seems to me probable that when, in v. 19, 20, he exhorts the Thessalonians not to " despise prophesyings," and not to " quench the Spirit," these warnings were prompted by the sort of discredit which was thrown on unusual manifestations of the Spirit, by the irregular and not entirely honourable conduct of those enthusiasts who, while desirous of acting the part of prophets and of privileged instruments of the Holy Spirit, neglected the simplest duties of their earthly calling. St. Paul feared that such conduct might create a feeling of repulsion on the part of the majority in the Church, and might lead to their depriving themselves of the blessings resulting from a normal use of these spiritual gifts. But how are we to understand his teaching on the second coming of Christ ? He, as well as the Church, appears to consider it as being close at hand ; he even seems to think that he, Paul, will be among those surviving believers who are to witness the event. " We," says he, " that are alive, that are left unto the coming of the Lord . . . shall, together with them (those risen from the dead) be caught up in the clouds" (iv. 15, 17).

The whole primitive Church, including the Apostles, certainly expected this event to take place sooner than has proved to be the case in reality. Christ had foretold that it was to be, but not *when* it was to be ; He had expressly declared that He did not Himself know the day of His return, and this is the more striking from its contrast with the words in which He announced that the destruction of Jerusalem should happen in the time of the generation then living. (See Matt. xxiii. 35-37, and Luke xi. 49-51, where none of the difficulties can be found which have been adduced with regard to Matt. xxiv. 34 and Luke xxi. 32.) Our Lord had often spoken of the Bridegroom as "tarrying," as perhaps only coming "in the morning" when no one would be expecting Him any longer (Mark xiii. 35). But in order to describe the moral state of the Church during that period of waiting, he had added that, by reason of the very uncertainty about the day, His disciples were to hold themselves in readiness *every* day; that they were to be like unto servants waiting for their master, having their loins girded and their lamps burning, and ready, when he should knock, to open unto him immediately (Luke xii. 35, 36). By a not unnatural mental process, the primitive Church turned this spiritual state of expectancy into an actual awaiting of an event that was soon to take place. She was led to do this by the prophecies

of the Old Testament, which, in describing the end of
the days, always showed the judgment of the pagan
world as following close on that of Israel, so that
it seemed impossible to fancy a new epoch in history
beginning after the judgment on Jerusalem, or to
imagine a heathen world Christianised and having
nothing more to do with Israel. Prophecies only show
the future foreshortened, as it were, the great epochs
being brought near to each other and the intervals
left out. For prophecy is not history, and sometimes
appears guilty of chronological mistakes which are,
nevertheless, deep moral truths. With regard to the
words by which the Apostle seems to rank himself
among those still living at the time of Christ's advent,
if we take literally the expression "*we* that are alive,
that are left," we must apply it to all the believers
who were living at the time when St. Paul wrote the
Epistle, and maintain that he expected none of them
to die until the Lord's return, which would be making
him guilty of an absurdity. The words " *We that are
alive*" must evidently be applied, not to the Christians
living (at the time then present), but to those who
would be alive at the Lord's coming ; this St. Paul still
further explains by adding the words, "*that are left*
(at that time). Therefore these words, "that are alive
that are left," must be considered not as describing, but
rather as explaining, the pronoun *we :* " We," I mean
those "that are alive, that are left" at that time. In
other words : Those among us Christians who will

be alive at that supreme moment. Otherwise, how
could the Apostle, in other epistles, rank himself
among those who will be raised from the dead (1 Cor.
vi. 14; 2 Cor. iv. 14; Phil. iii. 11), and again, in other
places, use an undecided mode of expression (2 Cor.
v. 6-10; Phil. i. 21 and following verses; Phil. ii.
17)? He is evidently only sure of one thing: that
there will be two classes of believers—those that shall
be raised from the dead, and those whose bodies shall
be changed at the same moment; but to which of the
two classes he will belong, he knows not, nor could
he decide the question without determining what,
according to his belief, is to be left undetermined.
For, to speak of himself positively as forming part of
either the one or the other, would be, in the one case,
to fix the day of Christ's second coming within the
space of his own lifetime, or in the other to declare
that it would *not* take place within that period. He
would thus be himself doing what he clearly forbids
others to do (v. 1-2).

It was probably only a few months later that St.
Paul supplemented this first epistle by a second, which
has also been preserved to us. It is addressed to
the Church at Thessalonica, in the same way as the
first one, by Paul, Silvanus, and Timothy, which proves
it to have been dated from the same visit to Corinth
during which the first was written, since only then
did these three men happen to be together. Some
have tried to prove that the Second Epistle to the

Thessalonians was really written first; but this critical fancy has not met with approval, and, in fact, the Apostle expressly mentions his first letter in this second one: "Hold the traditions which ye were taught, whether by word, or *by epistle of ours*" (ii. 15). Moreover, in the Second Epistle hardly any allusion is made to St. Paul's stay at Thessalonica, while the First teems with such recollections (chap. i. 3), and is therefore surely the one which followed most closely on the Apostle's departure from that city. Finally, it must be evident to all, that the situation referred to in what we consider the Second Epistle, is in every way aggravated. Persecution has grown more vehement, for during the whole of the first chapter the Apostle encourages the young Christians by showing them, in the very sufferings they are called upon to endure, the pledge of their glorious deliverance at " the revelation of the Lord Jesus from heaven." The religious enthusiasm or excitement, of which the first symptoms were discernible in the former Epistle, has now taken a more alarming character. In the First Epistle St. Paul neither asserted nor denied the *proximity* of the Lord's return; he only declared that its *suddenness* would take the world unawares, and drew from thence the conclusion that incessant vigilance was one of the Christian's first duties. But in the meantime people's minds had become more excited. Prophets, in discourses which seemed to be dictated by the Spirit (ii. 2), had announced that the great consummation was not only imminent, but was, in some sense, already taking place. Words were repeated which were attributed to St. Paul; a letter was even circulated amongst them which was said, perhaps only by mistake, to have been written by him, and which expressed the same thoughts. Religious excitement had reached a sort of paroxysm; an ever-increasing number of Christians gave up all their worldly concerns and duties for the sake of living a life of contemplation, inquisitive idleness, and begging (iii. 7-13). In order, therefore, to abate the intensity of this carnal, rather than spiritual flame, the Apostle is obliged to make use of all the means at his disposal, and the two principal of these are instruction and discipline. He uses the first in chapter ii., and the second in chapter iii.

In chapter ii. Paul reminds the Thessalonians of what he had already taught them when amongst them, namely, that the glorious return of Christ must be preceded by a manifestation of a directly opposite nature, that of the *Man of Sin*. This is evidently the same personality spoken of in other parts of the New Testament as " *Antichrist.*" *Wrong* must reach its apex, in the union of human wickedness with diabolical malice, before *right* asserts its final power by the manifestation of holiness at once human and Divine in the person of Christ glorified (ii. 3-5). But the appearance of the Man of Sin itself pre-supposes two facts which have not yet been realised: *first*, the great falling away of humanity from God, who had revealed Himself both in the Jewish and the Christian dispensations; *secondly*, the overthrowing of a power which St. Paul mysteriously designates by the expressions, "*that which restraineth*" (neuter), and "*he that restraineth*" (masculine). Apostasy is at work already, no doubt, but it is only beginning; and as for the restraining power, only after its overthrow can Antichrist appear and take its place. Nevertheless there is reason enough for the believer to be watching continually, for since the *mystery of iniquity* or *lawlessness* which is finally to give birth to Antichrist, is already at work, none can consider themselves safe from the temptations and seductions which are to try them (iii. 7, 10-14).

Who is this "Man of Sin" of whom St. Paul says that he will "set himself forth as God, sitting in the temple of God," and that he will exalt himself against all that is called God, while calling himself God? (ii. 4). And what is this power which restrains him and which must previously be overthrown? It has been supposed that when he spoke of "the Man of Sin," the Apostle meant Nero, who was preparing to ascend the imperial throne, and that *he who restrained* was none other than the old Emperor Claudius, whose prolonged life was preventing his successor from taking possession of the supreme authority. But Nero was at that time a young man of the greatest promise, therefore the Apostle's words must be considered either as mere human foresight, and in that case how could he know beforehand of the change for the worse which was to take place in the prince's character, turning him into a persecutor of the Church? or else this is an actual prophecy, and then how could St. Paul have ascribed to him actions of which he was never guilty? for Nero never set himself up in the temple of God either in Jerusalem or in a Christian Church. Others again, more numerous than the first, have believed the words to allude to the papal power; in that case, who would be the restrainer? It might be the Roman empire, whose overthrow allowed of the development of the new and unexampled power claimed by the bishops of Rome. But the description given by St. Paul of the "Man of Sin" cannot, without a forced construction, apply to the Pope, at least such as history has as yet shown him to us. Never has a Pope called himself God, or set himself above God or even above Christ. Up to the present time the Pope has merely claimed to be the representative of God on earth, Vicar of Christ, and governor of the Church in the name of her Lord. It may be otherwise in times to come, but the nature of the papal power must then have changed, and we cannot argue upon such a possibility. The "lying wonders" which St. Paul attributes to Antichrist have been thought to correspond with the boasted miracles of the Roman Catholic Church; but we must not forget that, in the text, St. Paul's expression "lying wonders" does not mean false miracles, but real wonders produced by

diabolical agency and destined to support falsehood.
It appears to me that the term Antichrist, given elsewhere to the " Man of Sin," puts us on another track.
This denomination is essentially Jewish, as is also
that of " Man of Sin," taken from Daniel ; it may be
translated either as the *Messiah's Adversary* or as *Rival-
Messiah*, and this second meaning seems the most
natural. Whence is such a being most likely to come ?
Evidently from the midst of the same people among
whom the Messiah Himself appeared. It therefore
seems to me probable that the false Messiah will be
an outcome of degenerate Judaism, and that the Jewish
nation, putting itself at the head of the great falling
away or apostasy of Christian humanity, towards the
close of its existence, will then give birth to its false
Messiah, the very ideal of man's natural heart, which
has rejected the true Christ. With a daring impiety
such as can only belong to him who has turned his
back on a holy destination, some Jew wonderfully gifted
will, by raising the standard of atheistic pantheism,
proclaim himself the incarnation of the Absolute, and
draw after him the great mass of mankind by promis-
ing a golden age. He will have no trouble in obtaining
credit in the midst of the dissolution and anarchy then
prevailing in the world. And how will this state of
things have been brought about ? Doubtless by an
interior social revolution, which will be no other than
the overthrow of *the restrainer*. We know what the
opposing force was which frustrated every attempt on

the part of the Jewish false Messiahs at the time when the Apostle was living. It was the strength of the Roman legions which crushed the Hydra-head of revolt among the Jews. Since that time, the laws which regulate society have maintained themselves on much the same basis as that laid down by the Roman power; but should this present order of things come to be overthrown, room would thereby be made for a despot who could turn to advantage the anarchy which would be the natural result of such a revolution. One glance at the course pursued nowadays by mankind in general, is sufficient to convince us that the fatal term, prophetically spoken of by St. Paul, is fast approaching.

The Apostle adds to his teaching, in the last chapter, a measure of discipline. He knew there still existed in the Church of Thessalonica a sound majority on which he might rely for support in his endeavours to put down the aberrations of the *disorderly*. Already, in his First Epistle, he had called upon all true believers to admonish these enthusiasts, and to bring them back to the life of work and duty from which a Christian ought never to depart. He now advises them to go still further, and if there remain some who, after having been exhorted, return not to a quiet, sober life, to note those men and to withdraw themselves from them. They must not, however, neglect to admonish them as brethren from time to time, and to urge their return to orderliness within the Church. The Apostle ends by giving a token whereby the Thessalonians may ascertain in future the authenticity of the Epistles attributed to him, so that the case alluded to at the beginning of chapter ii. might not occur again.

We shall not here touch upon the objections raised for the first time by a modern school against the genuineness of these two Epistles. They are quite insignificant, and are recognised as such by several theologians belonging to that very school. The characteristic feature of these Epistles, compared with those written afterwards by St. Paul, is the preponderance of the eschatological element, that is to say, of subjects relating to the end of the present order of things and to the final triumph of the Church. This has been explained as an instance of the progressive nature of the development of the Apostle's conception of Christianity. It has been said that at first St. Paul was still under the dominion of the Jewish ideas about the Messiah which so greatly influenced the hopes of the primitive Church, and that his attention had not yet fixed itself on the relation existing between law and grace. This would be the reason why the word *law* does not occur in either of these two Epistles ; and the primary character of " Paulinism," as a transition between the apostolic teaching from which St. Paul had started, and the broader conception at which he finally arrived, would be thus indicated to us.[1]

---

[1] Sabatier : *St. Paul*, pp. 101, 102.

But those who speak thus forget one thing, which is that both the Epistles to the Thessalonians belong to the *second* missionary journey, and must therefore be dated later than the great dispute at Antioch and the Assembly called the Council of Jerusalem, where the question relating to the freedom of the Gentiles with regard to the Mosaic law was fully discussed and solved with the concurrence of St. Paul. More than this, the altercation between Paul and Peter when the former expounded before the latter and before the whole assembled Church of Antioch (*before them all,* Gal. ii. 14) what he considered the truth with regard to the inefficacy of the law, and the free gift of salvation by the death of Christ, can only have been separated by a very short interval from the time when these Epistles were written; for this scene is related by St. Paul to the Galatians about the autumn of the year 54 as a bygone event, and both these Epistles were written in the year 53. At the time when St. Paul wrote them he had therefore arrived fully at that conception of the Gospel which is developed in his subsequent letters; and if he does not speak of it to the Thessalonians, it is not because a full understanding of it has not yet been granted to him, but because here, as usual, he keeps strictly within the limits of the question to be treated, and of the distinct and providential need which has caused him to take up his pen. St. Paul has often been represented as a fiery steed, clearing the roadside hedge and galloping over hill and dale to return at length on to the straight road;[1] but this is mere fancy. Never was a mind more master of itself or more severely logical than was the mind of Paul. At Thessalonica, Judaism had not yet tried to penetrate within the Church, to appropriate the Gospel to itself, and to alter it so as to suit Jewish ideas. What has been called " Judeo-Christianity" did not therefore exist as yet in this city, and there was no need for St. Paul to attack it. The question of the means of grace not having been raised, and the Apostle's teaching being accepted just as he gave it, it seems natural that subjects relating to the Christian's hope should have been those most discussed, and should have rendered necessary some further teaching on the part of the Apostle, which he gave by means of these Epistles. This teaching evidently presupposes a general knowledge of the gospel truths, which must have been given by St. Paul during his stay at Thessalonica. St. Luke, in the Book of the Acts of the Apostles (xvii. 3), thus sums up the Apostle's teaching given by word of mouth : he " reasoned with them from the Scriptures, opening and alleging, that it behoved the Christ to suffer, and to rise again from the dead." These are also the truths of which St. Paul reminds the Thessalonians in his First Epistle, as being well known to them (iv. 14), " If we believe that Jesus died and rose again, even so them also that are

---

[1] See Henry Ward Beecher, *Homiletic Review*.

fallen asleep in Jesus will God bring with Him." Thus he had not exclusively taught Christian eschatology; salvation, obtained by the blood of Christ, had been then, as it was afterwards, the central point and leading idea of his preaching. The verses (i. 9-10) which are frequently quoted to prove the contrary, and to restrict St. Paul's teaching in this city to the two Jewish elements of monotheism and the coming of the Messiah, prove nothing, because this summing up of the faith of the Thessalonians is made by the Thessalonian Jews themselves, whose report is here quoted by St. Paul.

Modern thought oscillates between two contrary currents. According to some, the world, overridden by evil, is hastening onward to its ruin ; it would have been better for it never to have existed ; the *being* ought never to have prevailed over the *non-being*, and the best thing humanity can do for itself is to labour for its own destruction and that of the universe. This pessimist current is opposed by another, which believes everything to be for the best, dreams of nothing but progress, and imagines that only a defective social organisation prevents the world from enjoying a golden age. Brightly indeed does the prophetic elevation of thought, contained in both these Epistles, shine forth when compared with these human intuitions or imaginations. It certainly does not ignore evil, but, on the contrary, sees deeper into it than our darkest pessimists, and sees it resulting in a general revolt against moral

law—a revolt which will give birth to the Man who
is to concentrate in himself all the venom of evil
dwelling in degenerate humanity, and to be the absolute
incarnation of sin. It sees this Man establishing for
a time his sovereignty over the world, even to the
extent of being worshipped as God. But if prophetic
revelation paints the future in colours as dark as the
sternest pessimist could desire, it none the less gives
full satisfaction to the most brilliant hopes of the
optimist. The reign of the Man of Sin (the last effort
of evil) will be immediately succeeded by the reign of
Christ (the last effort and triumph of right), and by the
absolute sovereignty of the will of God, good, accept-
able, and perfect. So does God's purpose (whose
mouthpiece St. Paul is) embrace both the opposite
poles between which the double movement of contemporary thought is divided. Though far surpassing
them in elevation and breadth, it reconciles what there
is of truth in each ; and this knowledge is not for the
Apostle a mere subject of prophetic contemplation.
The mystery of iniquity is already working, says he,
speaking of his own times ; he sees the final apostasy
preparing ; he evidently does not know how long a
time will be needed for its full development, but he
sees it beginning and he shows how it will terminate.

What does he mean by this ? He has no idea of
satisfying idle curiosity, he has a moral, practical end
in view, which is that, from this time forward, each
believer should take care not to give way to mere

excitement. As a man, mindful of the thunder of a still distant waterfall, takes heed that his boat be not carried away by the force of the current, so there is no single hour in the Church's existence during which her children can afford to be heedless, and not to keep a strict account of the spirit by which they are influenced in their conversation, their reading, their whole life. The two goals—darkness and light, the holy and the profane—are clearly pointed out. While, therefore, it is evident that these two Epistles were written in view of local and temporary circumstances, they nevertheless appeal to Christians of all ages. They set before us in vivid contrast the dark midnight of human existence, and its glorious midday. "Wait and hope," they say; "Watch and fear."

2

CONFLICT BETWEEN LAW AND GOSPEL IN GALATIA

(Galatians)

SCARCELY two years had passed since St. Paul had been required to interpose at Thessalonica in order to recall some over-excited brethren to the wisdom of the just, when it became necessary for him to write also to the Churches of Galatia in vindication of Christian liberty, which was seriously threatened among them. Just what the Act of Emancipation was to the slaves in the English colonies, was the Epistle to the Galatians to the primitive Church. It marked a new stage in its development. This Epistle is the manifesto of the spiritual enfranchisement won by Christ for all believers. It was by studying and appropriating this Epistle, that Luther was enabled to strike off the fetters weighing down the spiritual and moral life of one section of the Christian world. In this Epistle he found the secret of his own deliverance; hence he declares himself "wedded" to this letter, and called it his "Catherine Bora." Taking this as his weapon, he plunged into the fearful conflict with the papistry and religious materialism of his time. This was the pebble from the brook, with which, like another David, he went forth to meet the papal giant, and smote him in the forehead.

In our own time, this Epistle has again been brought into prominence by a man of genius of a very different order. It is from this Epistle mainly that the leader of the Tübingen school, F. Baur, has derived his most specious arguments, in support of the idea which forms the basis of his system of criticism. His idea is, that there was a radical opposition of principle between St. Paul and the twelve Apostles. This very suggestive idea, originating in the brain of the *savant*, and becoming diffused first among theologians, has in our day found its way down to the masses of the people, and has contributed, with other causes, to undermine their Christian belief.

So mighty an influence, then, for good or evil, is this Epistle to the Galatians, as it is rightly or wrongly interpreted.

Who were these Galatians, whose name points directly to the Celts, Gauls, or Gaëls? History tells us that somewhat later than the middle of the third century before Christ, a king of Bithynia, in Asia Minor, called to his aid some tribes of Gauls; and that these tribes, mingled with some of Germanic origin, were settled by him in the centre of the peninsula, in the fertile plains watered by the river Halys, now the

Kizil-Irmak. Living there in the midst of the old Greek populations, they adopted their language, and hence this province received the name either of *Galatia* or of Gallo-Græcia. The attempt recently made by the theologian Wieseler to establish the Germanic origin of the Galatians, and to represent their conversion as the beginning of the Christianisation of the Germanic peoples, has totally failed. The relation between the name of *Galatian* and that of *Celt*, the declaration of Justin that one of the tribes that had come to settle in the country, the Techtosages, had Toulouse as their capital, and other facts too numerous to be detailed here, leave no room for doubt that the Galatians came originally from Gaul; and if Jerome, who had visited that country, thought he discovered certain resemblances between their language and that of the inhabitants of Trèves on the Rhine, this coincidence (which might indeed have been only imaginary) is easily to be explained by the declarations of Cæsar and Tacitus, who tell us that the inhabitants of Trèves were themselves at this time of Gallic origin.

The Galatians had built for themselves three cities of some celebrity,—Ancyra, the best known, Pessinus, and Tavium; and it was probably to the Christian congregations in these cities that Paul addressed the letter to which our attention is now directed. In the midst of the pagan population there was found, especially at Ancyra, a large and wealthy Jewish colony. In the famous bronze tablet, called the *Monumentum*

Ancyranum, which is let into the wall above the altar of the temple of Augustus at Ancyra, and on which is inscribed a copy of all the decrees passed by the monarch in favour of the inhabitants of that city, special mention is made of the rights and franchises granted to the Jewish population of the country.

The foundation of the Church in these regions is not narrated in the Book of Acts; hence certain writers have supposed that the Churches at Galatia were no other than those founded by Paul and Barnabas on their first missionary journey into the more southerly provinces of Asia Minor. This seems the more probable from the fact that Augustus, after reducing Galatia to a Roman province in the year 26 B.C., extended the name of that province to Lycaonia and Pisidia, the very regions into which Paul and Barnabas carried the Gospel on their first missionary tour. Nevertheless, the theory does not seem to us admissible. In the first place, such administrative denominations are not rapidly adopted into the popular speech, which St. Paul uses; in the second place, it is a positive fact that in Acts xvi. 5, 6, Luke distinguishes Galatia from the more southern provinces. Lastly, there is this yet more conclusive argument derived from the Epistle itself, that in chap. iv. 12-15, St. Paul alludes to an illness which had detained him in Galatia, and had thus led to the foundation of the Churches in that province. Now it is certain that the mission of Paul and Barnabas was not in consequence of any illness, since they were

sent out by the Church at Antioch, entirely with a view
to preaching the Gospel to the Gentiles.

Since then we cannot assign the foundation of these
Churches to the first missionary journey, it must be
assigned, at the earliest, to the beginning of the second
journey, the time indicated in the words (Acts xvi. 6),
"When they had gone through Phrygia and the
region of Galatia. . . ." Paul was then travelling
with Silas and Timotheus. He was attacked with an
illness which, judging from certain expressions he uses
in his Epistle, must have been of a humiliating and
repulsive character (Gal. iv. 14), "*that which was a
temptation to you in my flesh ye despised not nor rejected*,"
and which detained him some time among these people.
They showed an extraordinary love for him ; they
opened their hearts to the Gospel, and several Churches
were founded (Gal. i. 2). It is evident from the
Epistle that these Churches were composed mainly of
Gentiles (chap. iv. 8, v. 2, vi. 12). But it may be
assumed that some among the Jews recognised Jesus
as the promised Messiah (iii. 28, iv. 3). We cannot
explain why the founding of this Church is not mentioned in the narrative in the Acts. Perhaps Luke
was not sufficiently acquainted with the details of
Paul's sojourn in Galatia, to attempt a narrative of it.
In the same way, Luke makes no mention of Paul's
journey into Arabia at the beginning of his ministry,
though Paul himself refers to it in the first chapter of
this Epistle.

After accomplishing his mission in Greece, from the autumn of 52 A.D. to the summer of 54, and after visiting Jerusalem and Antioch, as was his custom at the close of each of his mission journeys, Paul passed again through Galatia on his way to Ephesus, where he was to carry on his third mission. Luke says indeed (Acts xviii. 23) that "having spent some time at Antioch, he departed and went through the region of Galatia and Phrygia in order, stablishing all the disciples." These closing words are very suggestive. They show first, that the Church had really been founded by Paul on his previous journey; for it cannot be doubted that he was at least its chief founder. (Comp. Gal. i. 8, iv. 13, 19.) This expression, " stablishing all the disciples," indicates that difficulties had already arisen among these young Churches, and this conclusion is confirmed by certain expressions in the Epistle, in which Paul alludes to the earnest warnings he had already addressed to them. Thus in chap. i. 9 he says: "As we have said before, so say I now again, If any man preacheth unto you any other gospel than that which ye received, let him be anathema." And again (chap. iv. 16): "So then am I become your enemy, because I tell you the truth ?" And again (chap. v. 21): "I forewarn you, even as I did forewarn you, that they which practise such things shall not inherit the kingdom of God." The Apostle hoped, however, that he had left the Galatians confirmed in the true faith of the Gospel, and in the way of Christian holiness. "Ye were running well," he says to them (chap. v. 7). It was then a sad surprise and grief to him to hear, soon after his arrival at Ephesus, that troublesome persons had been in Galatia and had so quickly shaken the faith of the Christians.[1] Who were these disturbers of the Churches? It is easy to divine. Those same Judaising teachers who had previously troubled the Church at Antioch, had now travelled into Galatia, swooping down like birds of prey upon every place where the new life, awakened by the preaching of Paul, was asserting itself. The Galatians had lent an ear to these new teachers. They were on the point of submitting to the rite of circumcision by which they would be identified with the Jewish people (chap. v. 2, 4). Already they were observing the feast days fixed by the Mosaic law (chap. iv. 10). They had come to look with suspicion upon Paul himself. Their Apostle seemed to have become their enemy (chap. iv. 16). These strangers had come between him and them and had separated them from him (chap. iv. 17). They accused him of modifying his teaching to suit the people with whom he had to do (chap. i. 10); and the poor ignorant Galatians listened to such calumnies! All the fruit of the Apostle's labour was thus in danger of being brought to nought. "I am afraid of you, lest by any means I have bestowed upon you labour in vain" (chap. iv. 11).

---

[1] "I marvel that ye are so quickly moved," etc. (chap i. 6).

Such was the situation when St. Paul took up the
pen. These words may be taken here in a literal
sense, for what he says in chap. vi. 11, rightly understood, implies that Paul, contrary to his custom, wrote
this letter with his own hand, evidently with the
intention of impressing on the Galatians the great
importance which he attached to what he had to say.
The Epistle to Philemon is the only other Epistle thus
distinguished.

In order to carry their point the adversaries of Paul
had begun by raising doubts in the minds of the Galatians as to his apostolic authority. As Paul was not
one of the twelve Apostles chosen by Jesus Christ,
they asserted that he was merely an evangelist who,
after receiving the knowledge of Christianity from the
Twelve, had lifted up his heel against his teachers;
and in order to please the Gentiles, whose Apostle he
claimed to be, was preaching a Gospel opposed to the
apostolic model. The Twelve, they said, continued to
observe the Mosaic law, as Jesus Himself had done,
and made it incumbent upon the new converts; while
Paul, on his own authority, arbitrarily broke every
yoke, and baptized all the Gentiles who believed,
without requiring them to be circumcised or to keep
the law of Moses.

The question of Paul's authority as an apostle obviously lay at the root of the matter. It is with this
therefore the Apostle begins his letter. It is treated
in the first two chapters. In the very words with

which he opens (chap. i. 1-5) he refers to this disputed point, declaring that if he had not been made an apostle during the life of Jesus on earth, he had been so made by the Risen Jesus, and herein his apostleship was assuredly not inferior to that of the Twelve (v. 1). Then by introducing (v. 2) all the brethren who were with him at Ephesus as co-senders of this letter, he adds their testimony to his own as to this purely personal matter. After this preamble, the Apostle, omitting the usual thanksgiving, proceeds at once to express the sorrowful surprise which filled his heart. " I marvel that ye are so quickly removing from him that called you in the grace of Christ, unto a different gospel" (v. 6), and he pronounces a curse upon those who have thus troubled them. For, he says, the Gospel he preached to them he had received from Jesus Christ Himself. When, from a persecuting Jew of the straitest sect, God made him an apostle of the Lord Jesus, no other apostle had any part in his conversion nor in the ministry which followed. For three years he preached both at Damascus and in Arabia without having seen one of the apostles, simply declaring the Gospel which he had received by revelation from the Lord Himself, that he might be the minister of the Gospel to the Gentiles.

To this primary fact, which vindicates his entire independence, as an apostle, of the Twelve, he adds a second in the early part of chapter ii. He shows

that his authority as an apostle had been clearly
recognised by the other apostles themselves, when he
went up to Jerusalem to discuss with them his
methods of evangelisation among the Gentiles. He
had then taken with him, undoubtedly of express
design, a young Christian named Titus, of Gentile
birth and uncircumcised, in order to ascertain whether
he would be received at Jerusalem into the fellowship
of the Christian community. A formidable opposition
was raised by one party composed of false brethren
privily brought in, who tried to force upon the Gentiles
the observance of the Mosaic ritual. But this attempt
failed.[1] The apostles themselves refused to add
anything to St. Paul's Gospel teaching ; and not only
did they endorse the doctrine by which he exonerated
the Gentile believers from all legal bondage, but they
recognised his apostleship as of equal authority with
their own, admitting that the Gospel of the uncir-
cumcision was committed to Paul as the Gospel of the
circumcision was to Peter. This did not at all imply,
as has been asserted, that these were two different
Gospels, Paul being the apostle of one and the Twelve
of the other, which would be equivalent to two different
ways of salvation, and two opposing Christianities.
On the contrary, they recognised that it was *the same
God* (chap. ii. 7, 8), who had intrusted the Twelve

---

[1] It seems to me impossible to accept, with M. Renan, the reading
of the Cantabrigiensis and of Tertullian, which omits the words
οἷς οὐ δέ at the beginning of verse 5.

with the ministry of the Jews, maintaining the old legal ceremonies, who had commissioned Paul to preach the Gospel to the Gentiles without these observances. And in token of their complete equality as apostles and of their true oneness of spirit, they gave the right hand of fellowship to Paul and Barnabas, as workers together with them in one and the same cause. This solemn recognition on their part, must put to silence all the accusations of Paul's adversaries in Galatia.

To this second decisive fact, Paul adds a third, which should satisfy the Galatians, not only of his dignity but of his competence as an apostle, namely, the contest which he had had with Peter himself at Antioch. Peter had been taught by the vision given to him at Joppa (Acts x.), that he was not to regard as unclean the believing Gentiles who did not observe the Mosaic ritual. But this vision did not decide the question whether the believing Jews should or should not hold themselves free from such obligation. In the assembly at Jerusalem (Acts xv. and Gal. ii.), there had been a general consent on the point of not imposing any Jewish ceremonials on the Gentile Christians; but the believing Jews had been tacitly left *in statu quo*, so that they would still continue to keep the law of Moses. During his stay in Antioch, in a Church composed for the greater part of Gentiles, Peter yielded to the broad and generous impulses of his heart, and to the permission he had received from

God when he went to the house of Cornelius (Acts x. 28). He fraternised freely with these new brethren, and unhesitatingly set aside the legal observances which would have separated him from them. But, recalled to order by brethren who came from Jerusalem, he suddenly drew back and refused longer to eat with any but Jewish Christians. Then Paul, before the whole assembly, vigorously pointed out the inconsistency of his conduct, and openly laid down the principle, that in the cross of Christ was contained the abolition of the law, not only for the Gentiles, but for the believing Jews (chap. ii. 19, 20), "For I through the law died unto the law, that I might live unto God. I have been crucified with Christ." We may gather from Paul's silence as to the effect of this argument, that Peter had nothing to reply to it.

This then is the gist of the first part of the Epistle. How was it possible, after three such facts, that the Galatians should call in question the reality of Paul's vocation as an apostle, his apostolic dignity and qualification for his high office ? But important as was this preliminary point, it was, after all, only a question of competence and therefore of form. It was needful to go to the root of things. Was the enfranchisement of the believers both Jew and Gentile, which Paul had preached in Galatia, a truth or an imposture ? The adversaries of the Apostle had powerful arguments to urge—the example of Jesus Christ Himself, who had to the end observed the law—the example of the

apostles, who still observed it ; the Messianic promises
of the Old Testament which proclaimed salvation only
to the Jews, thus implying that the Gentiles must
needs incorporate themselves with the Jewish nation
by the rite of circumcision, and the acceptance of the
Mosaic code ; finally, the many passages in the Old
Testament in which the perpetuity of the law was
declared to be like that of the ordinances of the heaven.
The fabled labours of Hercules were light compared
to the burden laid upon any one who would undertake,
in face of such arguments as these, to defend the cause
of Christian emancipation from the law. It is to this
arduous task the Apostle devotes himself in the second
part of his letter (chap. iii. iv.).

He commences by appealing to the experience of
the Galatians themselves. The graces of the Holy
Spirit had been manifested in their Churches. He
asks, Did you receive these gifts by virtue of any legal
rites, or through simple faith in the Crucified One ?
The facts themselves give the answer. Their regeneration took place under the simple preaching of
the Gospel, and before any one had hinted that they
must be subject to rites and ceremonies (chap. iii. 1-5).
After this introduction, the Apostle goes into the
question itself.

There is in the Scripture one great model example
of justification, the case, that is, of the man Abraham,
who, though still a sinner, was placed, in relation to
God, in the position of a just man. How did he

obtain this privilege? The Book of Genesis tells us.
He believed the promise of God, and this act of faith
God counted to him for righteousness. Now God
Himself has made this example of Abraham the type
of the way of Justification for all men, saying: "All
nations shall be blessed in thee," consequently in the
same way (chap. iii. 6-9). And it is easy to understand why God acted in this way. If He had annexed
the gift of righteousness to the fulfilment of the law,
the gift would have been nullified. For the law of
Moses proclaims a curse on any one who breaks it any
way whatsoever, and this is done by all men; so that
if Christ had not been made accursed for us we should
all be under the curse. How then could the blessing
promised to Abraham come upon us either as Jews
or Gentiles? We must cling, then, to the means by
which Abraham himself was justified, that is, to simple
faith (chap. iii. 10-14).

This becomes still more evident if we consider that
the promise of justification and salvation was made to
Abraham and to his spiritual seed many centuries
before the giving of the Law. How then could this
gift, coming so long after the original promise, suddenly annex to the fulfilment of the promise a condition
of which no mention was made at the first? Even
between men no such thing would be permissible. An
engagement being once made, no new clause can be
afterwards introduced to modify it. Here St. Paul
draws attention, in passing, to the fact that the promise

made to Abraham referred to *one seed*, not to many. Many interpreters have imagined that Paul means here to point to Christ Himself as the *one seed* in opposition to the multitude of individuals composing the Israelitish nation, as though Paul was ignorant of the collective sense of the Hebrew term which signifies posterity. But it is enough to read Rom. iv. 11, 12, 16; ix. 6–8, in order to be convinced that Paul knows and applies the collective sense of the term used both in Hebrew and Greek. The opposition which he brings out in the verses before us is not between the Christ as an individual and the multitudes of the Jewish people, but between the *spiritual seed* of faith, which alone is heir to the promises, and other lines of Abraham's descendants, of an altogether different character, especially that to which his adversaries referred, the seed of Abraham according to the flesh, *i.e.*, the Jewish people as such. God, in making His promise to Abraham, had not contemplated for one moment, two seeds different, but both equally legitimate, the one by faith, the other by the flesh, two hostile families of justified and saved ones. He had ever contemplated but one seed, the characteristic of which is the ever fresh reproduction of the faith of Abraham, and which is all virtually contained in Christ, who is the Head of which it is the body (chap. iii. 15–18). This interpretation is brought out very clearly in Rom. ix. 6–8.

But what end, then, was to be served by the law, if its fulfilment was not a condition of salvation ? By making those who were subject to it conscious of the contradiction between their feelings and actions and the Divine holiness, it prepared them to accept, when the fulness of the time was come, the only true way of salvation—Christ, by faith in whom they become children of God, and whether Jews or Gentiles, compose that one spiritual family, that true seed to whom the promises belong, and which is all one in Christ Jesus (v. 28). In the argument in chap. iii. 19–29, which we have thus summed up, there occurs a passage which is thought to be one of the most difficult in the New Testament, and of which Dr. Jowett asserts that there are already four hundred and thirty different explanations. After saying in verse 19 that the law was ordained through angels by the hand of a Mediator, namely, Moses, the Apostle adds in verse 20, " Now a mediator is not a mediator of one, but God is one." What does this mean? Taking the whole drift of the passage, the intention of the Apostle can be nothing else than to bring out the inferior part assigned to the law in relation to the promises made to the patriarchs.[1]

---

[1] The promises made to the patriarchs, as we have just seen, hold out salvation to man on no other condition but that of faith, while the law does not deal directly with the gift of salvation, and is only a means of preparing man to receive it. Assuming this point of view, we may take the remark in v. 20 in two leading senses, according as we attach to the word *mediator* the sense of *intermediary* between two contracting parties, or that of representative of one of the contracting parties, including a number of individuals. As

The conclusion to be derived from the preceding argument is given at the beginning of chap. iv. 1-11. The law having been only a means of preparing the people to accept the salvation which should be one day wrought out for them in Christ, its use ceases with the manifestation of Christ and the offer of salvation. And it is as absurd for those who have once received Christ to place themselves again under the yoke of the law, as it would be for the heir of a great estate, having attained his majority and entered on the legal possession of his property, to place himself again under the tutelage of his guardians.

The application thus becomes more direct. The

---

to the application of this term of mediator to Moses, not to Christ, this seems beyond question. In the first sense, there is only need of a mediator where there are two contracting parties; hence, there is none where God has given the promise. God acted directly in person with Abraham. Now as God is one (with Himself) and cannot fail of His word, the promise is thus perfectly assured. The law, on the contrary, which is given by means of a mediator between God and the people, supposes two contracting parties; and since it is possible that the second party (the people) may fail to fulfil their engagements, it follows that the contract may possibly be annulled. In the second sense: a plurality of persons can only act through one representative, who acts on their behalf; it must then be the angels who gave the law, not God, since God is one and hence would need no intermediary. This second sense seems to me incomparably the more simple. On the former explanation we must take the word *one* first in the numerical sense (one alone), and then in the following proposition in the moral sense (always one with Himself), which is very forced. Then again, we are compelled to admit that the law and the promise are compared with each other as two real means of salvation, which is contrary to the whole of St. Paul's arguments.

Apostle speaks to the heart of these Galatians. Why should they be afraid to shake off the yoke of the law under which they are voluntarily placing themselves, when they see how Paul, who was by birth under the yoke, had shaken it off for their sake? Was he seeking their hurt in giving them this counsel? Had they done him some ill which might tempt him to lead them into error? On the contrary, had they not shown him the tenderest love? Had he made himself their enemy by frankly telling them the truth when he was among them? No! but he has jealous rivals, who have thrust themselves between him and them, and he travails again in birth for them till he sees them delivered from this delusion and settled in the truth of Christ (chap. iv. 12-19).

Finally, as if by a sudden inspiration, he tries another argument. He says, "You who desire to be under the law, do ye not hear the law?" and he reminds them of the hatred of Ishmael, the son of the bondwoman, to Isaac, the son of the free wife, and the casting out of the slave's son, which soon followed. Such in these days, he says, are the relations between the slaves of the law who have come to trouble you, and the free children who receive the adoption of sons by faith. And the day will come when the slaves will be cast out of the house of God by the Divine judgment. This application of the story in Genesis has often been regarded as a sort of rabbinical allegory, because men have failed to see that at the basis of the two facts thus correlated by the Apostle, lies one and the same permanent law of the kingdom of God—the law of natural enmity between the flesh and the spirit, the hostility which breaks out whenever and wherever, under any form, these two principles encounter each other in the progress of the Divine work. This is no arbitrary and artificial allegory, in which two facts are linked together simply by reason of some outward and accidental analogies.

It is then demonstrated from the Old Testament itself—that Divine document in the name of which Paul was accused of falsifying the Gospel—that the law counts for nothing in the moral act by which man is justified before God, any more than it had any part in the act by which Abraham received the promise. But here another question arises: Will not man, if thus set free from all external law, become the prey of his carnal instincts? And will not this absolute liberty as regards the law degenerate into licence? Quite the contrary, replies the Apostle; and he proves it in the third part of his letter (chap. v. 1—vi.10), "With freedom did Christ set us free; stand fast, therefore, and be not entangled again in a yoke of bondage," by those who seek to persuade you, and who slander me, as though I preached to others another Gospel than that I have declared to you. . . . They are false teachers, and will receive their punishment whoever they be (chap. v. 5-12).

Only be careful to render always, as the complement of your spiritual liberty, that which is equivalent to the fulfilling of the whole law—the voluntary submission of yourselves by love, which the Holy Spirit will work in you. From this will spring the spontaneous fulfilment of all the obligations imposed by the law. Thus, placed under the energising influence of the Spirit, you will keep the flesh under without the restraint of any law. The fruits of the Spirit will take the place of the works of the flesh, as "the old man becomes crucified with Christ" (chap. v. 13-26).

A series of exhortations follows, such as was doubtless demanded by the state of these Churches after the painful crisis and fierce struggles through which they had been passing (chap. vi. 1-10).

In conclusion the Apostle expresses the deep concern for the welfare of the Galatians, which had prompted him to write this long letter with his own hand. He complains of the bad faith of his adversaries who, while trying to enforce circumcision, do not themselves keep the law, and contrasts their conduct with his own utter devotion to the cross of Christ. Lastly, he reminds them, by one pathetic allusion, that the man whom they are grieving by their defection is one who bears in his body the marks of the Lord Jesus.

If we take a general view of this very powerful letter, we find it groups itself around three leading ideas :—

The Apostle of liberty; called and qualified, no less than the Twelve, by Christ Himself.

The Doctrine of liberty; proclaimed by the Old Testament no less than by the Gospel.

The Life of liberty; the holiness of which is even more effectually secured by the law of love proceeding from the Holy Spirit than by the law of Moses.

This Epistle may then be fairly called the Act of Emancipation of the slaves of the law in all ages. In our day this is no startling idea. We have become familiar with it through the writings of the Apostle. In order to estimate its extent and significance, we must go back in thought to the times in which this religious and moral conception sprang like a new creation from the mind of the Apostle, which was opened by the Holy Spirit to receive the knowledge of Christ and His work. This short Epistle to the Galatians was, then, like a lever powerful enough to lift the world from its old foundations and place it upon a new basis.

One is ready to ask somewhat curiously, whether his letter, begun in indignation (chap. i. 6), continued in a strain of wondering pity (chap. iii. 1), and closing with expressions of tenderest love (chap. iv. 19), fulfilled its purpose, or whether after all it failed. M. Renan tells us that the Apostle, having dictated it in one breath, sent it off instantly without re-reading; and he thinks that if Paul had taken one hour to reflect, he would not have let it go in this form. M. Renan suggests many things which, if they were true, would make us hopeless of any good effects from this letter of the Apostle. Happily there are other considerations to reassure us. Two years later, the Apostle, when arranging for a collection to be made in Greece on behalf of the Church at Jerusalem, writes to the Corinthians (1 Cor. xvi. 1), " Now concerning the collection for the saints, as I gave order to the Churches of Galatia, so also do ye." We are certified, then, that the Christians of Galatia had placed themselves again under the guidance of the Apostle, and had recognised both the validity of his apostleship and the truth of his teaching. The letter had then done its work.

It remains for us to enquire into one special point which is not without importance if we would come to a right understanding of the Epistle to the Galatians, and indeed of Paul's ministry generally.

Who were these adversaries of the Apostle, who, after troubling the Churches of Antioch and Cilicia, now threatened to frustrate his work in Galatia ?

In Acts xv. 1 they are described as certain men who came down from Judæa (to Antioch), and in v. 5 they are introduced in these terms : " There rose up certain of the sect of the Pharisees who believed, saying, It is needful to circumcise the Gentiles, and to charge them to keep the law of Moses."

From the sequel of the narrative in the Acts, it is evident that this proposal was rejected by the apostles and the elders and Church at Jerusalem. Baur and the Tübingen school maintain that this narrative in the Acts is incorrect, and ought to be rectified by that of St. Paul himself (Gal. ii.). They hold that the apostles themselves shared in the wish to make circumcision and the Mosaic law binding upon the Gentiles. It was they themselves who tried to compel Paul to have Titus the Gentile, whom he had brought with him to Jerusalem, circumcised before being admitted into the Church there. This is the special argument of Hilgenfeld, who has treated the subject with much ability.

It is said in Gal. iv. 2 that Paul absolutely refused to have Titus circumcised because of the *false brethren privily brought in* who tried to bring him into this bondage. St. Paul refused *because of them*, says Hilgenfeld; it follows then that the refusal was not addressed to them directly. And if not, to whom then was it addressed but to the apostles?

This seems a fair argument, but it proves the very opposite of what is intended. If, indeed, the *false brethren* privily brought in had demanded the circumcision of Titus in concert with the apostles, and on grounds on which they were all agreed, why should Paul have refused, because of the false brethren, not because of the apostles?

But even supposing the apostles had really desired Paul to have Titus circumcised—which is nowhere said and cannot be proved—they would in any case have asked it in quite another spirit and for quite other reasons than those urged by the *false brethren ;*

and it was because the reasons advanced by these false brethren, and by them alone, were incompatible with the Apostle's principles, that he absolutely refused to accede to their demand. There was then an essential difference between the motives of the false brethren and those of the apostles. What was this difference? This is not hard to understand. The false brethren said, "Circumcision is essential; without it there is no salvation for the Gentiles" (Acts xv. 1-5); while the apostles, supposing they had urged the same thing upon Paul, would have said, "Doubtless you are free in this matter; but if you can yield the point, do so for the sake of the Church's peace, and out of consideration for those among us whose consciences would otherwise be wounded." If the request had been made to Paul in this way, as a free concession, he might have yielded out of Christian deference to others, for circumcision was to him a matter of indifference from a moral point of view (chap. vi. 15). He could practise it or set it aside as seemed best for the kingdom of God (1 Cor. ix. 19-22). But here were false brethren, who would have abused any concession, and would, without fail, have construed it into an obligation to which he had been compelled to submit; and this would have been made a precedent which would ever after have crippled him in carrying the Gospel of Liberty to the Gentiles. Hence the Apostle's inflexible refusal. This is the explanation of vers. 3, 4. The Gentiles generally at Jerusalem were not required to be circumcised, so that even (οὐ δέ, ver. 3) the Gentile Titus, who was there present in the midst of that assembly of Jewish Christians, was not compelled to submit to the rite, and that (διά δέ, ver. 4), precisely because of certain false brethren who would have exalted its observance.

The position then is perfectly clear. At the two extremes were, the false brethren on the one hand, and St. Paul on the other. The former insisted on the acceptance of the law by the Gentiles, and their incorporation with the Jewish people, as a condition of salvation. The Apostle, on the contrary, considered not the Gentiles only but the believing Jews themselves as freed from the law of Moses, the law being abolished for them by the Cross of Christ (chap. ii. 19). Between these two extremes there were various shades of opinion, as was the case at the time of the Reformation and in all such great revolutions of thought. First, there were the Twelve, who, like the great mass of the Judæo-Christians, continued to observe the law, but who were not desirous, as the false brethren were, to make it incumbent upon the Gentiles. This is sufficient proof that they did not regard these legal observances as necessary to salvation, but simply as an act of piety becoming a Jew, and from the fulfilment of which only God Himself could release them. This they expected Him to do on the return of Messiah. Of the Twelve, Peter, when he was among the Gentiles, even went so far as to hold himself free from the

Levitical law concerning clean and unclean meats, preferring to it the higher law of Christian brotherhood. Had he not been taught this lesson by his vision at Joppa? (Acts x. 10-16, 28, 29.)

James, on the other hand, seems to have held the Christians of Jewish origin bound to a rigorous observance of the Mosaic law, even when mixing with Gentiles. This comes out clearly from Gal. ii. 12, where we are told of certain who were sent from James, and who, coming to Antioch, recalled Peter to order. It must be admitted that James had on his side at least the tacit consent of the conference at Jerusalem (Acts xv.). If he carried too far, and interpreted too strictly, the conclusions there arrived at, it must be borne in mind that he was not an apostle, and that the Lord had had reasons for not calling him to this service.

But why does St. Paul give to the ultra-legalists the name of false brethren, and speak of them as *privily thrust* in ? What right can he have to call in question their sincerity and their discretion ? It is not difficult to find in the Epistle the answer to these questions. We see, from what he says (chap. v. 11), " But I, brethren, if I still preach circumcision, why am I still persecuted ? then hath the stumbling-block of the cross been done away," that the adversaries of Paul did not persecute him really for the preaching of the cross, but simply because he would not, in preaching among the Gentiles, add to it the obligation to be circumcised.

These false brethren had only accepted the Gospel as
a means of extending over the whole world the reign
of the law, and they would but too gladly have
welcomed the immense missionary influence of the
Apostle, if they had been able to turn it to account as
a means of spreading Mosaicism among the Gentiles.
It was solely because Paul would not lend himself to
this manœuvre, that they pursued him with their
hatred, and hindered his work in every way possible.
Hence Paul calls them "false brethren." They looked
at Christianity only as a means of bringing about the
triumph of Judaism, and if they professed to believe
in Jesus as Messiah it was only in order to advance
the triumph of Moses and the kingdom of Israel among
the Gentiles. With them, the law was the end, and
the cross the means. Could Paul consider such faith
sincere?

When to the epithet "false brethren" Paul adds
"privily thrust in," he does not refer to their having
unwarrantably joined themselves to the Church, for
this would be mere repetition, and St. Paul never
repeats himself; but he refers to the fact that they
had come to the Church at Antioch, not as brethren
desirous of being instructed and edified with the rest,
but as spies, bent on finding out what was passing
in the young Church, and particularly desirous to see
how Peter, Barnabas, and the other Jewish Christians
comported themselves. This is what Paul intends
when he says that they were come "to spy out our

liberty which we have in Christ Jesus, that they
might bring us into bondage" (chap. ii. 4). The
Epistles to the Corinthians will give us yet further
information as to these converts from Pharisaism,
whose hearts had remained the same under the Gospel
as under the law—indeed, had become worse. When
the "old man" assumes the part of the Christian, he
becomes two-fold more the son of Gehenna. It is not
enough for the old serpent to change his skin—he must
needs die.

3

OPPOSITION TO PAUL AT CORINTH
HIS ULTIMATE TRIUMPH

(1 and 2 Corinthians)

NEARLY two years had passed since the Apostle
Paul had vindicated the cause of Christian liberty
in Galatia (early in the year 55), when at the Passover
season 57, toward the close of his ministry in Ephesus,
he was led by circumstances of unusual gravity to write
the letter which has come down to us in the canon of
the New Testament as the First Epistle to the Corinthians. It is generally supposed that this letter was
followed a few months later by that known to us as
the Second Epistle to the Corinthians. We shall show
that a very much longer interval must have elapsed
between the two letters.

But however this may be, the two writings are
closely linked together by the subjects of which they
treat. Both bring vividly before us the testing time
through which the work of St. Paul had to pass. The
Church of Corinth was the most brilliant crown of his
labour, but it was also that which he had the greatest
difficulty in defending against the inroads of moral evil
and the attacks of his adversaries.

The first Epistle brings before us the commencement of the struggle; the second, its happy issue. Between the two intervened days of anguish, such as the Apostle never experienced in any other stage of his history. Hence in no other of his letters do we get such an insight into his deepest feelings—the warmth of his heart, the keenness of his intellect; in a word, into his whole idiosyncrasy. Just what the great rifts in the earth's surface are to the geologist, revealing to him its hidden depths, such are to us these two Epistles, in which with emotion long repressed (in the first letter), but at length finding vent (in the second), he lays bare to the Church of all ages the recesses of his spiritual life.

But it is not the Apostle alone whom we here learn to know as nowhere beside. It is also the primitive Church in the early manifestation of its new life and creative power, and at the same time in its early errors and the experiences of its tumultuous youth.

In Galatia we saw the Gospel striving to break the weary yoke of Mosaic observances by the introduction of a spiritual Christianity. At Corinth, on the other hand, we see the new religion at issue with the licence of the Greek spirit, and find the Apostle enforcing the principles of Christian discipline necessary to regulate these wills so impatient of all control. If after eighteen centuries we are able to realise vividly to ourselves what was the life of the Church in the days of the Apostles, we owe it primarily to these two letters. The German *savant* Weizsäcker was therefore justified when he spoke of them as "a fragment which has no parallel in ecclesiastical history."

An interest of a secondary nature attaches moreover to the first of the writings. Through the circumstances of the case, the Apostle was led to treat in it of a number of heterogeneous subjects. We know how acute is his logic when he has one question before him for discussion, when he has to sound and analyse one subject, to demonstrate or refute one thesis. Of this we have an example in the Epistle to the Galatians, and we shall come to one even more remarkable in the Epistle to the Romans. But when he sat down to dictate his First Epistle to the Corinthians, he had before him nine subjects, all of them important, all except one of a practical nature, and all wholly distinct. Will he be able to bind all these together in one connected chain of argument ? or will he for once abandon logic ? Were he to do this, Paul would be no longer Paul ; and we shall find it a task of no small interest to trace the skill with which he classifies and connects subjects so widely differing.

The City of Corinth

The city of Corinth, "one of the glories and lights" of ancient Greece, had been destroyed by the Romans about two centuries before the time when the Apostle visited it. Already for more than a century it had been rebuilt. Inhabited largely by foreign settlers, among whom were a number of Romans, as well as by the descendants of the old Greek population, and possessing also a Jewish colony, it had rapidly risen to great prosperity, like those cities of the United States which have grown in the course of a few years from mere villages to huge emporiums of commerce.

It has been calculated that Corinth was, in the time of St. Paul, a league and a half in circumference, and had a population of from six to seven hundred thousand inhabitants, of whom two hundred thousand were free-men and the rest slaves. This rapid development was due to its privileged position on the isthmus which separates the Ægean from the Ionian Sea, and to its two harbours, Cenchreæ, by which it had free communication with Asia, and Lechæum, whence its ships sailed westward. In addition to the extensive commerce secured to Corinth by this unique position, it had various sorts of industries. Nor was it lacking in the culture of the fine arts and of the wisdom of the Greeks. It had its schools of rhetoric and philosophy, and it was its boast that no one could walk along any street in Corinth without encountering a sage. In spite of all this wisdom and culture, however, the morals of the city were notoriously corrupt. The temple of Venus, which crowned the citadel, was a sort of monument of the vices of the city. The expression, "to live like a Corinthian," had become a proverb through the whole of Greece.

Into the midst of this brilliant but dissolute city the

message of salvation was suddenly carried at the close
of the year 52. Let us picture to ourselves a man of
about fifty years of age, in the garb of an artisan
entering this busy city, and going through its streets
in search of a workshop where he might earn his daily
bread. Who could have imagined that this man,
apparently so insignificant, carried with him the leaven
which was to infuse new life into that whole mass of
moral corruption?

St. Paul was not long in finding a fellow-worker with
whom he could carry on his business. This was a
Jew named Aquila, lately come from Rome with his
wife Priscilla. They received the gospel from the lips
of the working man who had come to lodge with them,
and from that time they were his faithful co-workers
in the great cause to which he had devoted his life.
It has been said that Aquila was already a Christian
when he came from Rome to Corinth; but the text
of the Acts is opposed to this assertion, which is often
advanced only in order to prove the Judæo-Christian
character of the Roman Church in its origin. For
about two years Paul carried on his business as a
tent-maker and his apostolic ministry side by side.
He began by preaching Christ in the Jewish synagogue, as his custom was. "To the Jew first, afterwards
to the Greek," he himself said in his Epistle to the
Romans (Rom. i. 16). After some time he had the
joy of welcoming two of his fellow-labourers, Silas and
Timotheus, whom he had left behind or sent back

to Macedonia, to visit and strengthen the Churches
recently founded in that province. Encouraged by the
presence of his two friends, he redoubled his preaching
labours, till his adversaries became so exasperated that
he was compelled to retire with his adherents into a
neighbouring house belonging to one of them, in order
there to carry on his work without interruption.[1]

In the First Epistle to the Corinthians he himself
describes how he felt at this trying time. " I was with
you," he says, "in weakness, and in fear, and in much
trembling" (chap. ii. 3). When speaking to the Jews
he was wont to take his stand upon the writings and
prophecies of the Old Testament. Now in addressing
the Greeks, lovers of wisdom and eloquence, one would
think he might be tempted to attract them by more
elaborate forms of oratory and by the profundities of
speculative philosophy ; but the severe and holy
simplicity of the Cross forbade him to have recourse
to such methods. He stood therefore all unequipped
before those curious Greeks who came to hear him,
and in preaching to them nothing but Christ crucified
he had to rely solely on the " power and demonstration
of the Spirit," with which God might be pleased to
accompany the message.

Nevertheless a great multitude of believers joined
themselves to him. Among them were " not many
wise men, not many mighty, not many noble " (chap. i.

---

[1] See Acts xviii. 1 (and fol.).

26, etc.), but hearts broken by a sense of sin, who found in Christ crucified "the wisdom of God and the power of God."

Thus passed the two years which the Apostle spent at Corinth, in the midst of the perpetual conflicts and crosses which he enumerates in Acts xviii., and in consequence of which, shortly before Pentecost (54), he departed for Jerusalem and Antioch, leaving behind him the largest and most flourishing Church he had yet founded. We have substantial grounds for placing the composition of the First Epistle to the Corinthians three years later, towards the close of St. Paul's stay in Ephesus, in the spring of 57. Indeed, it is from Ephesus that he writes. This is evident from what he says (1 Cor. xvi. 8): "But I will tarry at Ephesus till Pentecost"; and also from verse 19 of the same chapter : " the Churches of Asia salute you." The note appended to this Epistle in the old version, "This Epistle was written from Philippi," arises from a misunderstanding of the expression, "When I shall pass through Macedonia, for I do pass through Macedonia" (chap. xvi. 5). This expression, " I pass," has been taken to signify that he was there at the time of writing, while really it only indicates the plan of St. Paul's proposed journey.

The time when this letter was written is indicated by the following facts. Paul has with him Apollos, who came to join him at Ephesus, after having visited Corinth (chap. xvi. 12). Now this Alexandrine

teacher was only converted by Priscilla and Aquila (at
Ephesus) in the course of the year 54. After that he
had gone with letters of commendation from them to
Corinth, where his ministry had been very effective
(Acts xviii. 24–28), and he had then returned to
Ephesus. All this must have occupied a considerable
time, say two years at the least. We arrive at a still
more exact date if we remember that towards the close
of his stay at Ephesus St. Paul resolved to transfer
his ministry from the East to the West, and that in
preparation for this great change he sent two of his
helpers, Timotheus and Erastus, into Greece, to visit
the Churches there (Acts xix. 22). This voyage of
Timotheus into Macedonia and Achaia is twice mentioned in the First Epistle to the Corinthians. From
these passages we learn that Paul wrote after the
departure of Timotheus for Greece, but that his letter
was intended to reach Corinth before that young
disciple, doubtless because the letter would go direct
by sea from Ephesus to Corinth, while Timotheus made
a northerly circuit, passing through Macedonia. This
coincidence clearly fixes the date of our Epistle. It
must have been written about the close of Paul's
sojourn at Ephesus, shortly before Pentecost, in the
year 54 (1 Cor. xvi. 8). These conclusions are confirmed by what the Apostle says at the beginning of
chapter xvi., with reference to the collection made in
all the Churches for the poor saints at Jerusalem. We
see from the two chapters which the Apostle devotes

to this subject in the Second Epistle to the Corinthians (chaps. viii., ix.), and from the reference to it in the Romans (chap. xv. 26-33), that he had resolved to make this the closing act of his ministry in the East; and it was doubtless with a view to stirring up the benevolence of the Churches that, as we have already observed, he had sent Erastus and Timotheus into Greece.

Three years then had not passed away since St. Paul left Corinth when he wrote the first canonical Epistle to that Church. What had been transpiring in that time? and what were the circumstances which led him to write in such a strain?

Circumstances Behind the Writing of the Epistle

The first important event had been the arrival of the brilliant Alexandrine teacher Apollos. We are told in the Acts of the Apostles (chap. xviii. 27, 28), that having been commended to the Church of Corinth by Aquila and Priscilla, he "helped them much which had believed through grace: for he powerfully confuted the Jews, and that publicly, showing by the Scriptures that Jesus was the Christ." By his oratorical gifts and his knowledge of the Scriptures Apollos led many of the Jews into the faith, and gathered around him a considerable party in the Church. The admiration of which he became the object was no doubt accompanied, on the part of some, by invidious comparisons with the true founder of the Church. The devoted friends of Paul were hurt at this, and took occasion to assert very emphatically their preference for the great Apostle who had brought them out of darkness into light. This rivalry would have been comparatively unimportant but for an element of a graver nature which was soon introduced. Did the Apostle Peter himself come to Corinth? This seems scarcely probable, for his ministry among the Jews in the East kept him fully employed for a long time in that region; but we know that Christians of Jewish extraction, living in Gentile lands, continued to attend the yearly feasts at Jerusalem (Acts xxi. 20-22). Many Christians from Corinth would no doubt do this, and would thus have the opportunity of meeting the Apostle Peter, of hearing his accounts of the life of the Lord, and seeing the fruits of his labours. Nothing could be more natural than that they should form an ardent attachment to him personally, and draw a comparison between him and St. Paul, to the disadvantage of the latter. Now Peter continued to observe the ordinances of Moses, while Paul attached very little importance to the old ritual. Those who on this account preferred Peter to Paul would not intend to make the Mosaic ordinances binding on Gentile Christians. Peter himself did not do this. They simply followed in the track of the Apostle Peter, observing the law of Moses themselves, without binding the same yoke upon the Gentile believers.

Nevertheless it appears that there were at Corinth other members of the Judaising party, who, on what they considered to be the authority of Christ Himself, went further, not only than Paul or Apollos, but even than Peter. In reply to those who said, "I am of Paul, and I of Apollos, and I of Cephas," there were some who had the boldness to say, "And I of Christ" (1 Cor. i. 12). One is fain to ask by what right they dared make such a claim, to the exclusion of the rest. Did they pretend that by vision or direct inspiration they were under the special guidance of the glorified Master, and thus had equal authority with the Apostles, or might even place themselves above them ? It would rather seem, from some passages in the Second Epistle, that this group of Christians was in connection with emissaries sent from Jerusalem, who pretended to have known the Lord during His life on earth, and to possess higher illumination as to His person and work than either St. Peter or St. Paul. From these passages, and from the place which St. Paul assigns to these men in the enumeration of the four parties, we gather that they must have formed, so to speak, the extreme right of the Judaising party. Taking their stand on the example of Christ, who had observed the law to the very end, and on such sayings of His as these, "I am not come to destroy the law, but to fulfil," and, "Ye have one Master, even Christ,"—they protested against the concessions made to Paul by the Twelve with regard to the Gentile converts, and sought to nullify them by establishing among the Gentiles a sort of Christianity compatible with the Jewish monopoly, which they would maintain at all costs. These people had gained access to the Corinthian Church, and there formed the fourth party, which said, "I am of Christ."

We see at once how melancholy a change had passed over the Church of Corinth since the Apostle's departure. But this was not the only danger to which this community, once so flourishing, was exposed. The levity of the Greeks, checked for a time by the seriousness of the Gospel and by the presence of Paul, had again asserted itself in many of the Christians. The love of money, impurity of life, a return to heathenish festivals, were all endangering the work of God. Some even dared to justify themselves by Paul's favourite maxim, embodying the principle of Christian liberty on indifferent matters, " All things are lawful for me " (1 Cor. vi. 12), and made this a cloak for licentiousness. Those who were not carried away with these errors asked themselves what was the right course to pursue under such circumstances. There had already been an interchange of letters on the subject. The Apostle had replied, to the question put to him, that there must be no association with those who conducted themselves in this manner. The Corinthians had replied that in that case they must needs go out of the world (1 Cor. v. 9). In order to clear up this difficult question, and others relating to marriage, to the behaviour of women in the assemblies, to the right use of spiritual gifts such as the gift of tongues and the gift of prophecy, it was thought well to send three deputies to Ephesus, and these men—Stephanatus, Fortunatus, and Achaicus—were at this very time with St. Paul, and were awaiting the return of Timothy before starting again for Corinth (I Cor. xvi. 17, 18).

Lastly, the Apostle had received from another source information as to the state of the Church. A lady named Chloe, either a Christian from Ephesus who had been staying in Corinth, or a native of Corinth who had come to Ephesus, had brought Paul news of the Church. It was particularly through some of her household that Paul had heard of the party names which were so harmfully dividing the Church (I Cor. i. 11).

Thus much we are able to ascertain of the events which had been transpiring at Corinth from the time of the Apostle's leaving the city to the writing of this First Epistle. Must we yet add to these circumstances, as many do, another visit of Paul himself to this Church ? Reference is indeed made in several passages in the Second Epistle to two visits made by Paul to Corinth, which would imply that Paul had visited the city a second time since the foundation of the Church. But we have already expressed our conviction that the first and second canonical Epistles are separated by a much longer interval than is generally supposed, and it is to this interval between the first

and second letters that we assign the second visit.
Else why does the Apostle make no allusion to it in
his first letter, but refer exclusively to circumstances
connected with the founding of the Church? We
have now before us the general facts preceding the
writing of this letter, and may proceed to study it in
detail.

A Study of the Epistle

This letter, which is called the first, but which
was, in reality, the second, begins, like all the other
Epistles (except that to the Galatians), with a greeting
and thanksgiving. These are contained in the first
nine verses. As usual, this introduction, while taking
in part the form habitual with Paul, has certain special
features corresponding to the state of the Church.
Holiness, as the seal of all true Christians, the *oneness*
of the Church, based upon a common adoration of the
name of Christ, are features on which Paul dwells,
not without intention, in the salutation (chap. i. 1-3).
And the marked omission in his thanksgiving of
any reference to the moral fruits of the Gospel, while
he speaks of the gifts of utterance and of knowledge, with which the Church was enriched, is very
significant. This will be made the more striking
by a comparison with the corresponding passages in
the Epistles to the Thessalonians (1 Thess. i. 3;
2 Thess. i. 3, 4).

As we have said, the Apostle had to treat in this

Epistle nine topics altogether heterogeneous. How has he managed to blend such a variety of subjects into anything like harmony? He refers first to the dissensions which had sprung up in the Church; that is to say, if we may use the expression, he begins with the *ecclesiastical question*. A little reflection will show how wise he was in doing so. It was necessary that at the very outset he should vindicate his position in relation to the entire Church before commencing the directions he had to give on the various matters which were to follow. He deals with this very delicate personal matter in the first four chapters. He explains first of all how he is led to speak of it. If he mentions the household of Chloe as his informers, it is probably that the Corinthians may not suppose that the news was brought by the three messengers of the Church who are with him at the time. After describing the internal dissensions in the Church, and pointing out how utterly inconsistent they are with the sole sovereignty of Christ (chap. i. 12-16), he strikes at the root of the evil by showing that it arises out of a false conception of the Gospel. The Corinthians have been thinking of the Gospel as wisdom, a system adapted to satisfy the intellect, while it is in truth *salvation*, a Divine power to rescue man from perdition (chap. i. 18). No doubt God had appealed first to man's reason, revealing Himself to it in a way full of wisdom, in the works of creation. But man not having understood this revelation under the form of wisdom, God has humbled his proud reason by dispensing with it, and now offers him salvation by a method which looks like folly, even by the cross of Christ. Hence not many wise and mighty men joined the ranks of the believers at Corinth. And how little had he, Paul, the preacher of the Cross, attempted to have recourse to excellency of speech or of wisdom in declaring his message (i. 18 ; ii. 4, 5)! Not that there is not Divine and glorious wisdom contained in the Gospel. The Apostle well knows how to display this to the eyes of those whose ripened Christianity fits them to receive it (chap. ii. 6). But this sublime wisdom, which God imparts by His Spirit to His servants, that they may declare it in inspired words to those who are spiritually-minded, the Corinthians are not in a fit state as yet to receive. Therefore the Apostle has kept them to the elements of the Gospel, like children who must be fed with milk (chap. iii. 1-4).

From the true nature of the Gospel Paul deduces that of the Christian ministry. A preacher of the Gospel, such as himself or Apollos, is not a wise man, the head of a school ; he is simply the servant of Christ, the one Lord (v. 5). Hence it is absurd to set up any rivalry among the servants of God, as though they were not all engaged in the same work. For himself, he is well content to have carried out at Corinth the commission given to him, namely, to lay the foundation stone of the Church, which is Christ Jesus, leaving it to others to build upon it, which is a more difficult and delicate task. For it is possible for men to build with bad materials, or even to destroy while they think they are building up; and thus, not only their work, but they themselves may be in danger of being burnt up. The Church does not belong to its teachers; the teachers belong to the Church, and the Church belongs to Christ alone, as He to God (chap. iii. 6-23).

St. Paul is not therefore at all troubled at the things said about him in Corinth. God, the Searcher of all hearts, will try his work, as well as the work of his opponents and critics (chap. iv. 5). St. Paul explains all this as though he were speaking solely of himself and Apollos, because he would have the Corinthians learn the general lesson, not to run wild after one teacher, to the disparagement of another. They have given place to spiritual pride. They seem to be sailing on a flood-tide of glory, while the Apostles, the founders of their Church, are left behind and subjected to all the sufferings and reproaches of the present time. The contrast thus sharply drawn might well make the Corinthians blush for their folly. Paul adds that Timothy is about to come to them as his messenger. He will seek to set them again in the right way. Then Paul himself will come, if the Lord will; and he asks how he will find them—puffed up with vain words, or still witnessing to the living power of the Gospel? (chap. iv. 6-21.)

The argument against human wisdom, which forms

the basis and the substance of this first part of the
Epistle, has often been supposed to apply to Apollos
and his method of preaching. This is, we think, a
grave mistake. Apollos, far from being a mere
philosopher, was a powerful interpreter of the word
of God (Acts xviii. 25-28), and St. Paul associates
him closely with himself in several passages (chap. iii.
5, 6; iv. 6). How then could it be to him that Paul
applies such a word as this, "God hath made foolish
the wisdom of the world"? It is quite clear moreover, from chapter xvi. 12, that Apollos was even
more indignant than Paul himself at the conduct of
the Corinthians with regard to him.

From the ecclesiastical question, treated in the first
part of the Epistle, the Apostle passes to a subject
of somewhat kindred nature—a question of discipline
which had arisen out of a case of scandalous impurity.
It has often been said that the Apostle is here dealing
with the vice of impurity itself. This is not so. He
does not touch on that subject till chapter vi.
Previously to that, he is speaking of the course of
conduct the Church should pursue when any scandals
arise in her midst. It is only an accident that in this
instance the cause of offence is an act of impurity.
There has been a case of fornication in the Church,
and such fornication as was not even among the
Gentiles. In face of so black a deed how does this
Church, so proud of her gifts of utterance and of
knowledge, comport herself? She seems to have

passed it indifferently by. But Paul at a distance hears of the crime, and " being absent in body, but present in spirit, judges him that had wrought this thing." Rebuking the neglect of the Church, he charges her that, " being gathered together," with his spirit and the power of the Lord Jesus, such a one be delivered " unto Satan for the destruction of the flesh, that the spirit may be saved in the day of the Lord Jesus."

After this terrible denunciation, the Apostle asks what can be the cause of this effeminacy and laxity of morals pervading the Church at Corinth. He is sure that there must be some old leaven of malice and wickedness deadening their spiritual life. He suggests that it is spiritual pride. Yet when once Christ the paschal Lamb has been sacrificed for us, the life of His Church should be one continual paschal feast, in which no leaven should be found. He does not indeed wish to set up a wall of outward separation between the faithful and sinners in general; for then, as they themselves had objected, they must needs go out of the world. No; it is those who are called Christian brethren, and yet fraternise with sin, against whom he would warn them. The Church is bound to show, by refusing to keep company with such, that it does not recognise this connivance of professing Christians with sin. The Church must judge her members, as Israel of old judged offenders against the law of God, stoning them to death. The Apostle points out in this chapter two ways in which this judgment may be passed. First, there may be a collective appeal to God, that He would Himself visit the guilty (chap. v. 2). Second, the breaking off all intercourse of the faithful with the offender. I see nothing like a formal excommunication in either of these proposed measures, nor indeed throughout the chapter. The act by which the Apostle delivers the offender to Satan is not excommunication. Excommunication is not destroying the body with the view of saving the soul. The question of discipline treated in chapter v. forms the link between the ecclesiastical question (chaps. i.-iv.) and the questions of morality discussed in the succeeding chapters (vi.-x.). These are four : going to law, impurity, marriage, and the eating of meats offered to idols.

From the matter of discipline the Apostle passes to the question of Christians going to law with one another before the Gentile tribunals. He would shame the Corinthians for so forgetting the obligations of Christian honour. Is it so, he says, that you, who are to judge the world and the angels, you who pride yourselves on your wisdom, cannot find one wise man among you who shall be able to decide a petty question of *meum* and *tuum* between brethren ? Should they not blush at having any such disputations among themselves ? Nay ; are they not defrauding one another, forgetting that they which do such things shall not inherit the kingdom of God ? (chap. vi. 1-11).

But there are even graver evils among them. They

have misconstrued and taken up as a general maxim words which the Apostle had used in reference to one particular thing. "All things are lawful for me," they say. Yes ; anything is lawful, but for a Christian man to alienate his liberty, and bring his soul into bondage to sin. Yet this is what the Corinthians are doing by indulging in impurity of life, as though that were as legitimate as eating and drinking. They have forgotten that the body of the believer is to be a temple of the Holy Ghost, the very Spirit of Christ dwelling in him, so that he is not his own but Christ's ; and that to desecrate this temple is to be guilty of the most deadly sin (chap. vi. 6-20).

From this subject the Apostle passes to one still more delicate and closely connected with it. This question, the advisability of celibacy or marriage, had been submitted to him by the Corinthians themselves in a letter to which he refers (chap. vii. 1). Perhaps a reaction from the laxity of morals at Corinth had led some of the new converts to regard marriage as a thing impure in itself. They probably confirmed themselves in this opinion by the example of Paul and of Christ Himself. The Apostle takes up first the question of the formation of the conjugal tie. He recognises the moral beauty of the position of the man who holds himself free from any such bonds and retains his complete independence ; but he admits that such a condition is not common, and is only safe for those who are specially called to it of God (chap. vii. 1-9).

He next examines the questions which may arise among married people, in relation to this subject. When some difference has arisen between a Christian husband and wife, or when one is converted and not the other, so that a Christian wife perhaps finds herself joined to a pagan husband, what course should be taken ? In the first case, the Apostle sanctions their separation, but forbids the Christian husband's marrying again. In the second case, he advises the Christian husband or wife not to break the conjugal tie, if the other is willing to maintain it, for the very willingness to do so implies a measure of acquiescence in the principle of Christian holy living, adopted by the new convert. As a general rule, the Apostle recommends Christians not to be impatient to change the outward circumstances in which they have been called, but to abide in their calling, even if it be that of slavery : " for he that was called in the Lord, being a bond-servant, is the Lord's freeman ; and he that was called, being free, is Christ's bondservant." Nevertheless, if opportunity offer for the slave to regain his freedom, he is justified in doing so (chap. vii. 10-24).

The third question touched on by the Apostle is that of the marriage of *young Christian girls*, a question which presented special difficulties, because, according to ancient custom, it was the father who decided absolutely the fate of his children, particularly that of his daughters. In Paul's view there were two arguments in favour of celibacy as preferable for

young Christian girls. In the first place, there were
the ever-increasing difficulties of the position, which
render the life of the mother of a family more and
more trying; and next, the greater freedom with
which a young girl can devote herself exclusively to
the Lord's service, without having to consult in everything the will of the husband to whom she has
surrendered her freedom. The Apostle extends the
application of these principles to widows (chap. vii.
25-40). It is evident that he does not look upon
celibacy as in itself a holier state than matrimony ;
he only points out that it offers more freedom and
facility for Christian service. The Apostle has been
often reproached for the manner in which he has
treated this subject ; but surely it would have been
scarcely possible to reply with more circumspection and
completeness to the difficult questions placed before
him.

The Apostle does not fail to recognise the element of
Christian liberty which enters into this subject, and
this forms the link between the foregoing passage and
that which follows. It seems probable that the next
question, that of the lawfulness of using meats that
had been offered in sacrifice to idols, may also have
been laid before the Apostle in the letter from the
Church. Portions of this meat were either eaten at
sacred feasts or offered for sale in the market. Many
Christians at Corinth felt some scruple in using such
food. It seemed to them dangerous thus to come

into contact with the impure spirit of idolatry. Others, on the other hand, who held broader views, were not afraid either to eat such viands, or even to partake of them at the banquets which their relations and friends held in the temple of the idol to whom the sacrifice had been offered. The Apostle takes up these questions in chapters viii.-x. He looks at them first simply from the standpoint of Christian charity, urging those who are stronger and more enlightened to remember that they should not by the imprudent use of their liberty bring sin upon the conscience of the more scrupulous (chap. viii.). Then he quotes his own example, to show the strong how they ought willingly to submit to privations for love of their brethren. He who as an apostle might have looked to the Churches which he had founded to support him, works for his livelihood with his own hands, that the Gospel may make freer way. On the same principle, while holding himself free from all legal observances, he yet submits to them when he can hope by this means to save one soul (chap. ix. 1-23). And in thus acting, he does not labour merely for the good of his brethren, but also for his own, which he would certainly compromise if he sought only to please himself. He reminds the Corinthians of what happened to the Israelites in the desert, when they gave the reins to their lusts and murmured at the privations which God designed for their discipline. In like manner will self-indulgence be fatal to the Christian life (chap. ix.

23-x. 13). This brings the Apostle to the point about which the Corinthian Christians were most concerned, the question of the lawfulness of taking part in heathen banquets. The time has come when this difficult question must be decided, and Paul draws the line with a very firm hand. The Christian who sits at the communion table places himself by that act under the influence of Christ, who presides unseen over the sacred feast. The Israelite who eats the meat of the sacrifice offered in the temple, places himself thus under the influence of the altar and of the worship of Jehovah. In like manner, he who sits at the idol feasts places himself under the influence of the spirit of the demons, which is the spirit of idolatry. Let the Corinthians themselves judge whether they can partake, side by side, of the table of the Lord and the table of demons (chap. x. 14-21). The Apostle concludes this discussion of principles with certain practical rules, addressed specially to the strong, as to the use of meats sacrificed to idols, winding up with this supreme law: "Whether therefore ye eat or drink, or whatsoever ye do, do all to the glory of God" (chap. x. 23-32).

The Apostle has now done with the moral questions, strictly so called, which had been brought before him, both those which he could decide positively—such as the going to law, and living in impurity ; and those which must be referred ultimately to Christian liberty —such as marriage and the eating of meats offered to idols.

He now passes to an altogether different order of subjects ; namely, those which relate to worship, and what might be called liturgical questions (chaps. xi.-xiv.). Of these he takes up three : the behaviour of women in the assemblies of the Church ; the removal of abuses in the celebration of the Lord's Supper ; the use of the gifts of the Spirit.

The Apostle begins with the one in which Christian liberty has largest scope. Woman, according to ancient usage, not only in the East, but also in Greece, was rarely seen abroad, and never under any circumstances played any public part. Even in the theatres, the women's parts were taken by men. Nevertheless it appears that in the Church of Corinth, led away by a false idea of freedom, they had begun both to pray and prophesy in the assemblies, no doubt on the plea that they were moved to do so by an irresistible impulse of the indwelling Spirit. The Apostle does not wish to put a violent stop to this spiritual movement ; but he endeavours to guard against its possible ill consequences, by requiring the woman who speaks to observe the utmost modesty of dress and demeanour. If she wishes to pray or prophesy in public, she must do so with veiled head, in token of her position of dependence with regard to her husband. This dependent position is a step in the Divine order which regulates the relation of the man to Christ, and of Christ Himself to God. The angels who watch over the worship of the Church, would be offended by any

behaviour on the part of woman inconsistent with a
relation allied to other relations so high and holy.
Woman's physical organisation is itself a testimony
to the modesty and delicacy which should be the law
of her life, for the long hair with which God has
endowed her is like a natural veil, indicating the Divine
will with regard to her (xi. 1-16).

In view of these arguments, it is impossible to say
that the Apostle's prohibition is based upon local and
temporary considerations, and is no longer valid. The
reasons which he assigns,—the relation of Christ to
God, the presence of the angels in worshipping
assemblies, and the long hair given to women,—are
facts which remain the same in all ages and in all
places.

There were other and graver irregularities in the
Corinthian Church. Adhering to the manner of the
first institution of the Lord's supper, it was the custom
of the early Church to celebrate it at the conclusion of
a brotherly meal. The viands for this banquet were
provided by the communicants themselves. The bond
of true brotherliness would have required that all these
viands should be placed on the table and eaten in
common. But instead of this, it became the practice
at Corinth for each guest selfishly to appropriate and
eat that which he had sent, so that the rich would
allow the poor sitting beside them to want, while they
themselves had enough and to spare ; and such selfish
and revolting conduct preluded the observance of the

Lord's Supper. The Apostle tries to make the Corinthians ashamed of their conduct, by reminding them of the institution of the Supper. It was not a feast intended to gratify the appetite, but a religious rite instituted by Christ to call up the most sacred of memories, and only to be observed in deep seriousness of mind. The violation of this rule would bring the condemnation of God upon them, as was already shown by the sickness which was ravaging their Church (chap. xi. 17-34).

By far the most difficult question yet remained; the right use of *spiritual gifts*. These supernatural powers, conferred by the influence of the Spirit, were based no doubt upon the natural aptitudes of individuals. They were personal talents, of which the Spirit made use in the regeneration of the persons themselves, and which became subsequently instruments for the propagation of the spiritual life. The Apostle enumerates as many as nine of these gifts in chapter xii. But the two principal ones, those which seem to have excited a sort of rivalry at Corinth, were the *speaking with tongues* and *prophesying*. The Apostle describes the former as a state of ecstasy in which the soul was filled with all the sweetness of the joys of salvation, and expressed this ineffable happiness by words unintelligible to those who heard them, and of which even those who uttered them had no cognisance. Yet it might happen that one of the hearers might be enabled to follow, and to give the interpretation; or even the speaker himself, when the state of ecstasy had passed, might be able to give an account of his or her experience. It is evident that this form of the gift of tongues differed materially from that on the day of Pentecost, for at Jerusalem no interpretation was needed. The language of the disciples was immediately understood by the hearers. Those who had the gift of prophecy exercised it in speech which could be at once followed by all. While, as the Apostle said, the one who spoke with tongues spoke to God, the prophet spoke to men. Filled with a sudden revelation, relating either to the requirements of the time, or to some phase of the future of the Church, he delivered his message in powerful words, designed to strengthen and encourage the assembly. The gift of tongues, from its altogether miraculous character, had strangely enlisted the sympathy of the Church. There was a third gift, which assumed a more unpretending form than either of the other two—the gift of teaching. The province of this gift was to unfold in a quiet, clear, and consecutive manner the truths of the faith. It is easy to imagine the sort of rivalry set up among these gifts. And it was this which called for the interference of the Apostle, and has secured to us the possession of the three wonderful chapters (xii.-xiv.) in this Epistle, in which he deals with this difficult question.

The Apostle begins by defining the sphere of the Holy Spirit's operation, and he does this by describing

the essential character of the work wrought by this
Divine agent; namely, to glorify Christ. He then
points out the unity and diversity of the manifestations
of this principle, and in this respect compares this
spiritual phenomenon to the organisation of the human
body, the life of which is *one*, while the members are
many. There is no room therefore for any exaltation
of the more brilliant above the humbler gifts, nor for
despising these, which are really the most indispensable. Each must desire just those gifts by which he
can best serve his brethren (chap. xii.).

This is the course enjoined by the supreme law of
love, that virtue without which all other gifts are
void, and which, with faith and hope, will outlive
the gifts of prophecy and teaching. Love is even
greater than its two companions faith and hope, since
through it alone are we made perfectly one with
God (chap. xiii.). In this pæan to Love, the Apostle
places the exercise of all the gifts under the control
of this sublime principle. And now, from this standpoint, he discusses the relative value of the special
spiritual gifts—speaking with tongues, and prophecy.
The superiority of the latter is now at once obvious.
In conclusion he gives some wise practical rules, by
which he seeks to stem that torrent of miraculous
gifts, which, swollen by the pride and vanity of the
Church of Corinth, threatened to desolate instead of
fertilising it. He adds one word with regard to the
function of teaching as regards women, condemning

it absolutely, and saying it is shameful for a woman to speak in the church (chap. xiv.).

One more subject—the most important of all—remained to be treated, and this the Apostle reserved for the close of his letter. It is a question of doctrine —the *resurrection of the body*. This is closely connected with the question whether Christ Himself rose again from the dead ; for salvation can only be realised by us as it was wrought out by Him. Now it is a fact, attested by the Apostles and by Paul himself, that Christ had appeared to them in bodily form, and that He was actually raised from the dead. If this was not a fact, the Apostles are false witnesses : nay, more, it follows that the salvation of mankind was not wrought out by Christ; for if He who in His dying bore our condemnation was not delivered by resurrection from the dead, then our condemnation remains, and the Christian, in sacrificing all for the life to come, is deluded by a false hope. This is the abyss of despair, into which we are plunged if Christ is not risen. But laying afresh this foundation broad and strong (which he had for the moment hypothetically denied) the Apostle sees rising upon it the whole glorious edifice of Christian hope : the resurrection of believers on the coming again of Christ; the ultimate destruction of death by the universal resurrection, after Christ shall have overthrown, in His millenarian reign, all His enemies ; and then the final act, when, the mediatorial reign being ended, Christ shall deliver up the kingdom to His Father, that God may be all in all to the sanctified believers.

Of what avail, he asks again, is it to be baptised for the dead, if the dead are not raised at all ? There is still much difference of opinion as to the meaning of this expression. To me it seems that the words which follow, point to the conclusion that the expression is a figurative one, meant to describe the martyr's sanguinary death. He who goes through this baptism of blood in order to join a glorified Church which has no existence, must be a fool. In that case, the true wisdom is to get as much enjoyment as possible out of the present life (chap. xv. 1-34).

But how can so strange a fact as the resurrection of a body that has become the prey of death and corruption be possible ? This is a question which human reason has asked itself thousands of times in view of the promises of the Gospel, and with regard to which the strong-minded have in all ages exercised their sarcasm. St. Paul replies to it by appealing to a familiar fact of constant recurrence,—the transformation of the seed, by the death which it undergoes, into a living and fruitful organism. The body raised from the dead is not the result of the gathering together of the molecules which formed the body that has gone to dust. Is there but one kind of body in the universe ? Does not a glance at the earth and the heavens show an infinite multiplicity and variety of organisms ? Thus the resurrection-body will differ completely from the terrestrial body from which it springs; for it is to be the organ, not merely of a living soul, but, like the body of the glorified Saviour Himself, of a principle of life of a higher order, of a life-giving spirit. A transformation of the body is indispensable in order that it may become partaker of the kingdom of God, and some such change must pass even upon those who have not tasted death and are alive at the return of the Lord. A glorious victory this, a full salvation, and one which we owe to Him who, by justifying us, has disarmed the law, and by sanctifying us has destroyed sin—the two pillars on which the throne of death was reared. Let us then be steadfast and immovable in the service of Him who has prepared for us so glorious a future (chap. xv. 35-58).

Such is this grand chapter, which we may doubtless take as a sample of that "wisdom among the perfect," of which Paul speaks in chap. ii. 7 and following verses.

It only remained for him to give the Corinthians the news and the commissions with which he usually closed his letters (chap. xvi.). These are, first, directions relative to the great collection then being made in all the Churches founded by him. Next, he tells them of his intention of visiting Greece before coming to them, a change on the plan he had at first proposed. Then he exhorts them to give a hearty welcome to Timothy, who will arrive shortly after this letter. He explains that Apollos was not willing to come to them just then, but would come some other time; and lastly, thanks them heartily for the joy he has felt in the visit of the three messengers of the Church, who are still with him when he writes, and who have brought him much spiritual refreshment. He sends some greetings, and then, just as he is closing the letter, and adding his salutation with his own hand, he puts in one awful note of warning, in the name of the coming Lord Jesus Christ—the anathema pronounced on any one at Corinth who loves Him not. Then comes the final salutation.

As we have gone through the pages of this letter, have we not felt ourselves living at Corinth, and at the same time at Ephesus, reading the very heart of Paul? We have been witnesses of the troubles of the Church, and of the fatherly solicitude of Paul for its welfare. We have learned through this one primitive Church to form an idea of all the early Churches, and we see that there is nothing ideal about them. We have followed the eye and the hand of the skilful surgeon, who knows so well how to probe and bind up its wounds. For every disorder he finds in the Gospel of Christ the true remedy. He begins the treatment of each subject by a long and detailed discussion, in which he sets forth all its aspects, and thus gradually carries with him the consciences of his readers. This is his aim, and it is only at the close of this thoughtful survey of the question that he gives some simple,

practical directions, generally introduced by the con-
junction *wherefore* (ὥστε) (see chap. iii. 21 ; vi. 20 ;
vii. 30; x. 31 ; xi. 33; xiv. 13 ; xiv. 39; xv. 58).
It has sometimes been asked, why, in relation to the
question of meats sacrificed to idols, he did not simply
solve the difficulty by the decree of the assembly at
Jerusalem (Acts xv. 23-29), and doubts have even
been thrown on the genuineness of this decree because
St. Paul did not thus appeal to it. It has not been
understood that what the Apostle desired to insure
was, not a merely legal obedience, but the free consent
of fully enlightened consciences (see chap. x. 15).
The most remarkable thing in the Apostle's teaching
is the lofty and far-reaching view which he takes of all
questions, in combination with the practical spirit,
the sober and balanced judgment, which always re-
solves them finally in the most natural and simple
manner.

In conclusion, we would call attention to that which
the Apostle leaves unsaid in this letter as scarcely less
admirable than what is said. The attentive reader
will observe on every page of this First Epistle to the
Corinthians traces of deep but repressed indignation.
Paul knows very well that strictures have been passed
on the apostolic teaching given by him to this Church
(chap. ii. 6 ; iii. 1, 2; iv. 1-5); that there are some
who make a mock of his promised visit, which he
is so often obliged to defer (chap. iv. 18-21); that
some call in question the genuineness of his Apostle-

ship, and are raising doubt about it (ix. 1-3); that others refuse to regard his exhortations as coming from the Lord (xiv. 38). A storm is thus gathering between him and his Church; this is evident. Thunder is muttering in the distance; yet the Apostle feels that it is not the time to give vent to his feelings. He possesses his soul in patience; and it is only from the study of the second letter that we learn how the crisis came at last, and how, above all the tumult of conflicting forces, Christ made His humble servant to triumph.

4

OPPOSITION TO PAUL AT CORINTH HIS ULTIMATE TRIUMPH (continued)

(2 Corinthians)

THROUGHOUT the whole of the First Epistle to the Corinthians, we hear as it were the distant mutterings of thunder, but the storm never bursts. In the Second Epistle it is raging in full violence around us.

The course of events between these two Epistles is usually explained in a very simple manner. St. Paul, we are told, remained some time at Ephesus in accordance with his expressed purpose (1 Cor. xvi. 8), " I will tarry at Ephesus until Pentecost." The tumult raised by the silversmith Demetrius, brought his sojourn in that city to an end sooner than he intended ; and he then fell back on the plan he had previously formed of going to Corinth by way of Macedonia (1 Cor. xvi. 5). He went first to Troas, where he hoped to meet Titus, who was coming from Macedonia and bringing him tidings of the Church at Corinth (2 Cor. ii. 12, 13). Failing to find Titus there, he went on into Macedonia, where he met him ; and in consequence of the good news which Titus brought, Paul sent him back to Corinth with this Second Epistle, in which he states his intention of coming himself shortly to the city with the purpose of wintering there. Everything is thus supposed to have taken place according to the plan indicated in 1 Cor. xvi. 5, 6, and thus scarcely six months elapsed between the two Epistles.

We cannot at all share this view. It seems to us that there are indications in this Second Epistle of a much longer interval between the two letters, and of the rise of much graver complications. We are especially struck with the intervention of a fresh co-worker with Paul, Titus the evangelist, and with the great importance attached to his person and mission. Hitherto the only evangelist mentioned had been Timothy, who, after visiting the Church at Corinth, was to have rejoined Paul at Ephesus, where the three delegates from the Corinthian Church were also awaiting him. The Apostle wished, no doubt, to confer with them over the report which Timothy would bring (1 Cor. xvi. 11). But here we find Timothy has suddenly vanished and everything depends upon Titus. It is upon him, not Timothy, that Paul is counting for the tidings which are to set his heart at rest as to the state of the Church. Not finding him, he is so anxious that he hurries into Macedonia to meet him. It has been conjectured that Timothy had been prevented from going to Corinth (indeed Paul only speaks doubtfully of his expected visit, 1 Cor. xvi. 10), and that after his return to Ephesus, Paul had sent Titus instead of him to Corinth. But how is it we find no hint of this in the whole of the Second Epistle, if it were really so ? Or, as an alternative, it might be conjectured that it was Titus, not Timothy, who had been the bearer of the First Epistle to the Corinthians. But then how is it that Paul makes no mention of him in that letter, but only of Timothy ?

Nor is this the only remarkable circumstance, supposing the facts to have been as suggested above.

In the Second Epistle to the Corinthians there are certain passages in which Paul alludes to a letter of severe rebuke which, with great pain to himself, he had been forced to write to them, and which was to serve instead of an intended visit. " I wrote this very thing, lest, when I came, I should have sorrow from them of whom I ought to rejoice. . . . For out of much affliction and anguish of heart I wrote unto you with many tears ; not that ye should be made sorry, but that ye might know the love which I have more abundantly unto you" (2 Cor. ii. 3, 4). In chapter vii. he says (8-10) that after he had sent the letter he rather regretted it ; but he regrets it no longer, now that he sees the effect it has produced. Would such expressions apply to the First Epistle to the Corinthians ? This seems to us impossible. That letter does indeed contain many stern passages, but none which would bear out such a reference as is here made. We should search in vain in the First Epistle for a chapter which must have been wrung from the heart of the Apostle with many tears. Further, it appears from certain expressions in the Second Epistle that the Apostle had received some grave personal offence from the Church of Corinth. He declares (chap. ii. 10) that he is quite ready to forgive him who has been guilty of the offence, and that if the Corinthians can forgive, so can he. In chapter vii. 12 he says that he has written to them "not for his cause that did the wrong, nor for his cause that suffered the wrong," but that they might know the earnest care which he, Paul, had for them in the sight of God. It has often been thought that the man to whom Paul refers in these passages was the one who had been guilty of incest referred to in 1 Cor. v.; but in that case the person who suffered the wrong could be no other than the father of the offender. But could Paul say in this case that he had not written for his sake that did the wrong? Does he not say that it was in order that his spirit might be saved in the day of the Lord Jesus that he had penned that fifth chapter? and could he here say that he regarded such a crime only from the standpoint of the wrong done to the father of the guilty man? Can we indeed suppose it possible that such an offence could have been committed in the very lifetime of the father? No; in these two passages the offended person can be no other than Paul himself. He means to say that he has not written this severe letter to get the man punished who had done him wrong, and thus to appease his own wounded pride, but for the good of the Church itself. Now how could the Apostle refer to the offence as done to himself, if he were alluding to this crime of incest? These passages must refer to some fact of which we find no trace in the First Epistle, and which must have taken place in the interval between the two letters.

We may refer further to three passages in the Second Epistle, which speak of Paul's expected visit to Corinth as the third to that city. So far as we have seen at present, this coming visit would be only the second; since after founding the Church at Corinth, Paul had taken up his abode at Ephesus, where, according to the narrative in the Acts, he laboured from that time without interruption. It has been sometimes supposed that before writing the First Epistle to the Corinthians he had made, from Ephesus, a rapid journey into Greece and Achaia, not mentioned in the Book of Acts. But there would surely then be some allusion to it in the First Epistle to the Corinthians, as he refers so frequently in that letter to the circumstances of his first visit. And how could it be said at Corinth that he dared not show himself there (1 Cor. iv. 18-21), if he had been there quite recently? Another conjecture has been, that the passages which seem to imply a second visit of Paul, refer only to a projected and promised visit which never really came to pass. This explanation might possibly be admissible for 2 Cor. xiii. 1, but cannot apply to 2 Cor. xii. 14. An attempt has indeed been made to translate this passage : " Behold this is the third time I am on the point of coming to you "; which would not necessarily imply that he had already been twice.   But the words which follow, " I will not be a burden to you," intimating as they do that again this time he will not accept the hospitality of any of them, do not admit of this interpretation. They imply that the two previous visits to which he refers in v. 14, were actual and not merely intended comings.   People do not live at others' charges in merely hypothetical visits.   The expression *"for the third time"* must refer then to the actual coming, and not to the being *on the point of coming*.   In chapter ii. 1 we find another passage no less decisive : " I determined this for myself, that I would not come again to you with sorrow," says the Apostle.   On his first visit, when he founded the Church, Paul had had abundant labours and trials from without, but for all that he would not have described that visit as a sorrowful one.   Between that first coming and the visit he was now projecting, there had then been another, very painful to him, and such as he did not desire to repeat.

If we now sum up the hints contained in the Second Epistle to the Corinthians as to the state of things in the Church as the result of the First Epistle, we shall be startled at the gravity of the situation.

There were certain men, whom we cannot fail to identify as those who with their followers claimed to be " of Christ " (see 2 Cor. x. 7 ; xi. 23), who attacked at once the apostleship, the character, and the teaching of the founder of the Church. " He has not even seen the Lord Jesus," said they, " and yet he gives himself out to be His apostle " (1 Cor. ix. 1 ; 2 Cor. v. 16). " He is so conscious of the inferiority of his position as regards the other apostles, that he dares not make himself chargeable to the Churches as they did (1 Cor. ix. 5 ; 2 Cor. xi. 7ff; xii. 13). He boasts of his disinterestedness, but so crafty is he that he manages to secure his own profit in another manner, by means of his messengers and collections which he gathers professedly for the poor at Jerusalem (1 Cor. xiv. 1-4 ; 2 Cor. i. 15, 16). He writes powerful threatening letters, but never comes to carry out his threats, or if he does appear, 'his bodily presence is weak and his speech of no account' (1 Cor. iv. 18; 2 Cor. x. 10). His letters are one long strain of boasting ; his head is turned with pride (2 Cor. iii. 1 ; v. 13 ; xi. 1). For the rest, his teaching is of little value. There are others immeasurably more gifted in speech (2 Cor. x. 10; xi. 6)."

What could the Apostle say or do after such crushing criticism as this ? There must surely be an end of him and his work. The Church must be left now to pass into the hands of his adversaries.

We need to realise to ourselves the gravity of the situation in order to understand the events which follow as we shall attempt to reproduce them, and through them to bring out the real meaning of this Second Epistle. The Apostle awaited at Ephesus the return of Timothy, and in consequence of the interviews he had with him and with the three delegates of the Church, he decided to revert to his first plan (which from 1 Cor. xvi. 5 he seemed to have abandoned), and to go direct to Corinth from Ephesus. This visit was a short and painful one, and Paul is referring to it (2 Cor. ii. 1) when he says, " I determined this for myself, that I would not come *again* to you with sorrow." The germs of disaffection towards himself had been growing. The severe and humiliating passages in his first letter had been craftily turned to account, and things had come to such a point that he was made the subject of gross insult without the Church raising a finger in his defence. Feeling that he could not himself insist on the reparation which was due to him, he went away to leave the Church time to act, saying however that he should come back again. He travelled into Macedonia, and perhaps as far as Illyricum on the shores of the Adriatic (Rom. xv. 19). He waited for news of the conduct of the Church. At length, hearing nothing to reassure him, he decided to write the severe and painful letter, watered abundantly with tears, of which he speaks in this Second Epistle. In it he made the Corinthians feel, what they ought to have felt without any such prompting—how much they owed to him ; and he gave them their choice between a rupture with him and the punishment of the offenders. The important mission of conveying this letter and supporting it, he committed to Titus, who was then with him. Then, having no more to do in Macedonia, and not being willing to return to Corinth while matters were in this position, he went back to Ephesus, where it would seem Timothy was grappling with a task beyond his strength. To this time refer the words in this Second Epistle (2 Cor. i. 23; ii. 3): "I call God for a witness upon my soul, that to spare you I forbare to come unto Corinth. . . . And I wrote this very thing (these severe reprimands), lest, when I came, I should have sorrow from them of whom I ought to rejoice."

It is, as we think, to this failure to come back as he had promised, that Paul refers in the justification which he gives of his conduct, 2 Cor. i. 17, 18.

At Ephesus Paul awaited, in much perplexity of spirit, the return of Titus. It was no doubt in this interval that the tumult was raised by Demetrius which nearly cost the Apostle his life, and to this time of trouble and deliverance he refers, as we think, in 2 Cor. i. 8-11. Having escaped this danger, the Apostle starts for the north on the route on which he hopes to meet with Titus. If to the two years and three months of his first stay in Ephesus we add the few months of this second visit, we get the three years during which, as he says to the Ephesian elders (Acts xx. 31), he had worked and watched for souls in that city. This unexpected prolongation of his stay in Ephesus seems to explain the singular expression (Acts xix. 22) with which the story of the tumult in the city is prefaced. "He himself stayed in Asia for a season." It would not have been possible for him to go west, leaving the Church of Corinth in such a position towards himself as it was at that time.

Arrived at Troas, he failed to find there Titus, the brother whom he was yearning to see (2 Cor. ii. 13): and in his anxiety (for the welfare of the most flourishing of all his Churches was at stake) he went into Macedonia to meet him. There at length they met, and the news from Corinth filled him with joy. Titus himself was quite reassured by what he had seen and heard, and Paul was so relieved that he resolved at once to send back this faithful fellow-labourer to convey the expression of his satisfaction, and to complete the work of reconciliation before the Apostle came again to pay one final glad visit to the Church and then to leave it for ever.

This Second Epistle to the Corinthians is then, properly speaking, the *Fourth;* for, as we have already seen, that which is called the *First* Epistle had been preceded by a letter which we have lost, and between the first and second we must suppose a third, which, like the first, has not come down to us, probably because both were altogether of a local and incidental character. If things took place at all as we have supposed, they imply an interval not of six but of eighteen months between the First and Second Epistles, namely, from the spring of 57 to the autumn of 58.

The Apostle, writing to the Church in the position we have described, had two main objects in view ; first, to testify his satisfaction and gratitude to the majority in the Church who had so warmly taken up his cause, and now rendered possible this happy visit to which he had so long been looking forward ; and next, to remove all the germs of disobedience and disorder which still remained in the Church, and which might again spring up to trouble him. In a word it may be said, his design was so to strengthen the spiritual bond which united him to the true-hearted majority in the Church, that the still disaffected minority might be powerless to break it. In addition to this, he may have had some special object in view, such as the success of the collection with which he was determined to close his ministry in the East, and which was to be to the Christians in Palestine the tangible proof of the new life awakened in the Gentile world.

In this way we explain the three parts into which this Epistle naturally divides itself. The first seven chapters are addressed specially to the section of the Church which was in sympathy with the Apostle, and their purport is to let them know how his heart has been exercised towards them under the recent crisis. This portion of the letter refers to the *past*. Chapters viii., ix. form a second part, the object of which is to encourage the faithful majority to take an active part

in the collection, which is already almost finished in
Macedonia.   It is with this view that he sends Titus
back to them with his letter.   This part of the Epistle
deals then with the time *present*.   Lastly, in chapters
x.-xiii. the Apostle, while still addressing himself to the
whole Church (because he will not himself create one
of those divisions for which he has been reproving
them), turns specially to the disobedient members,
showing them how they have been made the tools of
intriguing men, and how severely he will have to deal
with them if they persist in their hostile attitude and
wicked conduct till he comes again.   This third portion
relates to the *future*.

Such is the natural and simple division of this
Epistle.   For want of understanding this, doubts have
often been thrown upon its unity, and it has been
sometimes supposed to be a collection of fragments
composed at different times, with different objects and
even by various authors.

The whole Epistle follows the historical order.

Paul, and Timothy, who rejoined him in Macedonia,
address themselves expressly not only to the Christians
at Corinth, but to those of the whole province of
Achaia, over which the Gospel had spread since their
first sojourn in that district.   The Apostle desires first
of all that the Church should rejoice with him in his
wonderful deliverance from imminent death.   He is
referring, no doubt, to the tumult excited by Demetrius
at Ephesus.   He points out to his readers how under

God these painful experiences, through which he is
called to pass, become the means of making his ministry
more fruitful to the Church, so close is the spiritual
union between them (2 Cor. i. 1-11). After this he
explains the change in his purpose of coming to them,
which his enemies at Corinth had used as a handle
against him. It is generally supposed that the reference is to the change mentioned by the Apostle
(1 Cor. xvi. 5). But to us it seems that he is alluding
to a more recent change : for in the former case he
would have said (chap. i. 23), not " I forbore to come
unto Corinth" (οὐκέτι), but " I came not *yet* (οὔπω)
to Corinth." The word οὐκέτι (no more) implies
that he had been there once, but that he had not
returned as he had promised. And we have seen
already that after going from Ephesus to Corinth and
thence into Macedonia, instead of returning thence to
Corinth for the long stay he had promised, he had
returned into Asia and settled down again at Ephesus.
Why then did he not come back ? This is the seeming
inconsistency in his conduct which he must explain,
for he knows that it will be used against him. He
even resorts to a solemn asseveration, calling God to
witness, that, if he returned into Asia without visiting
Corinth, as he had promised, it was not through fickle-
ness or fear for himself, but because the state of the
Corinthian Church hindered him. He would rather
write the sharp things he has to say to them than come
and say them himself. This explains at once the reason

of his not coming back and the purport of that severe letter which he had sent them by Titus when he left Macedonia to go back to Ephesus (chap. i. 12—ii. 4). In reference to that letter, Paul speaks here *en passant* of the punishment of the guilty one administered by the majority of the Church, as the result of his letter, and urges that great indulgence be shown to him, lest Satan, who had tempted him to sin through arrogance, should now let him be swallowed up of overmuch sorrow. If the Corinthians forgave him, they may be assured that the Apostle forgives also. As we have already seen, such words could only refer to a personal offence committed against Paul himself, and not to the sin of incest (chap. ii. 5-11). From this explanation of the reasons which led him to go back to Asia without visiting Corinth, Paul passes to the account of his recent departure from Ephesus for Troas, and makes the Church feel the greatness of his love for her by his description of all the anguish of mind he was enduring at that time on her account. Not having met Titus at Troas, as he had hoped, he gave up his idea of evangelising in that district as the way opened, and in his anxiety hastened into Macedonia to meet Titus (chap. ii. 13). Here he lays open the depths of his soul to his readers. He shows them what are the feelings of a true servant of Christ in the fulfilment of his ministry. And first, he initiates his readers into the secret of spiritual power in that ministry, that they may see how needless it is for him to have recourse to the dishonest artifices which the preachers of a legal Christianity are obliged to use. In order to conceal the fact that the reign of law is over, they are constrained to employ some such means as Moses, who put a veil over his face that the people might not see the fading away of its glory.[1] The true servant of Christ beholds his Lord with unveiled face, and being clothed himself with the same beauty, he has nothing to hide (chap. ii. 14-iv. 6). In this admirable passage on the ministry of the spirit, as opposed to the ministry of the letter (of the law), there is the opening of the attack upon the Judaising teachers, but the battle, properly speaking, is reserved for the end of the letter.

Having once entered on the description of the apostolic ministry, Paul pours forth his thoughts and feelings in one broad rapid stream. While by the power of life and death attached to that ministry, the servant of Christ is raised above the ignoble artifices of the teachers of legalism, the *glorious hopes* which it inspires sustain the Apostle himself in the midst of his spiritual toil and travail, and make him triumph over all the discouragements which otherwise might overwhelm him. Everywhere he bears about with him the cruci-

[1] Not that the Apostle would thus insinuate anything against the character of Moses. When he acted thus, the time was not yet come for Israel to understand the transitory character of the legal economy and its future abolition. It was otherwise at the time when Paul wrote, and when his adversaries were seeking to prolong the Mosaic dispensation, which had really closed with the advent of Messiah.

fixion of Christ, but everywhere also he has part in
His resurrection ; and if, in the end, the body is worn
out in the strife and strain, he knows that God has
prepared for him another habitation eternal in the
heavens, in which he will soon enjoy perfect fellowship
with Him (chap. iv. 7-v. 10).

With a heart thus raised above all low and petty
motives, the Apostle sets himself to the task assigned
to him.   The baneful spirit of self-seeking has been
cast out of him as out of all those who truly experience
the redemption wrought for them by Christ.   Christ
died for all ; in Him then every believer is dead, as a
natural man.   There is in Christ only a company of
risen men with whom the old earthly relations have
passed away and all is become new.   Even Christ
Himself exists for them no more as an earthly, national,
Jewish Christ, but only as the spiritual, heavenly Christ,
in whom all old distinctions are done away, and He
alone remains as the centre of a new creation.   Marvellous indeed is the work wrought out by Him.   God
was in Christ first reconciling the world unto Himself,
and then by His ambassadors, the apostles, inviting
every man to come to Him who had borne the sins of
all, that they might be made the righteousness of God
in Him.   So sublime a task absorbs the whole soul of
him to whom it is entrusted, and leaves no place for the
satisfaction or glorification of self (chap. v. 10-21).

What remains therefore for the Apostle is to raise
his conduct to the level of so high a calling.   And this

is what he has striven to do, as he shows in chapter vi., where he reminds the Church of what he has done for it since its foundation; what sufferings he has borne for its sake, and what Divine strength has upborne him through such a diversity of trial. Unhappily, he does not always find in the Church, especially at Corinth, such faithful affection as he had deserved from them. The more his heart is enlarged, the more theirs seem straitened towards him. Why is this? Because he is obliged to ask of them the sacrifices which fidelity to their Christian profession demands? St. Paul is probably thinking here of what he had said to them before (1 Cor. viii.-x.), as to the necessity of entirely giving up the feasts offered to idols in the heathen temples. This injunction seems to have most irritated the Corinthians who thought themselves strong, and who were wont to say, "All things are lawful for me." The various interpreters who have thought that the passage from chapter vi. 2-vii. 1 of this Epistle ought to be omitted, have so judged because they have failed to perceive this reference.

After affirming in the opening of chapter vii. that he has done nothing which should relax the bond of affection between them and him, Paul turns in v. 4 to the joy that filled his heart on the recent arrival of Titus, whom he had met in Macedonia (4, 5). This forms a new starting point. So far he has been tracing things in order. This coming of Titus forms the goal. Paul had explained his return to Ephesus without staying at Corinth, then he had described his departure for Macedonia and waiting at Troas, then his meeting with Titus. The Apostle describes with effusion the joy with which his heart is now filled at hearing the good news brought by Titus. In order to give the Corinthians some idea of its intensity, he dwells on the sorrow that he had felt after sending off his former stern letter of rebuke. But now how keen is his thankfulness, as he hears how they have avenged his wounded honour. Henceforth he knows that he may fully rely upon them.

This forms the transition to the second part of the Epistle, in which he urges them to press on with the important work of the collection.

Macedonia has already done its share, while so far it appears the Corinthians had done nothing. He has therefore decided to send Titus to them with two deputies from the Churches of Macedonia, and he is the bearer of this letter. Paul did not wish to make this collection burdensome to them, but on the other hand he was sure that a rich blessing would come from it to themselves and the whole Church (chap. viii., ix.). The Apostle speaks of one of the two deputies who accompanied Titus as a man whose gifts as an evangelist had made him famous through all the Churches of Macedonia. It seems probable, as several of the Fathers thought, that this messenger may have been St. Luke, who had remained with the Church at Philippi after the departure of Paul, Silas,

and Timotheus. It is possible that the other may
have been Aristarchus, the Macedonian, who afterwards with Luke travelled with St. Paul to Rome.

Having thus reached the time present in this second
part of his letter, Paul now turns his eyes to the
future. The immediate future is his proposed visit
to Corinth. It is natural that all his thoughts should
be fixed on this goal of his desires, and he frankly
sets forth his feelings in the third part of the Epistle
(chap. x.-xiii.).

This clearly begins a fresh division, and Paul introduces it with the unusual formula : " *Now I Paul
myself.*" There is also a marked change of tone
in the verses which follow. From affectionate tenderness he passes to the severest irony. The abruptness
of the change is surprising. How could Paul utter
such cutting rebukes after just assuring the Church
of the joyful satisfaction he felt in its conduct (chap.
vii.) ? Some have gone so far as to suppose that
these last four chapters are the very severe letter [1]
previously sent by Titus to which the Apostle had
referred in chapter vii., and that it has thus come
down to us tacked on to the end of the later letter.
But it is impossible that this Second Epistle should
have abruptly terminated with chapter ix. ; and we
should be driven to suppose that some one had carefully expunged the end of the genuine letter to affix

---

[1] Hausrath, *Der Vier-Capitel Brief.*

to it another letter of quite a different tone. There
is no ground for such far-fetched hypotheses. We
see at once from chapter x. 2, where Paul speaks
of " some which count of us as if we walked according
to the flesh," that though he seems to be addressing
the whole Church, he is really speaking here only
to the disaffected party, and to the Church in so far
as it had allowed itself to be influenced by it. The
majority of the Church has returned, no doubt, to
a better mind; but there is still a rebellious minority,
whose opposition must be broken down, either by
means of this letter or by energetic action when Paul
comes. " Being in readiness to avenge all disobedience," he says, " when your obedience shall
be fulfilled." There are these two things to be done:
to secure on the part of the faithful a still more
complete submission, and on the part of the recalcitrant
a full surrender. This is the drift of these four
chapters, which thus connect themselves quite naturally
with the foregoing.

The Apostle implores them not to force him to use,
when he comes, the apostolic power which Christ has
given him. Doubtless there are among them those who
do not believe that he has any such power, and who
accuse him of being weighty and strong only while he
is at a distance, but in presence weak and contemptible.
He argues, however, that he has given in his ministry
irrefutable proof of his spiritual power. Was he not
the founder of this very Church of Corinth, into which

these his adversaries have obtruded themselves, entering into other men's labours ? " Not he that commendeth himself (by vaunting words) is approved, but whom the Lord commendeth," sealing his work by signs following.

Since his enemies disparage him, he is fain to defend himself, from very love to the Church, and in order to keep intact the spiritual bond by which he would have it bound to Christ.

Does he not see the converts turning aside from the doctrine he taught them, and receiving with open arms any who come preaching another Jesus and a different Spirit ? Yet, he asks, in what was he behind these new apostles for whom he was set aside ? There is only one thing in which they outdo him ; they take pay for their preaching, and get themselves maintained by the Church. In this respect alone will he own inferiority to these false apostles, who, like Satan, can clothe themselves as angels of light. Well then, since the Corinthians force him to it, and though it would be folly under any other circumstances, he will reveal to them the secrets of his soul's travail, and of his inmost life. And here the Apostle describes, with an incomparably graphic touch, all the privations which he has endured for Christ. He could, indeed, go on to tell them of more glorious things. The great city of Damascus was one day stirred to a frenzy about him, and sought to kill him. Then he had visions and raptures of revelation, in which he was caught up to the very third heaven. But to speak of these things is folly. If he must speak, let it rather be of the infirmities which humble him, and are, therefore, his safeguard. Such is that thorn in the flesh which he carries about with him, and about which the Lord said to him, " My grace is sufficient for thee." If he must glory, let him glory in those things which keep him weak, for then is he strong (chap. xi. 1-xii. 11).

From this picture, which he has felt constrained to draw in self-defence, he turns again to his adversaries, and to those members of the Church who had let themselves be carried away by them.

As there is only one point on which he has not made good his apostleship among them, namely, by receiving nothing at their hands, he will adhere to the same course of conduct when he comes again. Some had dared to say that this was only a pretence, and that he knew well enough how to get money for himself through his agents. Let them prove, then, that one of those whom he had sent had acted in this respect differently from himself. Those who bring this charge against him will do well to take heed and examine themselves, lest, after having been warned, the Apostle finds them when he comes, just as before, and is obliged to deal sharply with them, according to the authority the Lord has given him. He would rather show himself gentle and weak among them. Let them not force him to come with a rod; for if he can do nothing *against* the truth, he can do something *for* it. But his desire is, that in this coming visit all the weakness should be on his part, and all the strength on theirs (chap. xii. 11-xiii. 10).

The Apostle concludes with a short exhortation to joy, unity, peace; and with a blessing in the name of the Father, the Son, and the Holy Ghost, which, as an apostle of Jesus Christ, he substitutes for the old priestly benedictions. It was not then without reason that Paul commenced this section with the words, "I Paul myself." This part of the letter has been taken up with purely personal matters, but not by his own choice; the necessity was laid upon him.

It is natural to ask, Who were then these bitter enemies of Paul, who came to exert such an important and disastrous influence upon the Church of Corinth? They were evidently emissaries from without, for they had brought with them letters of commendation (chap. iii. 1). On their arrival they had taken advantage of the disunion which had already crept into the Church. Seeing that the more faithful disciples of Paul were treated with scant respect by those who were taken up with Apollos, and that these again were slighted by those who boasted of belonging to Peter's party, they took occasion to commend themselves as the only ones who really came in the name of Christ. What ground could they have for arrogating to themselves such a distinction? Baur and his school suppose that they took this title because they were sent by the apostles of Christ, and especially by James, the Lord's brother. Those whom Paul calls in this letter "*the very chiefest apostles*," must, then, be the Twelve, and it is from them that these Jewish emissaries must have received the "letters of commendation" mentioned in this Epistle. Pursuing this track, the famous leader of the Tübingen school has come to the conclusion that, in the early Church, Paul and the Twelve lived and worked in a spirit of mutual antagonism.

But it is easy to see the falsity of this idea. The Twelve, after having given the hand of fellowship to St. Paul, as he himself tells us (Gal. ii.), could not send out messengers from the Churches of Palestine, fortified with letters of commendation from them, to hinder Paul's work among the Gentiles.

Moreover, these men, who claimed to be specially "of Christ," did not set themselves to oppose the followers of Paul and of Apollos alone, but of Peter also (1 Cor. i. 12). Lastly, it is quite evident from 2 Cor. xi. 5, 6, that those whom the Church of Corinth seriously, and Paul ironically, called "the very chiefest apostles," were personages distinguished in some degree by their culture and eloquence ; for Paul says : " I reckon that I am not a whit behind the very chiefest apostles ; since though I am rude (ἰδιώτης) in speech, I am not in knowledge." These men were then exalted above Paul for their gifts of speech, just as Apollos had already been preferred to him on the same ground. How could this apply to the Twelve, who are themselves characterised as "unlearned and ignorant men" (ἀγραμματοὶ καὶ ἰδιῶτα, Acts iv. 13), and who were certainly far inferior to Paul in eloquence? The Apostle gives us to understand also that he had come behind these men in this respect; that he had not (like them) made himself burdensome to the Church (xi. 7 ; xii. 2). Now there can be no doubt that he is speaking of the Church of Corinth (xi. 20) when he describes the ill-advised conduct of these intruders in her midst. But the Twelve had never been at Corinth. It is not then the apostles at Jerusalem, but these new comers themselves whom Paul thus ironically describes, in language borrowed from their ardent partisans. In thus describing them, he stigmatises them as placing themselves not only above him, Paul, but also above those who in the ordinary language of the Church were called apostles, and especially above Peter. Some critics even of the Tübingen school have clearly seen that it was impossible to regard these adversaries of Paul as directly sent by the Twelve ; and they have ventured on the conjecture that they were rather men who had personally known Christ at Jerusalem, perhaps some of His kindred or acquaintance, who, going about to preach Him in the synagogues, had come as far as Corinth. We know, indeed, from 1 Cor. ix. 5, that the brethren of the Lord did go about as missionary evangelists. But we have no authority for attributing to them feelings of hostility to Paul, nor views differing from those of the Twelve.

The account which Paul gives of the Conference at Jerusalem (Gal. ii.) excludes, as is now fully recognised, any idea of hostility to the work of Paul among the Gentiles, on the part of James, the Lord's brother. He too had at that Conference recognised Paul as a divinely-called apostle, no less than Peter, and had given him the right hand of fellowship. Hence we conclude that these strange missionaries, who had formed a hostile party to Paul at Corinth, designating itself as "of Christ," came no doubt from Palestine, and probably from Jerusalem, but that like "the false brethren privily brought in," of whom Paul speaks (Gal. ii. 4), they did not belong to the Twelve, but acted independently of them, and even presumed to set themselves above them. They were probably of the number of those "priests" and "Pharisees" whom Luke mentions (Acts vi. 7; xv. 5) as having acknowledged Jesus as their Messiah. Having once entered the Church, these members of the Jewish aristocracy had hoped to take the direction of affairs into their own hands. They despised the apostles, as unlearned and ignorant men, and thought that they should shape as they pleased the work of Christian missions, the importance of which they recognised as a feature of the Messianic kingdom. They hoped, as we have seen in studying the Epistle to the Galatians, to make use of the conquering power of the Gospel as a means of extending the kingdom of the law in the Gentile world. Animated with this spirit, more legal than Christian, they set aside the apostles, and endeavoured to divert to their own ends the labours of Paul.

This, if we mistake not, was the party whose emissaries came to Corinth, furnished with letters of commendation. Since the conflicts in Antioch and Galatia, however, they had changed their tactics. They no longer spoke of circumcision, which would at once have repelled the Greeks, but they falsified even more thoroughly the spirit of the Gospel. Paul accuses them of preaching *another Jesus*, of introducing *another Spirit* and *another Gospel*. They are the tools of the serpent who beguiled Eve (chap. xi. 1-4). It is obviously at them that, in closing his first Epistle, Paul abruptly flings the challenge: "if any man love not the Lord, let him be anathema." This is all of which we can be sure. We do not know what was this new Jesus, this new Gospel, this new Spirit which they brought in. It would seem that it was something more than a doctrine in which legal elements were blended. The term, "*another Jesus*," suggests some new and dangerous theory of Christology, and I am disposed to think that it was at these neologists Paul aimed the vigorous arguments against human wisdom which we find in the first four chapters of the First Epistle to the Corinthians, and which have often been erroneously thought to apply to Apollos. However this may be, the Judæo-Christian character of these people is put beyond question by the passage 2 Cor. xi. 22, 23. It would appear, moreover, that they had not scrupled to ally themselves at Corinth with men of licentious life (chap. xii. 20, 21). All means seemed to them legitimate that would help to overturn the work of Paul.

We see now how wisely Paul proceeds in dealing with this deadly error. He first tries to strengthen all the links which unite him to the better part of the Church. Then, when he feels that the majority has once more rallied firmly in defence of his person and his apostleship, he attacks with all the energy of which he is capable, the rebellious party with its strange leaders, and sets before them his ultimatum.

What did these men do whom Paul had so menaced and stigmatised ? Did they await his arrival ? Did they resolve to hold out against him ? We doubt it. Either they left the place of their own accord, in consequence of this letter, or the Church made them go. Touched with the tenderness of those words : " I determined this for myself, that I would not come again to you with sorrow ; for if I make you sorry, who then is he who maketh me glad but he that is made sorry by me ? " it hastened to banish all the obnoxious elements that might have called for the stern exercise of the apostolic authority. The three months which Paul spent at Corinth during the winter of the years 58-59, were months of peace. Of this we have the proof in our hands. The Epistle to the Romans was the fruit of this repose.

In this second Epistle to the Corinthians we get the

fullest insight into the heart of the Apostle, so full of tenderness, human and Divine. From it we learn what were his views of apostleship, and of the Christian ministry generally. Nothing finer has been written on this subject than the passages in which it is treated in this letter. And if in the Epistle to the Romans we find the fullest statement of the Gospel and in the First Epistle to the Corinthians the most complete chapter on Church discipline, we have in this Second Epistle to the Corinthians the very mind of God with regard to the institution of the Christian ministry.

5

THE GOSPEL PREACHED TO THE CHURCH IN ROME

(Romans)

WHEREVER St. Paul founded a Church, he was careful to give the spiritual edifice as solid a foundation of Christian teaching as the circumstances permitted. We are told that at Ephesus, where he made a long sojourn, he held religious discussions every day for two years in the school of one Tyrannus, " so that all they which dwelt in Asia heard the word of the Lord" (Acts xix. 9, 10). We may be quite certain that what Paul thus gave was not a discursive, but a consecutive course of religious instruction. His mind was so logical that it could not fail to set its impress on his teaching.

The instructions which the Apostle thus gave in the Churches which he founded, extended over a very wide area, embracing even points which are often neglected by pastors in the preparation of their catechumens. Thus Paul reminds the Thessalonians that he had spoken to them, during his stay with them, of the coming of Antichrist, which was to precede the return of the Lord ; or rather of the existence of a power, the fall of which was to prepare the way for the manifestation of Antichrist. "Remember ye not that when I was yet with you, I told you these things?" (2 Thess. ii. 5).

Elsewhere he reminds them in detail of the practical duties which he had enjoined upon them. "Ye know what charge we gave you through the Lord Jesus" (1 Thess. iv. 2). At the commencement of chap. v. of the same Epistle he writes to them, that they do not need to be taught about the time of the return of Christ ; for they know themselves that " the day of the Lord so cometh as a thief in the night." He had, therefore, quoted to them the Lord's words on this subject, and had made these the text of his teachings.

In 1 Cor. vi. he says, as speaking to them of something of which they cannot be ignorant, "Know ye not that the saints shall judge the world?" "Know ye not that we shall judge angels?" This teaching which he had given them, he repeats in chap. xv. 24, 25, where he speaks of a time coming when Christ shall reign, and all enemies shall be put under His feet.

These indications show how thorough and minute was the instruction given by the Apostle to these young Churches.

How was it then with the Church at Rome, the capital of the Gentile world ? The Gospel had reached there before the coming of the Apostle to the Gentiles. The message had gone before the messenger. Other lips had brought it from Asia and from Greece, where it had already made its way. Little groups of believers had been gathered by the preaching of the Gospel, elementary as it no doubt was, and these believing companies were scattered about in different quarters of the great city. One of these little flocks met in the house of Aquila and Priscilla; another in that of Asyncritus and Phlegon; a third in that of Philologus and Julia (Rom. xvi. 4, 14, 15). These simple hearts had received with joy the good news of salvation, but they still needed such a solid course of instruction as the Apostle was able to give them. This, if I mistake not, was the real motive which led him to address to them this letter, which is altogether different in character from the rest of his Epistles, except perhaps, in some respects, the Epistle to the Ephesians. He was anxious, if possible, to settle the young Church upon stronger and deeper foundations than those yet laid. He gives the Romans by letter the Gospel which he had not been able (and let us thank God that it was so) to give them by word of mouth. After the death of a father or mother, the children are thankful for the occasional separations that had come between them and those beloved parents, for to this circumstance they owe the letters from them which are such treasured memorials. In the same way we rejoice that the Apostle was prevented from coming sooner to Rome, for to this delay we owe the Epistle to the Romans.

The motive which seems to me to have prompted

the writing of this Epistle, is far from being generally recognised. From a very remote period, and still more since the time of Baur, this Epistle has been regarded as a piece of ecclesiastical strategy. Paul (we are told) was desirous to free this Church from the Judaising spirit, more or less pronounced, which characterised it. Those who hold this view, suppose that Christianity had been brought to Rome by some Jewish pilgrims returning from Palestine, or by messengers from the Church at Jerusalem. We know that the Roman Catholic Church speaks of St. Peter as having come to Rome in very early times, to set up there the standard of the cross. According to the Tübingen school, Paul endeavoured to make himself master of this alien, or hostile position, in order to secure in the West, whither he meant to carry the Gospel, a standpoint corresponding to that which he found in the Church at Antioch, for his work in the East. But more recent investigation has brought out so distinctly the pagano-Christian composition of the Church of Rome, that this idea of the Epistle to the Romans is no longer tenable, and is now supported by very few writers.[1] The idea now is rather that the Apostle's object was to resist a Judaising invasion from the East, which seriously threatened the Church of Rome. The same troublesome party which had followed Paul into Galatia and Achaia, trying to bring

---

[1] Mangold, for example.

these Churches into the bondage of legalism, had come to Rome also, and had stirred up some to oppose the spiritual teaching of Paul. The Apostle writes this Epistle in order to meet this difficulty. This is Weizsäcker's opinion. But it appears to me that a comparison of the Epistle to the Galatians with this Epistle to the Romans suffices to make us distrust it. The polemical tone of the Epistle to the Galatians, written, as it is supposed by Weizsäcker, under circumstances analogous to those which prompted the Epistle to the Romans, is in such strong contrast with the calm didactic strain of the latter, that it is difficult to suppose the two were composed under similar conditions, or for the same ends. We may observe again, that in arguing with the Galatians, Paul takes as his starting-point the person of Abraham and the patri-archal origin of the Jewish covenant; while in the Epistle to the Romans, he goes back to the very beginning of the race, to Adam and his fall, as the occasion of the universal reign of sin and death. These two lines of argument bear the same relation to each other as the two genealogies of Matthew and Luke. So little is it the object of the Apostle in the Epistle to the Romans to emphasise the contrast between Judeo-Christian legalism and his Gospel, that he begins with a description of the corruption of the pagan world, which would be altogether irrelevant on such a supposition. It is not, as in the Epistle to the Galatians, the powerlessness of the law to save man, which is the prevailing thought in the Epistle to the Romans, though that comes in incidentally. It is the powerlessness of man, as such, to save himself, whether with or without the law, and the necessity of salvation by Christ, which is the great theme of the Epistle to the Romans.

But why then, we hear some one ask, are there so many passages dwelling emphatically on the incompetence of the law either to justify or sanctify? We reply: It must be borne in mind that even in treating of mankind at large, the Apostle could not omit the Jewish nation, and that in dealing with the question of salvation, he was under the necessity of paying particular attention to this people. Was it not the only nation with which the Lord had entered into covenant, and to which He had given the means of grace? the only nation, therefore, which had anything that could be added to or contrasted with the salvation which Paul preached? the only nation which could urge its peculiar claims in face of, and even in the midst of, the Church? It is none the less true that this antithesis holds only a secondary place in the Epistle. It is the *man*, whether Jew or Gentile, and not the *Jew*, whom Paul has in view. Hence he begins with a picture of the corruption of the Gentile world on the one hand, and of the Jewish nation on the other, that he may justify the sentence of universal condemnation which he then pronounces as the verdict of Scripture. And hence it is that in opposition to this universal condemnation, he lays such stress (chap. iii. 22) on the universality of the salvation offered in Christ. Therefore, also, in concluding the history of salvation, he uses these words : " God hath shut up all unto disobedience, that He might have mercy upon all" (chap. xi. 32).

This then is no controversy between Judaising and Pauline Christians. Paul is contrasting Christianity itself with the old pagan and Jewish religions, that he may show forth in Christ the one true and perfect salvation for the human race, lost as it was in its father Adam. The antithesis here is not, as in the Epistle to the Galatians, between Christ and Moses, but be-tween Christ and Adam. As De Wette observes, it was fitting that the Church of the world's metropolis should receive the Apostle's teaching upon so great a subject.

It seems to us probable that this grand conception of the Gospel formed the theme of the Apostle in his two years' course of religious instruction given at Ephesus, and that the Epistle to the Romans presents to us a summary of that teaching. The date at which the Epistle was written agrees with this supposition. It is evident from the Epistle itself, that the third mission of the Apostle to the East, his ministry in Asia Minor, was finished. He says so distinctly (chap. xv. 19-24): "So that from Jerusalem, and round about to Illyricum, I have fully preached the Gospel of Christ. . . . Now having no more place in these regions, and having these many years a longing to come unto you, whensoever I go into Spain, I hope to see you on my journey." Only before going thither he has to go again to Jerusalem, to take leave of the Church, and to hand over to it the collection which he had made on its behalf among the Gentile Churches. This definitely fixes the date of the letter. It was written at the close of his stay in Ephesus, and after the conclusion of the conflict with the Church of Corinth. Now at length Paul could make that stay in Achaia which he had so long planned (*see* 1st and 2nd Epistles to Corinthians), and enjoy three months' rest at Corinth (Acts xx. 3). This resting-time was fruitful of great results. It produced the greatest master-piece which the human mind had ever conceived and realised, the first logical exposition of the work of God in Christ for the salvation of the world.

It has often been asked, how it is that if this is the true character of the Epistle to the Romans, it contains absolutely no reference to Christology and Christian eschatology? We reply, in the first place, that this is not exactly the case. The humanity and divinity of the Saviour, though they are not treated directly, are evidently implied; the former in chap. v. 15, as well as in the whole parallel with Adam; the latter in chap. viii. 3, 32, and ix. 5. As to the eschatology, it is sufficiently and appropriately referred to in chap. xiii. 11, 12. But the main reason is this. Neither the doctrine of the personality of Christ nor of His second advent, formed the subject of the special revelation granted to Paul on his conversion. Jesus Christ "taught him by revelation" (Gal. i. 11, 12) that which he twice calls in this Epistle *his Gospel*,[1] and that which he describes (Eph. iii. 2, 3) as his *part* in the general apostolic revelation. Now it is this personal part, this Gospel entrusted specially to him, that Paul hands down in this Epistle. The work is worthy of the occasion which called it forth. The situation was a solemn one. The evangelisation of the West was about to follow that of the East. This Epistle, addressed from Greece to Italy, was like a bridge connecting the two parts of the ancient world, the link between the two great works of the Apostle of the Gentiles.

The general plan of the Epistle to the Romans may be traced in various ways. Not indeed that it is wanting in clearness. The ideas follow each other in close logical sequence, each one the legitimate offspring of its antecedent and parent of what follows. The great divisions of the Epistle are clearly marked. It is rather the grouping of the parts which is somewhat doubtful. Let us notice first, the series of well-marked divisions.

(1) We have the epistolary preamble (chap. i. 1-15), in which Paul reminds the Christians of Rome that as the Apostle of the Gentiles, he is also their Apostle, and that if he has not yet been to see them, it has

---

[1] This expression occurs again in 2 Tim. ii. 8.

been simply because he has been prevented by his work in the East.

(2) The second division contains only the description of the subject about to be treated—the Gospel as the true and only way of salvation for mankind, whether Jew or Gentile (v. 16, 17).

(3) The third division comprises the treatment of the first part of the subject indicated; it extends from chap. i. 18, to the end of chap. v. It includes three sections. In the first (chap. i. 18-iii. 28) Paul shows the lost condition of man without the Gospel; 1st, of the Gentiles (chap. i. 18-32); 2nd, of the Jews (chap. ii. 1-iii. 8); 3rd, of *all*, on the testimony of the Old Testament itself (chap. iii. 9-20).

The second section forms the antithesis of the first. In the midst of this darkness of fallen humanity a ray of light suddenly breaks forth. This is free pardon, justification by faith, based upon the work of Christ (iii. 21-v. 11), and offered to all as the way to salvation. 1st, The work of Christ is set forth as consisting in a manifestation of the Divine righteousness, so that he who consents to appropriate it by faith, thus becomes righteous before God, and this grace, being completely free, is placed within the reach of Gentiles as well as Jews (iii. 23-31). 2nd, This method of God's dealing in the Gospel is shown to be in harmony with the great example of justification in the Old Testament—the example of Abraham; for that patriarch obtained everything by faith—justification, his inheritance, posterity (chap. iv.). 3rd, This justification which the Christian obtains by faith is assured to him not only for the time present, but for the day of judgment, and consequently for ever. For it is accompanied by another grace which renders it permanent, the grace of sanctification (chap. v. 1-11).

Before describing this second gift, however, which makes the first immutably secure, the Apostle asks if the work of One like Jesus Christ can really extend its influence over many to such an extent as to justify all mankind. By a bold line of argument, he adduces, in proof of this power, the fatal influence which the one sin of Adam has exerted. If this sin of Adam's has been powerful enough in its effects to bring death upon all men, how much more shall the far mightier work of Christ bring in eternal life. This concludes the first division of the subject, that which deals with the fundamental fact of salvation, justification by faith. This part resembles the first day of creation, in the first chapter of Genesis. " *There was evening*," the long night of condemnation on Jew and Gentile; and " *there was morning*," the manifestation of Christ and of salvation. This was *the first day*. This first act is to be followed by many others, designed to complete the salvation of God.

(4) The fourth division is not less clearly defined than the foregoing. It extends from chaps. vi.-viii. In this the Apostle works out the theme indicated in vers. 9, 10 of chap. v., when, after having spoken of

reconciliation by the death of Christ, he adds the further gift of participation in His life. Having become, by faith in the atoning sacrifice, one with Jesus Christ, the believer shares at once in His death and in His risen life. The believer dies to the sin for which Christ died, and he lives to God, for whom alone Jesus lives in His resurrection life (chap. vi. 1-13). This effect of faith is produced in him by a moral necessity such that if he sought to evade it, he could only do so by denying the faith, and falling back under the old power of death under the law (chap. vi. 14-23). Being thus legitimately delivered by the death of Christ from the bondage of the law under which he was incessantly sinning, he is henceforward free to live in the new union with the risen Christ, a union in which he brings forth fruit unto God (vii. 1-6). Paul is here giving his own actual experience. He had himself lived under the law, and he knew that when the law came in contact with his moral life, it condemned it, and thus gave a sense of separation from God, and of spiritual death. In this state he was constantly striving to satisfy the requirements of the law, and to regain the favour of God. He did not succeed, and the result of all this fruitless struggle was an agonised cry: "O wretched man that I am, who shall deliver me out of the body of this death!" . . . "With the mind I serve the law of God, but with the flesh the law of sin." By his manner of expressing himself here, the Apostle gives the

impression that it would still be so with him at the
very moment when he is speaking, if he were left
to himself and separated from the salvation he had
received (chap. vii. 14-25). But this state of condemnation and powerlessness is no longer his. The
spirit of Christ, by imparting to him the holy life of
the Lord, has delivered him from spiritual death, and
made him capable of fulfilling the law spiritually, as
Christ Himself fulfilled it ; and this new life is to him
the pledge of future victory even over the death
of the body (chap. viii. 1-11). For just as eternal
death is certain for those who live after the flesh, so
the Divine heritage of eternal life is assured to the
children of God who live after the spirit (ver. 12-17).
The Apostle sets forth here the final issues of salvation—glory manifesting itself even in the outward,
corporeal, and material domain. A threefold sigh goes
up after this universal renovation ; the sighing of
nature itself, of the redeemed, and of the Holy Spirit ;
and this sighing will be heard, for it is in harmony
with the will of God, according to which those whom
God has foreknown as believers are predestinated to
bear the glorious likeness of His Son (ver. 17-30).
Having reached this culminating point, the Apostle
strikes the keynote of the grand song of salvation.
God is for us, therefore nothing which is against us
can break the bond formed between Him and us by
faith in Christ (ver. 31-39). This fourth division sets
before us, therefore, the destruction of sin and the

restoration of holiness, thus completing the work of justification, and preparing the way for our glorification. This is the *second day* in the Divine work of salvation, *Christ in us* carrying on and consummating the work of *Christ for us*.

(5) Here the fifth division begins, as it appears at first, somewhat abruptly. This division takes in chaps. ix.-xi. The Apostle has just been magnifying the grace enjoyed by the Church; but Israel, the chosen people, remains without, and shares in none of these high privileges. Is this possible? is it just? What end can be answered by it? If the salvation proclaimed by the Gospel is of God, ought it not to be, first of all, the portion of the chosen people? The Gospel which sets this great problem, must surely, if true, furnish its solution. This solution the Apostle gives us in these chapters (ix.-xi.).

And first of all, however real the prerogative of Israel as the chosen people, it cannot be of force to bind God against His will, or to make void His word. Now Scripture shows, by the example of Ishmael and Esau, both true sons of Abraham, and yet rejected, that to be descended from that patriarch, which is Israel's boast, is not in itself an assurance of salvation. There are spiritual conditions of salvation, failing which a man, even though an Israelite, is rejected and condignly visited with that punishment of having his heart hardened, which fell upon Pharaoh. But if these conditions are fulfilled, even by a Gentile,

they qualify the man to become the subject of the
infinite mercy of God, like Moses himself. It belongs
to God only to try the heart. Consequently He has
the right to exercise His Almighty power freely and
without human control ; to harden whom He would
punish, to bless whom He is pleased to save, for what
seems good to such a Being must be good. Just so
the potter, discerning the nature of the clay he has
to fashion, sets apart some for honourable and the
rest for vile uses. That which was then taking place,
the rejection of the Jews and the calling of the Gentiles,
had been so clearly foretold by the prophets, that none
should be stumbled at it (chap. ix. 1-29). Not only
then was the rejection of Israel possible, but it ought
to have been expected according to the Scriptures.
But is it just ? Were there sufficient reasons for so
severe a measure ? Yes, assuredly ; for notwithstanding its zeal for God, Israel had persisted in
resisting the Divine plan. With the coming of Christ,
the reign of the Law, and consequently the monopoly
of Israel, was to cease. Israel was obstinately bent
on perpetuating both. The work of Christ inaugurated
the era of a free salvation, by which the Gentiles were
placed on the same level as Israel. Moses himself
had clearly foreshadowed this revolution, when he
represented salvation as the gift of God, and not as
the reward of human effort. But Israel was unwilling
to give up its position of privilege, and was bent upon
maintaining it at all costs against the whole world.

It everywhere set itself against the proclamation of salvation to the Gentiles. It never grasped the meaning of the warnings of the prophets, of Moses, and particularly of Isaiah, who all foretold the coming rejection of Israel and the calling in of the Gentiles to take its place (chap. ix. 30-x. 21). Was then that glorious vision of a kingdom of Messiah of which Israel should be the centre, to vanish away for ever ? Were the promises of God to this people to be entirely and for ever annulled ? Nay, this could not be. In the first place, there were believers in Israel, as the example of Paul himself proves; and if the mass of the people was visited by a judgment of hardening for its pride, there was yet a faithful "remnant according to the election of grace" (xi. 1-10).

Nay, more ; the great body of the nation was itself one day to return and be reinstated in that kingdom of God from which for the moment it was shut out. Here the Apostle opens before us a long vista in the purposes of God. Israel, with its Pharisaic tendencies, could not have accepted Messiah without endeavouring to introduce into the new dispensation a strong leaven of legalism. Now salvation preached to the Gentiles under this Judaised form would infallibly have been rejected by them. It was necessary then that Israel, since it was incorrigible in these forms of error, should be blinded so as not to recognise Jesus as the Messiah at all, that so the Gospel, freed from all alloy of legalism, might make its way throughout the whole world. But what is the depth of the mercies of God ! This salvation, first realised among the Gentiles, will one day stir the rejected Jews to holy emulation, so that they will covet a share in the rich blessings enjoyed by the Gentiles, and will in the end receive the Christ by whom the Gentiles have been so blessed. And not only so, but this entering of believing Israel into the Church will be the signal for a spiritual revival and new fruitfulness throughout Christendom. Thus, as the casting away of the Jews led to the conversion of the Gentiles, so the conversion of the Gentiles will in its turn lead to that of the Jews. And this restoration of Israel will not be so hard of accomplishment as it might seem ; for there is still holy sap in that rejected vine, so that it will be grafted in again upon the tree of the Divine covenant more readily than the Gentiles themselves were grafted in. Nay, it may even happen that if the Gentiles indulge in proud boasting against the Jews, they may be for a time rejected as were the Jews.

As the final issue, we see all humbled, each in his turn by a term of disobedience, but all at last gathered in by the all-embracing arms of the Father's love. And as at the close of chap. viii. the Apostle burst into a jubilant hymn of praise over the assurance of salvation, so now he magnifies, in one adoring exclamation, the depth of the wisdom of God's ways with man.

(6) With chap. xii. a new division begins. The open-

ing words, "*I beseech you then*," fitly introduce its contents, which are the practical consequences which ought to follow in the lives of believers from the Divine works, the mercies of God just set forth.   These consequences bear on their conduct, first, as members of the Christian community (chap. xii.), then as belonging to the great human family (chap. xiii.).   Besides these two general applications of Christian principles, the Apostle makes one particular application to a difficulty existing in the Church at the time when he was writing (chap. xiv. 1-xv. 13).   The section of the Epistle which we are now considering, extends therefore from chap. xii. 1 to xv. 13.   Paul begins by laying down in the first two verses of chap. xii. the basis of Christian activity. This he represents to be the complete sacrifice of self made by virtue of a renewed mind which has become quick to discern, in every case, the will of God.   He next shows the twofold form in which this sacrifice is to be presented—first, as a member of the Church, by the faithful administration of the gift received, whatever it may be, with no ambition beyond its simple and conscientious use in all humility (ver. 3-8) ; next, by loving service of the brethren in all the relations of life, whether with the faithful or with the enemies and persecutors of the faith, so that all evil shall be overcome of good, that is, of love (ver. 9-21).   To this sacrifice of self in all humility and charity the believer is to add, as a member of the state, respect for the rights of others in all civil relations, whether by submission to authority of every kind, or by just dealing towards all fellow-citizens ; and this duty of fair dealing with all men the Apostle sums up as naturally implied in the bond of love (chap. xiii. 1-10). The Apostle concludes this exposition of the duties of the believer as a Christian and a citizen, by reminding him of the supreme motive by which he is ever to be sustained in his daily walk—the looking for the Saviour who is coming again, and for whose appearing the believer ought to be ever arrayed in pure garments, " putting on the Lord Jesus Christ " Himself (ver. 11-14). What follows relates to the relations of the Church with one particular group of believers who thought it their duty to abstain from meat and from wine. The Apostle urges the obligation of mutual forbearance. Those who abstain ought not to judge those who believe they have a right to use the things which others deny themselves ; and those who use them ought not to look with contempt on those who abstain, since in such matters every one is to be guided by his own conscience (chap. xiv.). That the strong should support the weak is a sacred duty laid upon them by the example of Christ Himself, and is it not the only means of realising the union in one spiritual body of believing Jews and Gentiles—those believing Jews to whom God has so amply vindicated His faithfulness to His promises, and those believing Gentiles whom He has freely loaded with His benefits (xv. 1-13) ? The Apostle closes his summary of Christian duty with this thought of the spiritual union between the two great families of mankind in the Church. The close of his teaching is thus fully in accord with its commencement (chap. i. 16, 17), in which Paul dwelt on the salvation offered by faith alike to Jew and Gentile. The Apostle anticipates in prayerful desire the harmonious hymn of praise which is to rise from the whole Christian community to the glory of the redeeming work he has been describing.

(7) The seventh and last division consists of concluding words corresponding to the preamble (chap. i. 1-15). After excusing himself for offering such teaching to this community which possesses within itself so many means of Christian instruction, but which nevertheless comes within his sphere as Apostle to the Gentiles, he tells the Christians of Rome how he is placed at the moment. His work in the East is finished ; he is purposing to go shortly into Spain, and hopes to take this opportunity of visiting Rome. Lastly, he tells them of his approaching visit to Jerusalem, to hand over to the Churches the collection made for them among the Gentile Christians, and thus to seal the bond of friendship between them and the mother-Church (chap. xv. 24-33). He commends the deaconess Phœbe, the bearer of the letter, to the kindly care of the Church ; he sends greetings to the various Christian workers whom he knew personally, having met them in the East, and who were now labouring for the spread of the Gospel in the capital of the world. Then

he warns the various groups of Christians against the Judaising agitators who have been so busy troubling one after another the Churches founded by him, and who will be sure to come to Rome as soon as they hear that there are Christian communities there. He concludes with greetings from the workers who are with him, and with a solemn prayer to God for this important Church, that it may be stablished in the truth of the Gospel " now made known unto all the nations unto obedience of faith."

Such is the Epistle to the Romans—this sublime effort of the human intellect to apprehend the thought of God in the salvation of mankind, and to give to the world its first clear exposition. How shall we distinguish, in this deep meditation on the things of God, the element of direct revelation given by Christ Himself, of which Paul speaks (Gal. i. 11, 12), from the natural workings of that rare intellect to which the Lord had been pleased to commit such a treasure ? May we say that the substance was given by revelation, the form produced by reflection ? It would be difficult to separate the two in this way. It would be better to say that Paul placed his intellect wholly at the service of Christ, to grasp and reproduce the Divine revelation. However this may be, we fail to find one gap in this great work, one break in its continuity. Everything is worked out in perfect order in this exposition of the Divine idea, as though by a law of inward necessity. But we note at the same

time, very distinct divisions in it. We have enumerated seven, the first and the last being of an epistolary
character, which marks them off from the rest; so that
they are like the envelope which contains the letter
itself. The interesting question with regard to these
five intermediate sections is, how to group them; that
is to say, what is really the plan of the Epistle, as
conceived in the mind of the Apostle. Various answers
may be given to this question. We may divide the
body of the letter, as I have done in the first edition of
my Commentary, into a doctrinal part (chap. i. 16 xi.)
and a practical part (xii. 1-xv. 13); subdividing the first
part into three sections—the one fundamental (i. 16-v.),
explaining justification by faith; the two others supplementary, intended, the one (vi.-viii.) to set forth the
holiness of the justified believer; the other (ix.-xi.)
to explain the history of salvation from this standpoint. Or, as I have tried to do in my second edition,
we may, while maintaining this great division into
doctrinal and practical, subdivide the former into two
sections, the one comprising chap. i. 16-viii., that is to
say the whole exposition of salvation in its three
essential phases—justification (i.-v.), sanctification (vi.-
viii. 17), and the future and certain glorification of
believers (viii. 18-39); the other setting forth the
historical progress of salvation among mankind (chap.
ix.-xi.). There is, however, a third mode of division,
perhaps preferable, and which I think I should adopt if
I were required to bring out a third edition. This

would be to divide the whole matter contained in the
five middle sections into three parts : first, chap. i.-viii.,
salvation ; second, chap. ix.-xi., the history of salvation ; third, xii.-xv. 13, the salvation-life. These
three prats would be like the central block of a great
building, the two epistolary sections forming the two
wings. Of course the only interest of such a question
arises out of the desire to understand what was the
idea present to the mind of the Apostle when he wrote
the Epistle.

And now let us pause for a moment before this great
structure, and try to count up some of the treasures
it contains. I do not speak here of the light which
flashes from it into the dark places of the heart of man,
showing his corruption, his powerlessness for all that
is good, and revealing at the same time the one way
of salvation set before him, by which he may climb
again the heavenly heights. I am speaking now of
the intellectual treasure contained in these sixteen
chapters, and which enrich with added treasure those
who have already found the kingdom of God and His
righteousness. In chap. i. we have a philosophy of
paganism which searches to the very depths that great
historical phenomenon, unveiling its hidden cause, and
explaining its fearful consequences. In chap. iii. we
have an explanation of the mystery of the cross which,
better understood, would have prevented many misconceptions and removed many intellectual stumbling-
blocks. In chap. v. we have a rapid survey of the

history of humanity based upon the two opposite principles of life which regulate the whole development of the race. In chap. vi. we have the outlines of a moral philosophy which admirably combines the two elements of liberty and necessity. In chap. vii. we have an inimitable psychological analysis of the condition of unregenerate man, both as to what remains of good in him and as to his inability to realise his good intentions. In chap. viii. we have a philosophy of nature, which recognises the abnormal and transitory character of creation as it is, and which in this painful phase of its existence, corresponding to the fallen estate of man, discerns the pledge of a future renewal of all nature corresponding to man's glorious restoration. In chaps. ix.-xi. we have a philosophy of history which sets forth the great contrast between Israel and the Gentile nations as the key which can alone explain the strange vicissitudes of national life, and unlock the mystery of their final issues. In chap. xiii. we have a system of political philosophy, which assigns to the State a basis no less Divine than that of the Church,— "the powers that be are ordained of God,"—but, at the same time, marks most distinctly the difference between the two societies, by the difference between the *love* which is the soul of the one (chap. xii.), and the *justice* which is the mainspring of the other. What we admire here is not so much this clear distinction between the State and the Church, since the Apostle would be naturally led to this by the hostility of the

State to the Christian community at that time; but rather his recognition of the possibility of a moral union between the two resulting from this very distinction. For what opposition could there possibly be between the two equally Divine principles of justice and charity? or between two communities based the one on one of these principles, the other on the other? As to an administrative union between Church and State, Paul never dreamed of it, because of this very distinction. The State may exact by coercion that which is its just due. But the Church asks the free surrender of self under the constraining power of love. The State cannot claim this. The Church alone can call it forth. Each of these two institutions has its proper sphere, and its special methods adapted for the work it has to do. This relation, which even the nineteenth century so signally fails to comprehend, Paul placed on its true basis.

Was not Coleridge right when he called the Epistle to the Romans " the most profound writing extant " ? It is a mine which the Church has been working for more than eighteen centuries, and from which it will go on drawing ever-fresh treasures till it is raised at length from faith to perfect knowledge.

6

THE FIRST INDICATIONS OF GNOSTICISM IN ASIA MINOR

(Colossians)

FOUR years had passed away since Tertius, Paul's amanuensis at Corinth, had laid down his pen, after writing, at Paul's dictation, the last words of the Epistle to the Romans. Grave events had taken place in the interval. The Apostle had been arrested in Jerusalem. For two years (59-61) the Roman governor had kept him prisoner in his house at Cæsarea. In order to escape from this captivity, which threatened to be prolonged, the Apostle had been constrained to have recourse to his privilege as a Roman citizen, and to appeal to Cæsar's tribunal. In the autumn of the year 61 he had embarked for Rome with other prisoners and a detachment of the Roman legion. Two faithful friends had accompanied him of their own accord, Aristarchus of Thessalonica and Luke the physician, who had both been his fellow-workers in the latter part of his sojourn in Greece. The story of their escape from shipwreck is well known, and how, after spending the winter in Malta, they arrived in Rome in the spring of 62. Although a prisoner, Paul enjoyed much greater liberty in Rome than at Cæsarea. His military imprisonment was exchanged for what was called *custodia libera*. He was allowed to hire an apartment at his own charge, and he was free to receive there any who wished to visit him. He also maintained constant communication with all the Churches of Greece and of Asia.

In the course of the two years which the Apostle passed in Rome in this position, he one day received a visit from an evangelist named Epaphras, who had come from Asia Minor, and who had preached Christ with much success in southern Phrygia. There, a few days' journey to the east of Ephesus, in the basin of the Lycus, an affluent of the Meander, is a mountainous region of great beauty. Above it rises Mount Cadmus, massive, picturesque, covered with eternal snows. At its feet runs the Lycus, near which formerly stood the city of Colosse or Colassæ. A little more to the west were the cities of Laodicea and Hierapolis; all three forming a triangle, of which the last named occupied the northern apex. At the present day the site of the two larger cities, Laodicea and Hierapolis, is only marked by a few ruins, while the vestiges of Colosse, a league distant from Chonæ (χῶναι, the funnel-shaped cavities in which the Lycus loses itself at intervals), are still less considerable.

This was the field of labour of the zealous and faithful

Epaphras. He had probably been one of Paul's converts during his stay in Ephesus. For whatever may be said, it is certain that Paul had never himself been in this region (Col. ii. 1). When, at the commencement of his third missionary voyage, he had gone from Antioch into Galatia and from Galatia to Ephesus, he had passed through northern Phrygia, but the basin of the Lycus lay on his left.

It must have been about the same time that Epaphras arrived in Rome that a great earthquake occurred in this district, and was felt with peculiar violence in the city of Laodicea. The exact year in which this catastrophe occurred is not known. Tacitus places it in 60-61; Eusebius in 64; according to Orosius it was still later, in 68. As the Apostle makes no allusion to it, we must conclude either that it did not take place till after the arrival of Epaphras in Rome and the writing of the Epistle to the Colossians, or that Colosse did not materially suffer, and rapidly recovered from the shock. Laodicea rose again from its ruins in the very year of its overthrow (*eodem anno*), and that by its own exertions (*propriis opibus*), as Tacitus tells us.

What we have just said rests upon the supposition that it was in Rome and about the year 62-63 that Epaphras came to visit the Apostle, with what special object we shall have to enquire presently. But many scholars place this visit of Epaphras to Paul at a much earlier date, namely during the captivity of Paul at Cæsarea, from the summer of 59 to the autumn of 61.

The reasons alleged in favour of this opinion are
some of them very weak and some simply absurd, and
cannot, as it seems to us, weigh at all against those
which can be urged in favour of the view we have
taken. We call attention, in the first place, to the
marked correspondence of style, thought, and circumstance between the Epistle to the Colossians and that
to the Philippians, in which the Apostle frequently
alludes to his state of captivity. Timothy, of whom
there is no mention during the captivity at Cæsarea,
has a share in both these epistles. The reference
which Paul makes (Col. iv. 11) to his fellow-workers
of Jewish origin, corresponds with what he says to the
Philippians on this subject (chap. i. 15-17). Now it
is quite certain that the Epistle to the Philippians
was written from Rome and not from Cæsarea. For
the Apostle says in it that he hopes soon to visit
Macedonia, while during his captivity in Cæsarea he
had no thought, either before or after his appeal to
the emperor, of going anywhere but to Rome and
the West.

His whole position, as implied in the Epistles to the
Colossians and the Philippians, is one of much greater
freedom than was permitted by the more severe form
of imprisonment at Cæsarea. There he was chained
by the wrist (Acts xxvi. 29), and was only allowed to
receive his relations or friends. Under these circumstances, instead of asking the Churches to pray for
him that he might be able faithfully to preach the

Gospel, as he does in writing to the Colossians, he would have been more likely to ask them to seek first that he might be set at liberty. In Rome, he was simply guarded by a soldier, and free access was allowed to all who liked to visit him. Thus he was able to discuss for a whole day with the elders of the Jewish synagogue. Now this position of Paul, which is described towards the close of the Book of Acts, corresponds exactly with that which we gather from the Epistles to the Colossians and to the Philippians. It could only be in the world's capital that Paul could write thus: "The word of the truth of the gospel which is come unto you, even as it is also in all the world, bearing fruit and increasing as it doth in you also" (i. 6). We know from these Epistles that Paul's apartment in Rome was what his prison-cell in Cæsarea never could have been, the head-quarters of the army of evangelists who were going forth under his direction to the conquest of the Gentile world.

But to return to Epaphras. For what purpose did he come to Rome? Did he simply wish to testify to Paul the love and concern of the Churches of Phrygia for the Apostle whom they had never seen in the flesh, but whom they loved in the spirit? Undoubtedly this was part of his mission, and it brought comfort to the heart of Paul (i. 8; ii. 1). But there were more urgent reasons for his undertaking so great a journey. The Churches which Epaphras had founded were troubled at this time by a doctrine which shook the very foundations of the Apostle's teaching as they had received it through Epaphras; and if this new school were to prevail, it would not fail to affect deeply the religious and moral life awakened in these young Churches. In order to understand the greatness of the danger which had led Epaphras to seek counsel of the Apostle, we must call to mind the particular circumstances of the district in which these Churches were placed. On the one hand, Phrygia had been from the most remote antiquity the seat of the worship of Cybele, the goddess of nature, or "the Great Mother"; a worship of a very wild and excited character. On the other hand, Judaism had taken a strong hold of the people of these districts. Two centuries earlier, the King of Syria, Antiochus the Great (224-187), had caused two thousand Jewish families to remove from Babylon into this region, in order to secure the submission of the inhabitants, who were disposed to revolt (Jos., *Ant.*, xii. 3, § 4).*

It is easy to understand that the combination of these two elements must have peculiarly predisposed the people to the adoption of doctrines at once legal and mystical, Jewish and superstitious. These are the very features of the doctrine against which Paul is arguing in the Epistle to the Colossians. On the one hand it presents a certain analogy with the Pharisaic Judæo-Christianity which, seven years before, had threatened to undermine the Churches of Galatia. It perpetuates the Jewish feasts, the observance of the

*Josephus. *Complete Works of Josephus.* Kregel Publications. 1962.

new moons and Sabbaths, and of certain rules relating
to food (ii. 16), possibly also of circumcision (ii. 11),
as obligatory on all believers. But at the same time
it is evident that, since the contests in Galatia and at
Antioch, Judaising heresy had assumed quite a new
character. We have already seen, in studying the
Epistles to the Corinthians, that in attempting to reach
the Greeks, Judæo-Christianity had stooped to unworthy
and carnal allurements, and had attempted to clothe
itself in a speculative garb, appealing especially to the
craving for knowledge, and attempting to introduce a
new Christology (2 Cor. xi. 4-6; 1 Cor. iii. 17-20).
This tendency we note also in the Epistle to the
Colossians. Paul calls the new teaching "philosophy
and vain deceit, after the tradition of men, after the
rudiments of the world and not after Christ." It is an
attempt to solve the problem of human life in a new
way, leaving Christ out of the solution.

From this it would appear that the Judaising teachers
who had come to the Church of Phrygia, while remaining attached to the observances of Mosaism, attempted
at the same time to give them a higher bearing and to
amalgamate them with a philosophic system. How
was this ? We can perhaps gather the answer from
the words of the Apostle, in which he accuses them of
taking pleasure in a voluntary humility and worshipping
of angels, intruding into things not intended for their
knowledge, vainly puffed up as they were by their
fleshly mind (ii. 18). This verse, which some of the

latest critics (Holzmann and von Soden) try to prove
is an interpolation, is really the key to the whole
Epistle. It is objected that there is no connection
between the worship of angels and the legal side of
the system. But from a Jewish point of view the
connexion is obvious. Did not Stephen exclaim before
the Sanhedrim, " Ye who received the law as it was
ordained by angels and kept it not!" (Acts vii. 53).
And Paul himself in writing to the Galatians, says,
" The law was ordained through angels " (Gal. iii. 20).
To revere the institutions of Moses was then to revere
the angels by whom they had been delivered to the
people, and consequently to assure the favour of those
higher powers, to place themselves under their pro-
tection, to render themselves worthy of their heavenly
communications and of the more sublime revelations
of which they were the mediators. By means of the
angels, Christians were to be initiated into that Divine
world with the mysteries of which angels were familiar,
and were to receive strength adequate to raise them
to the standard of perfect holiness. By not rendering
to the angels the worship due to them, and not observing
their ordinances, Christians might be deprived of their
assistance and have to remain in the position of Gentiles
—a position very inferior to that to which Israel had
been raised by means of the law.

There is another consideration of still greater weight.
In the opinion of the Jews, the Gentiles were under
the sway of diabolic powers, the angels of darkness,

to whom the idolatrous worship was offered. How could they be delivered from the dominion of these maleficent spirits? There could be but one way of escape; to place themselves under the leading of the angels of light, who alone could vanquish these unseen enemies of man. But for this end these heavenly spirits must be propitiated by scrupulous obedience to their precepts and by the worship which was their due.

Thus these two apparently diverse tendencies in the doctrine of the Judaising teachers at Colosse are easily reconciled; and the attempt so often repeated, to prove that we have in this Epistle two heterogeneous elements, falls to the ground. The argument has been, that the part of this epistle really written by St. Paul deals with a legalising Judæo-Christianity, differing somewhat from that of Galatia, but resting on the same basis. The other part of the epistle is said to be from the pen of a writer of the second century, and merely an interpolation. It is intended to refute the gnostic dualism of later times. The close relation which Judaism established between the giving of the law and the ministry of angels—a relation recognised by Paul himself (Gal. iv. 1-3)—forms the bond (disregarded by these scholars) between the legal and speculative elements of this new form of Judæo-Christian heresy.[1]

---

[1] Holzmann considers that out of the 95 verses in the Epistle to the Colossians, only 48 belong to the original letter sent by Paul. Von Soden thinks that only nine and a half verses (i. 15-20; ii. 10, 15, 18 *b*) are interpolated.

It will naturally be asked whether, as Pharisaism was unquestionably the basis of the old Judæo-Christianity antagonistic to Paul, so there was also a latent tendency in Judaism to produce this new form under which Judæo-Christianity manifested itself at Colosse? The question suggests itself the more forcibly, because certain elements in the doctrine of the new teachers at Colosse do not seem to arise naturally out of the law of Moses taken by itself. Thus Paul speaks of scruples in relation to certain drinks (ii. 16). Now there is no prohibition of this kind in the law, except the prohibition to priests to drink wine when about to perform their duties. We must suppose then that these Judæo-Christians at Colosse, like those in Rome (Rom. xiv.), were under other influences than those of the law of Moses alone. And it is interesting to inquire whether at this period we shall discover in Judaism ascetic tendencies, like those which, as we have just shown, prevailed among the Judæo-Christians at Colosse.

The most remarkable development of Judaism in this direction is Essenism. The sect of the Essenes took its rise probably in the middle of the second century before the Christian era. At the time of Paul it had become a powerful body. It would be erroneous to conclude, from the passage of Pliny referring to this sect, that it was confined to the solitudes around the Dead Sea. The Essenes, who, as Philo tells us, numbered at that time 4,000, were spread all over Palestine, and were found in large numbers in the cities and villages of Judæa. They must have been very numerous in Jerusalem, for Josephus speaks of a gate which was called "the Gate of the Essenes," probably because it adjoined the house belonging to the order.

The Essenes formed in fact a caste apart. They lived together and had all things in common. The products of each one's labour belonged to the order, which provided for his wants. There were three principal degrees among the Essenes, entered by successive stages of initiation. They bathed many times a day, particularly before meals, and after contact with any object regarded as impure, or even when a member of a higher degree had been touched by one of the lower. The food was prepared by superiors designated for the work, and partook of the character of an offering to God. The Essenes might not eat of viands not prepared in this way and sanctified by prayer. It is not certain whether they abstained altogether from wine and meat,—some writers hold the one view and some the other. That which *is* certain is that they held in abhorrence sacrifices of blood such as men offered in the Temple at Jerusalem. Hence they were excommunicated. But they maintained, nevertheless, the bond of union with their nation and with its worship, and sent every year offerings to the Temple. They abstained, as a rule, from marriage, though there were a few married men among them. They took no oath except the vow by which they entered the order. By this they were bound under the most terrible sanctions to fulfil all their duties towards God and their fellow-men, not to reveal to the uninitiated the things which they had been taught, and particularly to keep silence about their books and the names of the angels. They were very scrupulous in the observance of the Sabbath, and revered the name of Moses as the most sacred after that of God. Any one who spoke evil of Moses was to be punished with death. Like officiating priests, they were generally clothed in white linen. Just as the Pharisee was a development of literalised Judaism, so we may say that the Essene was the quintessence of Pharisaism, but with an added element of mysticism which seems to indicate some other influence at work than that of Judaism. The morning invocation addressed by the Essenes to the sun, their numerous lustrations, and the large development given by them to the doctrine of angels might suggest that they had come under Parsee influence. The rejection of sacrifices of blood is in harmony with the Hindoo spirit. The wearing of white garments, and the repudiation of marriage and of oaths, are features of the school of Pythagoras. It is difficult to decide between these various influences, which may indeed all have made themselves felt at this time on the life of the Jewish nation.

Somewhat later other off-shoots of Judaism give similar indications. Thus the doctrine of Cerinthus,

who lived in the apostolic age, was a blending of
Oriental theosophy and Jewish legalism. Some say he
attributed to angels the creation of the world. In any
case, he regarded Jesus as the son of Joseph, a pious
Jew, with whom the Divine Christ was momentarily
united. Cerinthus taught the permanent obligation
upon Christians of the Jewish ceremonial law.

Still later, at the commencement of the second
century, we note the appearance of a strange sect
bearing clearly the impress of its Oriental origin, but
arising out of the midst of Judæo-Christianity. Its
leader, Elxaï (God hidden), brought from Persia a new
doctrine contained in a book which had fallen from
heaven. Christ Himself had appeared to Elxaï as
a gigantic angel, accompanied by the Holy Spirit, His
sister. This Christ is, according to Elxaï, a creature.
He becomes incarnate again and again. Men are
united to Him by baptism, calling to witness the seven
elements (ἐπὶ τῇ τῶν στοιχείων ὁμολογίᾳ), namely,
heaven, water, the holy spirits, the angels of prayer,
oil, salt, and earth. There are auspicious and ill-fated
days; good angels preside over the one and bad angels
over the other. The Sabbath and the third day of the
week are to be observed, and nothing must be begun
on the days ruled over by the evil angels. The
Elkesaïtes used incantations by means of chanted
formulas (ἐπῳδαί), also invocations to demons (δαιμονίων
ἐπικλήσεις). They had a profound contempt for the
Apostle Paul.

The appearance of this sect at the beginning of the
second century reveals, like those of earlier date, and
others which we might mention, the existence of tendencies at once legalising and mystical in the midst of
the Judæo-Christianity even of the first century. Consequently we cannot wonder at the intrusion into Asia
Minor of a doctrine such as that described in the
Apostle's polemics as we have sketched them.

Let us now follow the thread of the Epistle itself, and
see how the Apostle fights the old enemy under the
new mask. He has now to contend with legalism not
as a meritorious ground of salvation, but as an ascetic
means for attaining a state of sanctification and higher
illumination. That which would strike the Apostle
most painfully in this new doctrine was the absence of
Him who should be all in all—of Jesus Christ, who in
the Apostle's eyes was Himself *Salvation*. By their
doctrine of the mediation of angels, the new teachers at
Colosse set aside Jesus the one Mediator. As the
Apostle says, they did not hold *the Head*, the vital
principle of the whole body (ii. 19). We can understand how, in this Epistle, he directs all his attention to
this central point—Christ ; what He is, what He has
done, what we have in Him. Christ being once reinstated in His true place, the false doctrine will naturally
fall to the ground.

Hence it is that after giving thanks for the work
done by Epaphras at Colosse (i. 1-8), and referring to

the intercessory prayer which he is constantly offering
to God for his converts, that the work may be carried
on unto perfection by Him who had translated them
out of the power of darkness into the kingdom of the
Son of His love (9-14), Paul passes on at once to his
main subject—the person and work of Christ; the
supreme dignity of the one, the boundless extent of the
other. This passage (15-23) opens the first, or what
might be called the didactic part of the Epistle, which
goes on to the end of chapter i.

Christ, regarded in His relation to God, is He in
whom God reveals Himself, as the soul of a man comes
out in his face. Christ, regarded in His relation to the
world, was before all things, for He was the Son
begotten not created. And not only was He before all
things, but He was the *Author* of all things. "For by
Him were all things created that are in heaven and
that are in earth, visible and invisible, whether they be
thrones or dominions or principalities or powers. All
things were created by Him and for Him, and He is
before all things, and by Him all things consist"
(15-17).

That which He is to the universe He is, in a special
sense, to the Church, with which He stands in a still
more intimate relation. It is by His death and resurrection that the Church has been called into being, and
from the bosom of His glory He imparts to it His
glorious life, as the head gives life and leading to the
body (18, 19).

And He thus in all things, material and spiritual, has the pre-eminence, because it pleased the Father that in Him should all the fulness of created things dwell and be consummated. God has made all things by Him, because He would that all things should be for Him. This leads Paul to set forth the work of Christ, by which this bringing together of all things in Him is made possible. He speaks here of the reconciliation not only of things on earth, but of things in heaven, by the blood of the cross. Does he mean then to teach that Christ died for the reconciliation of the fallen angels also, or for the justification of angels not fallen but imperfect in the eyes of the Holy, Holy, Holy God ?

Paul does not add here τῷ Θεῷ, *with God*, as he does in 2 Cor. v. 18-20, but says only εἰς αὐτόν, with or in relation to Him. The thought thus expressed may therefore be understood without necessarily going beyond the sphere whether of Biblical teaching in general or that of the Apostle in particular. The angels, as we have seen, were the Divine mediators in the giving of the law. How then could they have beheld without deep sorrow the countless transgressions both of Israel and of mankind at large ? How could they have acquiesced in a general amnesty which would set at nought the Divine threatenings unless it were accompanied by a solemn tribute paid to the holy law of God by the shedding of atoning blood ? As it is the blood of the Son of God which makes it possible

for a holy God to pardon, so it is the blood also which
reconciles the holy angels both to a pardoning God and
to pardoned sinners, and brings them into harmony
with the Divine plan of mercy.   Thus the cross brings
together in one all these divergent wills in heaven and
on earth, and inaugurates the return to the final unity
which is God's design for the universe.   By it the first
and the second creation are blended in one and the
same work (21-23).   Thus those orders of angelic
beings whom the teachers in Colosse prided themselves
on knowing, whom they perhaps, like Cerinthus,
regarded as the creators of the universe, to whom they
assigned the part of mediators between God and man,
(thus derogating from the sole mediatorial prerogative
of Christ), were, in Paul's argument, reduced to their
true position as His creatures, existing only for Him,
reconciled to men through His atoning death, and thus
brought into harmony with the purposes of God.
How significant this reversal of the parts !

This is the groundwork of the whole Epistle.   To it
the Apostle adds two very important though subordinate
thoughts.   First, that the Colossians and the Gentile
Christians in general have their own place in the great
whole of a world made new by the cross, and that this
place will be perpetuated to them if they continue in
the faith which has brought them into it (21-23).
Second, that it is by the ministry of Paul who now
writes to them, that the portion of this glorious plan
which concerns the Gentiles at large and them in

particular is to be wrought out. To the sufferings by which Christ accomplished their salvation, it is given to him to add, as a complement, those which at the time of his writing and throughout his whole life he is enduring, in order that he may carry this blessed message to the ends of the earth, and may bring the Church, the body of Christ, to the measure of His perfect stature (24-29). In the words "if ye continue in the faith grounded and stedfast," we have an indication of the danger that threatened the Colossian Church. This apprehension takes still more definite shape from the commencement of chap. ii., and forms the natural transition to the second or polemical part of the epistle.

Paul has just reminded the Colossians of what Christ is and what He has done. It only remains for them to apprehend what they possess in Him and in His work, that they may see the futility of the things which some are urging them to add to this great and perfect salvation.

The Apostle begins by expressing his concern for them, for though he has never seen them, he is nevertheless their apostle. He has heard that a doctrine is being preached to them which is called philosophy, but which is in reality only vain deceit; for it is based upon the traditions of men, and points to outward observances as of saving efficacy, instead of to the work and teaching of Christ (ii. 1-8).

These outward observances Paul calls by a name

which we shall meet with again in the second century, in the doctrine of the Elkesaïtes. He speaks of them as the rudiments or elements of the world. This term he had already used (Gal. iii. 9) with the epithets "poor and beggarly," and the following verse, in which Paul speaks of the Jewish feasts, of the observance of "days and months and seasons and years," shows to what he was referring in the word *elements*. He means that these were outward and earthly things upon which these teachers were trying to build up the religious life. The meaning is obviously the same in the Epistle to the Colossians. In Col. ii. 16 he refers to feast days, such as new moons and Sabbath days. Then in ver. 20 he again uses the same expression, "*rudiments*," applying it to the minute regulations of the false doctors: "Touch not, taste not, handle not." This leaves no doubt as to the thought that was in his mind in ver. 8. The philosophy against which he would put the Colossians on their guard is false in two aspects. First, in its origin. It does not confine itself to re-introducing the ordinances of Moses; but enforces also the arbitrary and purely human prescriptions which had been added by the rabbis, and of which Jesus speaks in almost the same terms as the Apostle: "Ye have made void the word of God because of your traditions. Well did Esaias prophesy of you, saying, This people honoureth Me with their lips, but their heart is far from Me. But in vain do they worship Me, teaching as their doctrines the precepts of men" (Matt.

xv. 6-9). Then this philosophy is false as to its
substance. It connects salvation with external rites
of a material nature, without relation to the moral life
of man. Not so with the true gospel, the wisdom of
which is "after Christ." This Paul shows when he
sets forth all the fulness of that salvation which is
given us in the person and by the work of Christ,
described in chap. i. (ii. 9-15). All the *fulness* of life
and of Divine perfection dwells in Christ under a bodily
form ; if then we are united to Him we have all fulness
in Him, and have no need to seek anything from those
principalities and powers, of whom He is Himself the
Head (vv. 9, 10). The consecration which the Jew
received through the circumcision of the flesh, the
Colossians received in a more excellent way, through
baptism, which by uniting them to the death and resurrection of Christ, made them die inwardly to sin
and live again in Him with a new life (ii. 11-13).
What folly to wish after that to bring them back to
circumcision ! Who would circumcise a man who had
died and risen again ? There are three characteristics
of this new life possessed in Christ—the forgiveness of
sins, which the old sacrifices could never procure ;
freedom from the threatenings of the law—the hand-
writing which God has Himself annulled, nailing it to
the cross of Christ ; lastly, deliverance from the power
of the evil spirits which ruled the pagan world, but
which were despoiled by Christ of their power and
glory, He triumphing openly over them in His cross

(ii. 13-15). The first of these verses shows the reason
for the abolition of ceremonial worship ; the second
shows the uselessness, as far as the believer is concerned, of all legal institutions ; the third is intended
to free the believer from all superstitious fear of the
maleficent power of the angels of darkness. As he has
nothing to seek from the good angels, so he has
nothing to dread from the bad. Paul now contrasts
this description of the glorious standing of believers in
Christ with the method of the spiritual life set before
the Colossians by their new teachers.

To these men, pardoned, enfranchised, endued with
a new life, divinely kept, are now presented, as saving
ordinances, certain sumptuary regulations and the
observance of sacred days—things which had some
sort of value before the coming of Christ, but which
are empty and meaningless since His manifestation
and the living union of believers with Him (ii. 16, 17).
The new teachers enjoin the worshipping of angels ;
they dazzle the Christians with the suggestion of new
revelations to be obtained through these celestial
spirits. They pretend to have access to a higher
world by visions which are only the effect of carnal
excitement (18) ; and they do not cherish the union
with the glorified Christ, that Head of the body who
alone imparts a power of vital growth to all the
members (19). But, says Paul, *you* who have been
raised together with Christ, are no longer under the
dominion of material elements. Your spiritual life no

longer depends on the things you touch, taste, and handle. These three prohibitions laid upon them : " Handle not, nor taste, nor touch," apply probably, the first to marriage, the second to the use of certain foods, the third to contact with material objects. We find various examples of such prohibitions among the Essenes. But all these petty regulations which deal only with the perishable element of our nature are after all but a tribute, such as ill becomes the believer, paid to the powers of the flesh (22, 23). Being once risen with Christ you have but one thing to do, to live as men raised from the death of sin, seeking only those things which are above in that higher world in which you already live with Christ, while awaiting your own manifestation with Him in glory (iii. 1–4).

Hence, instead of enforcing these purely outward observances which are of no avail, the Apostle urges the Colossian Christians to mortify all sinful inclinations. Instead of an imaginary rapture with the angels, he urges them to share the risen life of Jesus by the holy aspirations of a heart at one with Him. This leads him on to the third and practical part of the Epistle (iii. 5–iv. 1).

However real is this death unto sin and union with the glorified Saviour wrought in the Christian soul, it is but a beginning, and the task of the faithful through the rest of their earthly life is to labour for the perfecting of this work, both by putting off more and more the evil tendencies of the old corrupt heart (5–9) and by putting on the new nature which makes them all one in Christ (10–14).

This is the twofold task of the individual Christian. But the Colossians have also a duty as a Church. They are to be at peace one with another, and to promote each other's edification and joy by psalms and hymns and spiritual songs (15, 16). The bondage of fear under which their heretical teachers would have placed them, certainly could not have conduced to this end.

Lastly, from the life of the individual and of the Church, Paul passes to *family* life. This is the first time we have found him touching on this subject. In the Epistle to the Romans he had spoken of the duties of the Christian as a member of the State (Rom. xiii.); doubtless because he was addressing himself to the Christian community which inhabited the political capital of the world. In the Epistle to the Colossians, he sets forth the duties of family life, probably because the new teachers with their false spiritualism had spoken doubtfully of the sacredness of marriage. He begins by laying down in ver. 17 a general principle which includes all he has to say. " Do all in the name of the Lord Jesus." He then proceeds to apply this principle to the various relations which constitute family life, and first of all to the central relation—that of husband and wife (18, 19). Next to the inner circle of parents and children, and lastly to the outer circle ot the home life, the relation of masters and servants (iii.

22–iv. 1). This concludes the Epistle. All that remains is the sending of special messages of remembrance and greeting (iv. 2–18).

He enjoins the Colossians to be stedfast in prayer, and specially to intercede for him. He urges them to be wise and considerate in their dealings with the unconverted around them (2–6). He tells them that Tychicus his beloved fellow-labourer is shortly about to visit them, and that Onesimus will come with him. He calls Onesimus his "faithful and beloved brother," being anxious to assure a welcome for him. He does not say much of himself or of how he is placed, because all this these two messengers will tell them by word of mouth (7–9). Then follow messages from his fellow-labourers, and first from three who were Jews by birth and the only ones among his countrymen who had remained faithful—Aristarchus, who had accompanied him from Cæsarea to Rome ; Mark, who had come thither to join him ; and Jesus Justus. Mark was cousin to Barnabas, who out of love to this kinsman had separated from Paul. Mark was now on the point of leaving again for Asia Minor. Paul next mentions three evangelists of Gentile origin— Epaphras, the pastor of the Colossians, who never ceases to pray for them and for the Christians at Laodicea and Hierapolis ; Luke the beloved physician ; and Demas, to whose name he joins no honourable epithet, as if he already had a presentiment that he would be unfaithful (see 2 Tim. iv. 10 ; ver. 10–14).

Three commissions follow—a salutation to the Church at Laodicea, and to Nymphas in whose house it met ; then a direction to forward this letter to Laodicea and to receive from thence the letter written by the Apostle to that Church ; lastly a charge to Archippus, who was probably the son of Philemon and was taking the place of Epaphras during his absence.

The Apostle concludes with his own salutation, reminding them touchingly of his captivity, and desiring that grace may be with them all.

There is perfect logical unity in this Epistle. As the Epistle to the Galatians groups itself entirely around the idea of Christian liberty, in relation to the law, so the central idea of the Epistle to the Colossians is the perfect sufficiency of Christ for our salvation. As the Epistle to the Galatians contains, first an apology in which Paul proves the complete independence of his mission and of his teaching (the apostolate of liberty) ; then a didactic portion in which he shows the agreement of his doctrine with the Old Testament (the doctrine of liberty) ; and lastly a practical part which gives the picture of the life of the believers under the holy discipline of love (the life in the liberty) ; so the Epistle to the Colossians divides itself also into three parts, the first didactic, in which Paul sets forth the divinity of Christ and the greatness of His work ; the second polemical, in which he shows the Colossians all the fulness of the salvation which is theirs in Christ, and as a consequence the futility of the miserable

makeshifts for sanctification and higher illumination
which have been offered them ; lastly, a practical part,
in which he draws the picture of human life, especially
family life, renewed and sanctified by the life of Christ.
The objections to the general authenticity of this Epistle
are now altogether abandoned even by those who think
that it has been more or less interpolated. If the
Apostle's vocabulary differs considerably from that of
the previous epistles, this is not to be wondered at
where there was a mind so creative as that of Paul ;
and it is indeed accounted for by the entirely new
nature of the heresy he had to combat. He had to
deal with new dogmas—the mediation of angels and
their supposed hierarchy ; legal ordinances regarded
as an ascetic method by which the faithful might be
prepared to receive new revelations to supplement
those given by Christ. In dealing with such errors
the Apostle was constrained to employ a new vocabulary
largely derived from that of his adversaries. Any
forger attempting to pass off this Epistle as written by
St. Paul, would have scattered it thickly with expressions taken from his known epistles, such as " works,'
"justification," etc., which never occur in this letter.
Do we not feel, moreover, as we read the personal
references at the close of the epistle, which are so free
from any attempt at legendary amplification, that they
would have no meaning in an apocryphal writing,
composed long after the death of the Apostle ? In fine,
it would be hard for any writer to counterfeit so

happily an epistle of St. Paul's, and to reproduce the
vigour of thought and terseness of style which make
his writings so powerful.

All that the critics of to-day venture to do then
is to impeach the integrity of this Scripture. They
grant that the Apostle really wrote a letter to the
Colossians, and that this authentic epistle is contained
in the canon of Scripture. But they say that some interpolator of the second century got hold of the epistle
and introduced into it arguments against the gnostics
of his day, so as to lend to his polemics the authority
of St. Paul. They dispute, for example, the authenticity of the passage in chap. i. on the divinity of
Christ; of the passages relating to the invocation of
angels, etc. But it would be difficult to explain how an
interpolator could have so skilfully woven his thoughts
into the tissue of those of St. Paul, that the hiatus
is nowhere to be discovered. Beside, the apostolic
writings were not at the mercy of any chance writer.
They were deposited with the archives of the Churches
to which they were addressed, and we fail to conceive
how the interpolator could have disguised his fraud.
If he had made his interpolations on the original manu-
script, they would have been obvious to the first reader.
If he had substituted a new and enlarged MS. for the
old simpler one, the Church which read and re-read
the writings of the Apostle, and passed them on to
any Churches which asked for them (Col. iv. 16), would
have quickly discovered it. Again we ask, What is it

that the critics propose to omit? The grand passage on the divinity of Christ in chap. i.? But this is to the rest of the Epistle what the head is to the body. If we remove that we leave but a torso. Or are vv. 10, 15, 18 of the second chapter to be eliminated? We have seen what a necessary part they are of the whole argument of the epistle, and how closely connected with its fundamental thought.

At the basis of these criticisms, whether of the whole letter or of some of its more striking passages, there lies, I admit, one very just observation. The world in which the thought of the Apostle is moving, is no longer the same as that to which he was addressing himself in the previous epistles. In them he dealt chiefly with the method of justification, the way in which sinful man might attain to reconciliation with God. Now the subject is altogether different. Paul is addressing himself to Christians already rooted and grounded in Christ (i. 23), those who have died and risen again with Him (ii. 20, 21), and he unfolds before their view the treasures of wisdom and knowledge which are in Christ (ii. 3). He traces His Divine personality to its source. He shows the vast future consequences of His work, which after binding together Jews and Gentiles upon earth, is one day to bind together men and angels under the same headship. This universal operation of the work of Christ is connected with the supreme dignity of His person. He is the Alpha because He is to be the Omega. The foundation of the Church by the Risen Saviour is the commencement of a spiritual work by means of which the history of the universe is to be consummated. Christ and the Church; this is the key to the Divine plan in the government of the universe.

It is sometimes asked, were these sublime ideas, of which we get only glimpses in the earlier epistles, new discoveries to the mind of the Apostle ? Assuredly not. The divinity of Christ was from the very first an integral element of his teaching. It was as the Son of God that Christ had been revealed to him on the way to Damascus (Gal. i. 16). To this Christ, Paul, in his first Epistle to the Corinthians, had attributed the creation of all things, and the conduct of Israel through the wilderness. Of this Christ he had said in his second Epistle to the same Church, that He had emptied Himself of His Divine riches to enter into human poverty (2 Cor. viii. 9). Paul understood the Old Testament too well not to know that the appearance of the Christ was looked for by the prophets as the supreme manifestation of the *Angel of the Face*, the Adonai Himself (Mal. iii. 1).

But he was led to expand these truths by the new ascetic and mystical, we might almost say gnostic form which Judæo-Christianity was assuming at this time in Asia Minor. This treasury of sublime thoughts as to the relation sustained by Christ, first to the Church and then to the universe at large, was so present with him when he wrote his earlier letters that he distinctly alludes to it in the first Epistle to the Corinthians. What else can be the meaning of the declaration (ii. 16), " We speak wisdom among them that are perfect " ? Paul means to say that when he finds himself with believers who are strong and settled in the Christian life, he is not afraid to unfold before their eyes the higher wisdom contained in the appearing and work of Christ.

Such an occasion had arisen when he was called to write to these Churches in Phrygia, which false teachers were trying to bewilder with the glamour of a wisdom higher than that revealed in Christ. It is interesting to observe how St. Paul, as he rises to these heights in his Epistles to the Colossians and the Ephesians, stands on the same glorious summit as the Apostle John, and joins in the same anthem with him, though in other words. For after all, has not the figure of the head and the body precisely the same significance as that of the vine and the branches ? As he stands on this lofty height, St. Paul reaches up to, but does not go beyond, that which is most sublime in the teaching of Christ.

Would it be difficult to find among Christians of to-day, men who are eager for revelations of things behind the veil, higher than those which Christ has been pleased to give us, and who seek for them by methods which Paul would have described as the rudiments of the world ? Would it not be easy to find many Christians who make their salvation hinge on things which affect only the perishable part of our being, and interpose between themselves and heaven other mediators beside the One in whom dwells all the fulness of the Godhead ?

The letter to the Colossians was sent from Rome. Would it not be well to send it back to its cradle ?

7

THE MESSAGE TO THE GENTILE CHURCHES

(Ephesians)

JUST as there are double stars, consisting of two suns revolving round and enlightening each the other ; just as in the teaching of Jesus there are pairs of parables, in which the same truth is represented under two aspects, the one supplementing the other—for example, the parables of the leaven and the grain of mustard seed, of the treasure hid in a field and the pearl of great price, of the lost sheep and the lost piece of silver ; so in the apostolic correspondence there are pairs of epistles, so to speak, in which two aspects or the same subject are treated separately, in such a way as to set the whole question in a clear light.

Such is the relation between the Epistle to the Romans and that to the Galatians, as also between the two minor epistles of John ; and still more strikingly between the Epistle to the Colossians and that to the Ephesians.

Relationship of the Epistles

We have seen that when false doctrine was threatening to invade the Church of Colosse in Phrygia, the

Apostle set forth Jesus Christ the Son of God as Himself the Head of the Church, which is His body upon earth. In this way he sought to bring home to the Colossians the futility of the mediation of angels, and the uselessness of those Jewish ordinances under which some were trying to bring them into bondage. On this occasion the Apostle felt himself called to address another letter to several Gentile Churches in Asia Minor, of which the Church of Colosse was one. Paul had not himself founded these Churches, and had never visited them. For this very reason he felt all the more bound, as the Apostle of the Gentiles, to do something for these young Christian societies, which, planted in the midst of paganism, belonged to his apostolic domain.

This more general Epistle was intended at the same time to supplement that to the Colossians. In the earlier letter Christ was set forth as the Divine Head of the Church ; in this, Paul desired to show to these Gentile converts, that this new society into which they had been incorporated was as the earthly body of the heavenly Head. This was only repeating to the Church, under another form, the sublime truth which Jesus had taught His disciples under the figure of the vine and its branches. This letter is, if we mistake not, that which appears in our canon as the Epistle to the Ephesians.

It may seem strange that we should so describe a letter which we have already said was addressed to

Churches which, like the Church of Colosse, were situated in the interior of Asia Minor, many days' distance from the great metropolis of Ionia. Our reasons are as follows:

One cannot but be struck, in reading the letter commonly called the Epistle to the Ephesians, with the fact that in several passages the Apostle speaks to his readers as to Christians personally unknown to him. Thus in chap. i. 15 he says to them that he has " heard of the faith in the Lord Jesus which is among them, and which they show toward all the saints." And in chap. iii. 2 he expresses himself thus : " If so be ye have heard of the dispensation of the grace of God which was given me to youward " (that is, his apostleship to the Gentiles). In chap. iv. 21 he writes: " But ye did not so learn Christ ; if so be that ye heard Him, and were taught in Him, even as truth is in Jesus." Now Paul never could have written thus if he had been addressing the Church at Ephesus.

Another feature of this Epistle seems to make it highly improbable that it was intended for that Church ; namely, the absence of any personal greetings at its close. Can we suppose that Paul would not have mentioned the names of at least some of the members of this Church, with which he abode so long, if this letter was really intended for it ? To these two considerations there is a third to be added, which, from very early times, has struck attentive readers of this Epistle. In many ancient manuscripts the words "at Ephesus," in v. 1, are omitted after "the saints which are." This gave rise to a very extraordinary explanation. " *The saints which are*" was made to signify the saints who possess the true, celestial, eternal existence. But the words thus understood would be a philosophical expression such as we do not find anywhere else in Scripture. Unless we are prepared to admit that the words "at Ephesus" have been expunged for some unexplained reason, we must conclude from this omission that the name of those to whom it was sent was not mentioned in the original letter, and that the heading, "Epistle to the Ephesians," was added when the collection of St. Paul's Epistles was made in the Churches, and that it was based on a mistaken supposition. This we shall now proceed to show.

To whom did the Apostle really address this letter? and how can we account for the fact that their name was omitted in the superscription?

The first question is easily answered. There is so close and continuous a connexion between this Epistle and that to the Colossians, that they must have been written almost at the same time and addressed to readers who had much in common. This conclusion is confirmed by the singular expression, chap. vi. 21 : " But that ye also may know my affairs, how I do, Tychicus, the beloved brother and faithful minister in the Lord, shall make known to you all things." This expression, "that ye also," seems to prove, in the first place, that Paul was not addressing this letter to a

single Church, but to several, each of which was included in the "ye also"; and the idea is that they
should all, one after the other, receive from Tychicus
tidings of the Apostle. Colosse would certainly belong
to the group of Churches which Paul had in view;
for he uses a similar expression in Col. iv. 7: "All
my affairs shall Tychicus make known unto you, the
beloved brother and faithful minister and fellow-servant
in the Lord." Tychicus then was to visit in succession
all the Churches to whom this Epistle was addressed,
and to leave a copy of it with them, while giving them
at the same time *vivâ voce* tidings of the Apostle. We
should naturally look for this group of Churches, of
which Colosse was one, in the province of Phrygia.
Were such Churches actually found there? Assuredly.
In the Epistle to the Colossians (ii. 1), Paul says:
" For I would have you know how greatly I strive for
you, and for them at Laodicea, and for as many as
have not seen my face in the flesh." The Church of
Laodicea, and others, like that of Hierapolis (Col. iv.
13), which had been founded without the co-operation
of Paul, in this central district of Asia Minor, were the
objects of his peculiar concern. Is it surprising, that
while addressing to the Colossians a letter adapted to
their particular circumstances, he should have felt
anxious to send a second letter to these other Churches
to supply the lack of a personal visit?

This supposition is further corroborated by the
following fact. In the year 140, a young man of

distinction, Marcion, the son of a bishop of Pontus, in
Asia Minor, made a collection of the Epistles of St.
Paul, for the use of the Churches which he founded on
a basis opposed to the prevailing orthodoxy. We have
a list of the apostolic epistles which he admitted into
his canon. Among them was what we call the Epistle
to the Ephesians, but it appears as the Epistle to the
Laodiceans. It is not impossible indeed that Marcion
may have taken this name from the passage in the
Colossians (iv. 16), in which the Apostle charges that
Church to read the Epistle to the Church at Laodicea. But why should he take this to mean the
Epistle to the Ephesians ? Marcion must have had
some more definite reason for thus describing it. May
we not suppose that, in going from Pontus into the
west, and visiting on his journey the Churches of
Phrygia, he had found this Epistle in the Church of
Laodicea, as a letter addressed to that Church ? If so,
it is decisive that this Epistle was intended for one, or
more than one, of the Churches of Phrygia.

After this, it is easy to explain the omission of any
name in the superscription of the letter. All that we
have been saying suggests the following reply to the
question : When Tychicus left Rome for Asia Minor, he
had with him three letters, one to the Colossians, one
to Philemon, and this which we call the Epistle to the
Ephesians. This, as we have just shown, was to be
delivered to the Churches of Phrygia around Colosse,
all of which Tychicus was to visit. Now Tychicus

possessed probably only one copy of this letter. The
Apostle intended that he should have as many copies
made at Ephesus as he would require, in order that
each Church might have one addressed to itself. The
original letter remains in the archives of the Church of
Ephesus, just as Tychicus brought it, with no indication to whom it was addressed. In the copies the
blank was filled in according to the destination of each
letter. Marcion found at Laodicea that which bore the
name of that Church, and he therefore, in all good
faith, so catalogued it in his canon. But when subsequently the various Churches of Christendom were
desirous to possess it, they naturally sent to Ephesus,
the great seaport and chief city of that region, for
copies. Thus the Epistle came to be spoken of throughout Christendom as the Epistle to the Ephesians; and
the words "at Ephesus" were added to the superscription, though traces still remained of the original blank
left to be filled in. In fact, the words are omitted
in the two most ancient MSS. of the New Testament
now in our possession—the Vaticanus and the
Sinaiticus.

At the close of the Epistle to the Colossians, Paul
enjoins that Church to read the Epistle which was to be
sent to it from Laodicea, and to send on to that Church
its own Epistle. From all that goes before, it appears
evident that this letter which was to be sent to the
Colossians from Laodicea, was no other than our
Epistle to the Ephesians, which was the fitting supple-

ment to that which the Colossians themselves had
received, and which they were to forward to Laodicea.

The Scope of the Epistle

Let us now proceed to study the scope of this Epistle.
Chrysostom said, " That which the Apostle had nowhere else proclaimed, he reveals in this scripture."
This is true. In the First Epistle to the Corinthians,
Paul refers to a higher spiritual wisdom contained in
the Gospel; but he adds that he can only speak of it
among the perfect. Those whom he thus describes
were those who had come to the stature of full-grown
men in Christ, as he says again in Eph. iv. 13.
This wisdom was nothing else than the apprehension
of the Divine plan, and it is this which he sets forth
in the Epistle before us.

We have seen that the Epistles of St. Paul generally
begin with thanksgiving, the subject of which is the
work of God already accomplished in those to whom he
writes, and that this thanksgiving is followed by a
prayer in which the Apostle asks that the gracious
work may go on in their souls. After this, he passes
to the subject he proposes to treat. In the Epistle
before us he commences with thanksgiving and prayer;
but, if I may so speak, he never gets beyond this, and
all that he has to impart to his readers is included in
the outpouring of gratitude and desire, which runs
through the whole of the first three chapters. All that
follows from the beginning of chap. iv. is only the

practical application of this true apprehension of the
Divine work.

The thanksgiving turns on the treasury of heavenly
benedictions which God has opened to these Christians.
This Apostle traces the river of grace back to its source
in the eternal decree by which God has predestinated
believers to salvation and to adoption, in the person of
His well-beloved Son (i. 3-6).   Then he reminds them
of the cost at which this merciful design has been
fulfilled, "redemption through the blood of Christ" (v.
7) ; and through the revelation granted to the Church,
gives them a glimpse of the glorious consummation of
the Divine plan—the gathering together of all things,
both in earth and heaven, under the sovereignty of
Christ, the supreme Head of the universe (vv. 8-10).
After having thus glanced at the source, the means, and
the end, he goes on to show that this great plan is
already in process of fulfilment by the calling unto salvation, addressed by God first to the Jews, then to those
Gentiles who have believed and been sealed with the
Holy Spirit of promise (vv. 11-14).   This is the beginning of the gathering together of all things in Christ.
After thus descending from the heights of the Divine
intention to its application to his readers, the Apostle
proceeds to offer prayer on their behalf.   For after
their conversion there is much progress to be made.
Have they themselves grasped the extent of the change
which has been wrought and yet is to be wrought in
them ?   Have they sufficiently understood the grandeur

of the position to which their new faith entitles them ?
Have they considered the exceptional greatness of the
power which has been at work within them to effect
this change ?   It is upon this point the Apostle asks
that they may be enlightened (vv. 15-19).   It is essential for them to understand that that which has been
done and yet is to be done in them, is nothing less
than a transformation similar to that wrought by God
in the person of Christ Himself, when " He raised Him
from the dead, and made Him to sit at His own right
hand in the heavenly places."   From this glorious,
high throne, Christ is forming for Himself a body here
on earth, even the Church, filled with the fulness of
His life (vv. 19-23).   It is a similar work which God
accomplishes in believers, when, finding them "dead in
trespasses and sins," He "quickens them together with
(or in) Christ, and raises them up with Him" in such
sort that they live in Him in the heavenly places.
This is a fact already accomplished by grace on God's
part, by faith on theirs.   They are really saved ; and
that without any meritorious effort of their own, but by
the pure mercy of God, who places them henceforward
in a new relation to Himself, in which they may abound
in good works (ii. 1-10).

The Apostle now comes to the principal point on
which he wishes specially to insist with those to
whom he was writing.   Who were you, he says, you
whom God has thus dealt with, whom He has raised
like Christ Himself, from death to life, from the grave

to the throne ? Were you aforetime among His covenanted people ? Had you any part in the promises ? Nay, ye were " aliens from the commonwealth of Israel, and strangers from the covenants of promise, having no hope." Nevertheless God has brought even these Gentiles nigh to Himself by the blood of the cross, and has made them His people. He has broken down for them the wall of separation, the law, which rose between them and the Jews, and has thus brought together in one body these two races—till now so bitterly hostile—the Jews and the Gentiles. In thus reconciling both unto Himself and abolishing the enmity, He " has made in Himself of twain one new man, so making peace." He gives to both access to the throne of grace on equal terms (vv. 11-18). So far then from being any more strangers, they are " fellow-citizens with the saints and of the household of God," and are built up like living stones into the spiritual temple, founded upon Christ and His Apostles, to be a habitation of God through the Spirit (vv. 19-22).

Such is the greatness of the grace of which they are the subjects. St. Paul adds yet one more point which concerns him personally. In order to effect this incorporation of the Gentiles into the kingdom of God, there must be the creation of a new apostolate in addition to that of the twelve. This apostolate extraordinary is that with which Paul, the writer of this Epistle, and now a prisoner, has been invested. Unto him, who accounted himself "less than the least of all saints, was this grace given," that he "should preach among the Gentiles the unsearchable riches of Christ"; and that he should make all men see that the Gentiles were fellow-heirs, fellow-members of the body, and partakers of the "promise in Christ Jesus through the Gospel" (ii. 1-12).

He entreats them therefore not to be troubled by the tribulations he has to endure for so great a cause, which are a glory and not a shame to them. And here he again falls into prayer, and from his prison intercedes with God on their behalf. He gives them, so to speak, a glimpse into his prison cell, where on his knees and pleading for these Churches of Asia Minor which he has never seen, he asks for them that they may be strengthened with power through the Holy Ghost, that Christ may dwell in their hearts through faith, that they may be rooted and grounded in love, that they may have the inward illumination by which the gracious work of God will be revealed to them in all its height and length and breadth and depth, that thus they may be filled with the very fulness of God. What can he ask more? (vv. 13-21).

So far extends the utterance of praise and prayer, which, in the other Epistles, precedes the introduction of the main theme of the letter, but which in this instance includes it. The whole of the first part of the Epistle forms one hymn, in the midst of which the subject is intercalated. In the second part (iv.-vi.),

Paul only draws the practical conclusions from the premisses of grace which he has been magnifying. He makes the greatness of their Divine calling a plea for the holiness of life by which these Gentile Christians should walk worthy of it (iv. 1).

And first, as a Church, they are bound to maintain unity in the faith, each one consecrating to the good of the whole, the gifts he has received from the glorified Christ. It is for the growth and prosperity of His body, the Church, that the invisible Head has bestowed particularly the four essential gifts by which the body is to be raised to the perfect stature of its Head. He has thus given, first, apostles and prophets, whose work it is to lay the foundations of the Church; evangelists, by whose ministry it is to be extended; lastly, pastors and teachers, whose office it is to build up that which has been already begun. These heavenly gifts are the means by which the glorified Lord guards His body, the Church, from the seductive influence of false doctrines, and makes it grow up into the fulness of spiritual life (iv. 2-16).

From the life of the Church the Apostle passes to that of individuals. After reminding his readers of what they once were, he sums up all that he has to ask of them under two heads: he charges them to put off the old man, and to put on the new man created in the image of God (vv. 17-24). In order to give vividness to this idea, he proceeds to contrast each member of the new man with its corresponding member in the old. This brings out the eight following antitheses :

Falsehood—truth (v. 25).

Anger—forgiveness (vv. 26, 27).

Theft—doing good (v. 28).

Corrupt speech—words of edification (vv. 29, 30).

Bitterness—love (v. 31 ; v. 2).

Impurity—chasteness (vv. 3-14).

Unwisdom—wisdom (vv. 15-17).

Rioting and excess—spiritual joy (vv. 18-20).

We have observed these same contrasts in the Epistle to the Colossians (iii. 15-17) ; but there all the members of the old man were united as in one body, and contrasted with the new man as a whole.

Lastly, from the life of the individual the Apostle passes to the life of the family, which is to bear in all its relations the impress of Christian holiness. The parallel passage (Col. iii. 18 ; iv. 11) goes much less into detail.

The salient feature in this picture of a Christian family is mutual and voluntary subordination (v. 31). The Apostle refers first to the relation of husband and wife, which is compared to that between Christ and the Church (v. 22-23). This is the centre of the family life, and around it is formed first the inner circle of parents and children (vi. 1-4), and outside this the relation of masters and slaves (vv. 5-9).

But this ideal of Christian holiness in the life of the Church, of the individual, and the family cannot be realised without conflict; and this conflict is not simply that which arises from indwelling and encompassing sin. The Christian has also to fight against invisible foes, devilish suggestions, which cannot be withstood by his own unaided strength. Hence the Apostle invites his readers to put on the various pieces of armour which God has provided for their use. Three of these he describes under the figure of armour to be bound to the body: the girdle, the inward possession of the truth; the breastplate, the stedfast love of righteousness; the shoes, the determination to meet the enemy only with the gospel of peace. He next describes three dispositions under the figure of the movable parts of the armour: faith in the Divine promises, the shield; the glorious hope of salvation, the helmet; the use of Scripture to repel the assaults of the enemy, the sword. Lastly, he urges them to use that which alone can make any of these weapons effectual— prayer. This he asks on behalf of all the saints, and specially for himself, their Apostle, " an ambassador now in chains" (vv. 10-20).

Thus will the Church fulfil its task in the world, which is to overthrow the kingdom of Satan, and to set up on its ruins the kingdom of God.

The Apostle concludes, as usual, with some personal details. He tells his readers that Tychicus is coming, who will bring them tidings, and comfort their hearts. His wish is that peace and love may be established among them on the foundation of the faith. He desires that grace may be with all those who love the Lord Jesus Christ in uncorruptness (vv. 20-24).

The unity of this Epistle is self-evident. Its one theme throughout is the calling to salvation by grace, addressed as freely to the Gentiles as to the Jews. This theme is explained in the first part of the Epistle (i.-iii.), and enforced in the second (iv.-vi.). It is impossible therefore to regard this Scripture as merely a collation of earlier writings ; the piece of new garment would show some disparity with the old. But there is no such disparity. This observation suffices to set aside the opinion, learnedly maintained by Holzmann, that the Epistle to the Ephesians is only the expansion of a short letter addressed by Paul to the Colossians. He argues that some writer of a later date possessed himself of the shorter Epistle about the close of the first century, and manipulated it into what we call the Epistle to the Ephesians. A work thus composed of two heterogeneous elements could not fail to betray its origin by the want of that very directness, logical sequence, and unity which are so marked in this Epistle.

Critics of the same school point to the many parallel passages in the Epistle to the Ephesians and that to the Colossians, and ask how these can be explained, except on the hypothesis we have mentioned, supplemented by the following. The supposed writer of the Epistle o the Ephesians, after having amplified Paul's

original letter to the Colossians into what we call the
Epistle to the Ephesians, afterwards manipulated also
the original letter, using his own Epistle to the
Ephesians in the process. In this way the mystery of
the resemblance between the two canonical Epistles is
explained.

It seems to us that the problem can be solved in a
much simpler way. It is not impossible that two
completely independent and original writings may
coincide on certain points, both in substance and in
form of expression. If they treat of two very similar
subjects, if they are both by the same author, if both
were written at about the same time in his life, and
under the influence of the same feelings, it cannot be
wondered at if there are strong resemblances, both of
form and substance, between them. All these conditions are fulfilled in the two letters to which we are
referring. It is not difficult for us to picture to ourselves what was taking place at the very time when
they were written.

Epaphras has just come from Colosse to Rome.
There he finds Paul and Timothy. He tells them of
the new doctrine—a fusion of Essenism and Christianity
—which is threatening his Church. Paul meditates a
while. Then he says to Epaphras : "The best way to
cut the roots of this false speculation, with its ascetic
tendencies, is to remind the Church of Colosse of the
supreme dignity of Christ as the Head of the Church, in
the presence of which all the glory of the angels van-

ishes away.   Then to show them that the work of Christ
for the salvation of men is complete, that nothing is
to be added to it ; that baptism into His death is the
true circumcision, that the law is henceforth like a
cancelled charge, that the cross is the triumphant
chariot to which the powers of darkness are bound and
led captive.   All the legal ordinances and practices
enjoined by these false teachers will then be seen to
be vain.   The Colossians will understand that the true
death and the true resurrection are to be found, not in
their useless ascetic practices, but in sharing the death
and resurrection of Jesus ; and that all that remains is
to consummate these two spiritual facts by the daily
mortification of the old man, and the constant growth
of the new."

Epaphras gives his joyful assent to this plan of cam-
paign.   Then Paul asks what tidings there are from
the other Churches in the district.   Epaphras tells him
that they are walking in faith and in love (Eph. i. 15).
Though they are not exposed to the same dangers as
the Church at Colosse, it would be good for them nevertheless to be brought into direct personal relation with
the Apostle, and to receive from him some words of
encouragement.   It would be especially useful to urge
upon them the holiness which ought to characterise all
the family relations, upon which the heretics were
trying to bring discredit by a semblance of higher
spirituality in their mode of living.

Paul at once sets himself to his task, with the help

of Timothy (Col. i. 1). He first dictates to him the letter which has the most direct aim—the letter to the Colossians. Then, as Apostle to the Gentiles, Paul writes, in his own name only, the more general letter, with no polemical bearing, to the neighbouring Churches, to stir them up to adore the boundless grace bestowed upon them, and to urge them to a life becoming those so highly favoured.

Hence it comes to pass that the central idea of the Epistle to the Colossians is this: Christ the Head, from whom the body derives all its nourishment; while the central idea of what we call the Epistle to the Ephesians is the Church, the body which Christ fills with His Divine fulness, and raises to sit with Him in the heavenly places. Of these two thoughts, which supplement each other, the second was certainly suggested by the first. The first note struck woke the vibrations of the next; then followed a pæan of Divine harmonies. What could be more natural than that two strains thus suggested, should have many tones in common, though each set in a different key?

But it has been said again : The style of the Epistle to the Ephesians is wholly unlike that of the Epistle to the Colossians, or of Paul's other letters. Instead of the close, argumentative strain to which we are accustomed, we find here the full, swelling notes of a hymn. This rich and abundant phraseology has nothing in common with the broken, concise, uniformly sober style of the Apostle.

Yet there are passages in other Epistles, such as the close of the 8th and 11th chapters of the Epistle to the Romans, which show that Paul knew, not only how to teach and to discuss, but how to sing. He says himself to the Corinthians that he thanks God he can speak with tongues more than they all. Now the speaking with tongues was rather song than speech; it was the language of ecstasy. Can we be surprised if, in addressing Churches to whom he had no special teaching to impart or rebuke to administer, Paul should have for once risen to the exalted tones of a hymn, to magnify the grace which had wrought such great things for them?

The Epistle to the Ephesians is indeed a *tongue*, a tongue interpreted by Paul himself, and changed by this interpretation into a prophecy intelligible to all (1 Cor. xiv. 18, 19). The more I read and re-read this admirable letter, the more it strikes me that Paul himself tried to sum it all up in the words of the prayer (iii. 18), in which he asks God to give his readers to understand the dimensions of the Divine salvation,—that edifice of which God is Himself the Builder,—that they might be strong to apprehend with all saints what is its breadth and length and depth and height. The *length:* this he describes in chap. i., where he shows how the salvation of the world proceeds from an eternal decree, which was before all the ages, and the purport of which is to give the sovereignty to Christ in the dispensation of the fulness of the times. *The breadth:* he shows how the kingdom of God is gradually to embrace all intelligent beings: first, Jews and Gentiles—that is, all believers; finally men and angels, the sovereignty of Christ being thus co-exten-sive with the intelligent universe. *The depth:* he points to Christ going down into the dark abyss of death, to be set again on the highest throne by His resurrection and ascension. *The height:* he bids his readers look upon themselves as henceforth risen in Him, and seated with Him in the heavenly places.

Even Paul never wrote in grander strains than these, and to imagine that after his death another might have penned them in his name is to suppose that somewhere and somewhen there arose a second Paul, unknown to the Church, who has left no other trace of his existence but this single letter. It is far easier to believe that once in his life the Apostle of the Gentiles beheld in raptured contemplation, and magnified in this sublime language, the glorious work committed to him—the work of restoring the unity of the body of mankind, which from the time of Abraham had been divided into two great branches, thus herald-ing and preluding the time when all things in heaven and earth should be gathered together in Christ.

This is the keynote of the Epistle to the Ephesians, as of the Gospel of John. The two great Apostles thus meet on the topmost height of the Christian revelation.

8

THE FIRST ANTI-SLAVERY PETITION

(Philemon)

M. RENAN has called the Epistle to Philemon a *note*. It is indeed a letter in few words, but this very brevity only enhances the greatness of its contents.

There are other writings in the New Testament which might be described in the same way, as, for example, the second and third Epistles of John.

This group of short letters seems to have been regarded by the primitive Church as scarcely worthy of a place in the canon of sacred writings. Many Churches did not receive the second and third Epistles of John, and Jerome tells us that the Epistle to Philemon was rejected by many writers. From the absence of any approach to doctrinal teaching in this Epistle, they concluded that it was not by St. Paul, or that, if it was his, it did not belong to the canon, since it contained nothing by which the Church might be edified. This decision arose out of a narrow view of the canon, and the primitive Church, as a whole, did not ratify the verdict. Preserved at first as a precious relic in the family of Philemon, this apostolic document was subsequently placed among the archives of the Church at Colosse, in the house of one of its elders. We find the first mention of it, as forming part of the Pauline collection, in the writings of Marcion, son of the Bishop of Sinope in Pontus, who about the year 140 went to Rome from Asia Minor. Soon after this it finds a definite place in the Canon of Muratori, in the fragment found at Milan in the middle of the last century, which dates from about the year 170, and contains a list of the writings received and publicly read at that time in one of the Western Churches, either that of Italy, or more probably that of Africa.

We observe, moreover, that the Epistle to Philemon formed part of the Western canon, included in the old Latin translation, usually called *Itala*, and that in the Church most remote from this, the Church of Syria, it also found a place in the authorised translation of the Scriptures, the *Peshito*, in the latter part of the second century.

It is obvious then that the Church very early learned to appreciate the importance of this brief letter. It differs undoubtedly from the other writings of the Apostle, inasmuch as it refers to a purely personal and private matter. But this private matter came within the scope of the work which Christianity was to accomplish among men. And even if it had not been so, how full of interest for us must be the one opportunity supplied by this letter of studying the character of the Apostle Paul in this private relation which brings him into such close contact with our daily life.

We read in Col. iv. 7 that when the Apostle sent to Colosse the letter intended for the Church of that city, he entrusted it to one of his fellow-helpers named Tychicus, and that Tychicus was accompanied by another brother—Onesimus—whom Paul describes by the honourable terms, "faithful and beloved," and speaks of him as "one of us." It is impossible to doubt that this Onesimus is the subject of the Epistle to Philemon, and that it also was therefore sent to Colosse. If any doubt at all existed on this point, it would be set aside by the statement of Theodoret, a Syrian bishop of the fifth century, who says positively that "the house of Philemon at Colosse was still standing in his time."

In the city of Colosse, in the beautiful basin of the Lycus in Phrygia, there lived then at this time a rich citizen named Philemon. This man, as we gather from the Epistle, had been brought by Paul himself to the knowledge of Christ; and as Paul had never visited the Churches of the district in which Colosse was (Col. ii. 1), we must conclude that the rich Phrygian burgher had been converted by the Apostle at Ephesus during a visit which he paid to that capital. The wife of Philemon, we find from the second verse of the Epistle, was named Apphia, and as Paul mentions immediately afterwards in the same verse the name of Archippus, it is highly probable that this third personage was no other than their son.

Chrysostom indeed speaks of Archippus as a friend of the house, and Theodoret supposes him to have been a Christian teacher receiving the hospitality of Philemon ; but these suppositions are not so natural. To us it seems more probable that Archippus, as a young Christian and the son of Philemon, should have been entrusted (in the absence of Epaphras, who had gone to Rome to see Paul) with the care of the Church at Colosse, and that it was in order to make him feel the responsibility resting upon him, that in the Epistle to the Colossians Paul wrote these words : " Say to Archippus, Take heed to the ministry thou hast received in the Lord, that thou fulfil it."

The Greek and Roman names of this household show what a hold the authority of Rome and the culture of Greece had taken of the once barbarous nations of Asia Minor.

After saluting the three principal members of the family, Paul goes on to greet the Church gathered in the house. This does not mean simply the household of Philemon ; the name *Church* does not allow of such a restricted signification. On the other hand, the distributive preposition κατά equally excludes the whole body of Christians at Colosse. It refers rather to that portion of the Church which was accustomed to meet in the house of Philemon.

But it may be asked, if Paul was writing to Philemon on a private matter, why should he have addressed his letter to the section of the Church of which Philemon's house was the centre ? And out of this question arises another. Why should he have associated the name of Timothy with his own in such a letter ?

It must be admitted that the case of Onesimus interested in some degree the whole of the little community that was wont to meet in the house of Philemon. They had all heard of the wrongdoing and of the flight of his slave; and now that Onesimus had come back as a Christian, Paul wished to secure for him from them all the same brotherly welcome which he desired Philemon and his family to give him. Hence he wrote commending Onesimus to the confidence and love of them all. It was doubtless with the same end in view that he introduced the name of Timothy. Perhaps Timothy had himself visited Colosse. At any rate his recommendation would take away any semblance of favouritism or personal weakness on the part of Paul. That which Paul asked as the "prisoner of Jesus Christ," Timothy asked in the name of the Christian brotherhood ("Timothy our brother"), which united him to the Church at Colosse and formed a plea for the kindly reception of the new brother. We hear nothing further, however, of Timothy in the letter, and Paul speaks throughout in the first person singular, because it was really his affection for and personal interest in Onesimus which made him write.

What was the wrongdoing which had caused Onesimus
to run away ?   The Apostle refers to it in v. 18.   The
expressions used do not necessarily imply that the
fugitive slave had committed a theft.   They may be
explained on the supposition that he had·been guilty
of culpable negligence which had brought serious loss
on his master.   However this may be, it was the fear
of well-merited punishment which had caused Onesimus
to run away.   Where had he escaped to? and where had
he met Paul ?   Many commentators think that it was at
Cæsarea, in Palestine, where Paul was kept a prisoner
from the summer of 59 to the autumn of 61.   It is
urged in favour of this opinion that Cæsarea was less
distant from Colosse than Rome.   But a fugitive slave
does not seek to hide as near as possible to his master,
and it was far easier to get from Ephesus to Rome
than to Cæsarea.   The runaway would obviously be
much less likely to be found by his master in the
great capital of the world than in the little residence
of Cæsarea.   The other reasons urged in favour of
Cæsarea are still more feeble, and bordering on the
absurd, as the reader may judge by reading those
alleged by Meyer.   We have already observed, in our
paper on the Epistle to the Colossians, how much more
natural it seems to date that Epistle from Rome than
from Cæsarea, and this would suffice to decide the
question with regard to Philemon.   We find moreover
in v. 22 what seems to me an irrefutable argument to
show that this letter was written during the captivity

in Rome, that is, between the spring of the years 62 and 64.

Let us now turn to the Epistle itself.

A modern commentator has shrewdly observed that the Epistle to Philemon was a practical commentary on the injunction of the Apostle in the Epistle to the Colossians (iv. 6): " Let your speech be always with grace seasoned with salt." As we study the letter in detail, we shall be struck with the truth of this remark.

In the opening words vv. 1-3, the Apostle speaks of himself as the prisoner of Jesus Christ, delicately sub-stituting this description for the usual one, "servant of Jesus Christ." He is indeed at this time fulfilling his apostolic calling, not by active missionary labours, but by bonds and imprisonment.[1] This thought is well adapted to open the heart of Philemon to grant the request Paul has to make. He calls Philemon his " beloved and fellow worker," because when he became a Christian, he had placed his strength, his property, and his life at the service of the same work in which Paul himself was engaged—the salvation of men (v. 6). In v. 2 he gives Archippus a somewhat different title. He calls him his " fellow soldier," because, as Epaphras' deputy, he had to contend at Colosse for the truth, and specially to combat the false doctrine which threatened to invade the Church.

These opening words are followed, as usual in Paul's

---

[1] The expression is equivalent to "captive servant of Jesus Christ."

epistles, by thanksgiving for that which God has already wrought in the readers, followed by a prayer for the continuance and increase of the work (vv. 4-7). In v. 5 the Apostle says: "hearing of thy love," and not, as in the corresponding passage of the Epistle to the Ephesians (i. 15), "hearing of the faith in the Lord Jesus which is among you." The conversion of the readers of the Epistle to the Ephesians was an *accomplished fact*, of which the Apostle had been assured once for all, while the love of Philemon was a present and constant disposition of mind, the ever-new manifestations of which gladdened the heart of Paul. The Apostle adds, "and of the faith which thou hast toward the Lord Jesus, and toward all the saints." It is not without advertence that Paul brings out in this instance alone, the faith which a Christian should have, not only towards the Lord, but also toward those who belong to Him. He had spoken of faith in an analogous sense in 1 Cor. xiii. 7. "Love covereth all things, believeth all things." In speaking of the faith which Philemon has not only in the Lord, but also in the work of grace which the Lord can perform in the heart of the vilest of men, Paul is certainly thinking of the welcome he is about to ask for him who was formerly the unfaithful slave; which welcome must depend entirely on the confidence felt by Philemon in the work of grace wrought in Onesimus. A succession of disappointing experiences often produces among Christians, particularly among those who are older, a religious scepticism which paralyses love and kills enthusiasm. The good there is in the saints must be always, with their fellow Christians, a matter of faith. It was this faith toward all the saints which was about to be tested in the case of Philemon.

In thanking God for this gift bestowed on him, there is an implied exhortation that he should be faithful to it in the case in question. In v. 6 Paul gives the substance of his prayers for his friend Philemon.

"*The fellowship of thy faith*" must refer to the beneficent communications of which his faith is the source.[1] These become more and more abundant and effectual by the knowledge of the beauty and holiness of the work which God performs in Christians,[2] *to the glory of Jesus Christ*, through whom it is done. In desiring for Philemon a growing knowledge of the work of God in his brethren, Paul certainly wishes to prepare him to recognise with gladness and confidence the (to him) almost incredible change wrought in Onesimus. We see how free Paul's style is from anything that is stereotyped. Every word has its peculiar fitness. The language of the Apostle is the ever fresh garb of a truth ever new.

After this preamble the Apostle passes to the subject of his letter, the commendation of Onesimus to his master. But before making his request, as he does in v. 17, he carefully prepares the way (vv. 9-16).

---

[1] The active sense of the word κοινωνία is proved by Rom. xv. 26.

[2] The reading "*in us*" is certainly to be preferred to "*in you*."

In vv. 8, 9 he reminds Philemon who it is who makes this claim on him ; it is he who, as the apostle of Jesus Christ, might have all boldness to declare to Philemon the will of the Lord, and to enjoin him what was fitting to do under the circumstances. But he prefers to appeal to his heart, asking that of him as a proof of his love which he might have enjoined as a duty. His claims to the affection of Philemon are all comprised in that name *Paul*, which recalls to him so many memories, and in those two epithets which render its appeal still more forcible, "the aged," and "a prisoner." Paul's age at this time would be about fifty-five. His conversion took place in the year 36 or 37, and he could not have been then less than thirty years old. Had he been younger than this he would not have been competent to receive from the Sanhedrim the important commission entrusted to him. But the labours, the sufferings, the persecutions he had endured, had prematurely aged him, and he knew well how these two words, "aged" and "a prisoner," would touch the heart of Philemon.

After thus reminding Philemon who it is that asks, he goes on to speak of the one for whom he intercedes. He is careful not to name him at first, knowing what painful associations the name would call up. He begins by describing the close bond which his conversion had formed between himself as the spiritual father and this child whom he had begotten in his bonds. And only after this does he mention him by his name

Onesimus, which means "helpful," and which would be merely ironical if applied to the part played by him in the house of Philemon, but which has become now a true description, because of the kindly offices he has already done for Paul, and is anxious now to do for Philemon also if he will consent to forgive and receive him back. Paul is evidently playing here upon the name of the slave, but not as a mere *jeu de mots* to display his wit ; rather as a delicate way of recommending the faithful slave to his master, by substituting for the remembrance of his past failures the hope of the service he might now render. It is in this capacity of a servant who will prove himself in the future worthy of his name (helpful) that Paul sends him back.

The same idea—"profitable to thee and to me" (v. 11)—is worked out in the succeeding verses. Only we must rectify the unfortunate modification introduced by the copyists in v. 12—"thou therefore receive him that is mine own bowels," which is an anticipation of the request in v. 17. According to the best manuscripts, v. 12 ought to read simply, "whom I have sent back to thee in his own person, that is my very heart (or mine own bowels)." This expression is very common in Latin (*mea viscera, cor meum*), meaning that which fills my heart. The sense is : He is one with me in such a way that whatever you do to gladden him, my bowels will feel it as if done to myself."

Vv. 13, 14 enlarge on this idea of the value of Onesimus to Paul himself. He would fain have kept him in Rome, as an evangelist, all the more that his captivity rendered such help very needful to him. But he had refrained, not wishing to anticipate that which Philemon might feel prompted to do of his own accord, in granting the Apostle this welcome help. Paul does not wish to take Onesimus away from Philemon. If he is privileged to have his help, it shall be as a living proof of Philemon's affection for himself.

In v. 13 the Apostle says "that in thy behalf ($\acute{v}\pi\grave{\epsilon}\rho$ $\sigma o \hat{v}$) he might minister unto me." This explains vv. 15, 16, in which Paul enlarges on what Onesimus is to become to Philemon himself. Providence had perhaps permitted all that had happened in order that the temporary relation of master and slave, in which Philemon and Onesimus had stood to each other, might be exchanged for the eternal relationship of brothers in the Lord. Not that Philemon must on that account necessarily keep Onesimus with him; on the contrary, Paul has just hinted (vv. 13, 14) at his hope that Philemon might perhaps spare Onesimus to him. But in this way the master would really benefit by the service of his slave; for the services which Onesimus would render to Paul in his Roman prison would be the very same kind offices which Philemon himself would gladly do him if he could. This is the explanation of the words, " on thy behalf," in v. 13. In v. 16, Paul says, " a brother beloved specially to me, but how much more to thee, both in the flesh and in the Lord." These words show how little even slavery excluded the

gentler domestic affections. Onesimus is henceforward
beloved by Paul as by no one else ("specially to me")
unless it be by Philemon, in whom the old affection of
the master will now be reinforced by the new affection
of the brother in Christ ("both in the flesh and in the
Lord"). Before leaving this passage, which is one of
inimitable grace and delicacy, we may call attention to
the word "*perhaps*" at the beginning of v. 15. The
Apostle is going to try and show the good results of
the parting "for a season" of Onesimus from his
master. But it is always very difficult to interpret the
ways of Providence, especially when man's own mis-
doing has to be taken into the category of causes
working for good. Therefore, feeling that it might be
rather startling to Philemon to represent Onesimus'
offence in this light, Paul discreetly adds "*perhaps*."
God might no doubt have brought about the conversion
of Onesimus by some other means ; but as a matter of
fact He had condescended thus to overrule evil for
good.

After these preliminaries, each one of which has its
due weight in the balance, the Apostle at length comes
(vv. 17-21) to the request he wants to make. He has
reminded Philemon who it is that asks—Paul the aged
and a prisoner ; he has said who it is for whom he
pleads—his own son in the faith, and henceforth a
brother to Philemon, one capable of doing immense
service to the Apostle in the great work laid upon him,
and which is dearer than aught else to the heart of

Philemon also.   He thus comes in v. 17 to the request which is the keynote of this short Epistle.   " If then thou countest me a partner, receive him as myself." Let us imagine Paul arriving at Colosse and knocking at Philemon's door.   What rejoicings there would be through the whole household, alike in master and slaves !   What delight in all hearts, on all faces !   Just such a welcome he now asks for the wandering sheep that has come back to the fold.   His request is not only for pardon and complete restoration, but also for the welcome of a brother in the household of faith.

There remains however one dark spot on the picture. Onesimus had caused considerable loss to Philemon, either by his own dishonesty or by the results of his negligence.   In any case the loss had not been made good.   Here then Paul offers himself as security for the reparation which is still due.   " If he hath wronged thee at all, or oweth thee aught, put that to mine account."   This offer might scarcely appear serious. In order that his reader may see that it is so, Paul repeats emphatically, " I, Paul, have written it with mine own hand, I will repay it."

Some interpreters have supposed that Paul wrote only this passage of the letter with his own hand. This seems to me a strained and childish explanation. He meant to call attention to the fact that, the whole letter being written by himself, the offer contained in these last words was well guaranteed : " I will repay it : *I* (ἐγώ), Paul, have written it with mine own hand."

The past tense, "*I have written*," is a common form in Greek, by which the writer places himself by the side of the reader when the communication is received.

Bonâ fide as the offer is, it is clear that the Apostle thinks it impossible that Philemon will accept it; therefore he adds : "that I say not unto thee how that thou owest to me even thine own self besides"; which evidently implies that beyond the remission of this debt, Philemon owes himself, all that he is and all that he has, to St. Paul, inasmuch as he owes to him his eternal salvation.

In contrast to such unworthy conduct on the part of Philemon as demanding the payment of this debt by Paul (who has, even in that case, taken the burden upon his own shoulders and released Onesimus), the Apostle goes on to describe in loving words what he really expects from his old convert : "Yea, brother, let me have joy of thee in the Lord; refresh my heart in Christ." It is in Christ that he pleads; in Christ that he hopes to gain a hearing; and this granting of his request will remove any uneasiness he might have felt for his dear son Onesimus. He hopes for even more than the obedience to which he feels he has a just claim. He is confident that Philemon will do beyond what he asks. Are not these words sufficiently clear ? How can they have been misconstrued by so many commentators ? De Wette, who sees the idea of the enfranchisement of Onesimus already expressed in v. 16 (ὑπὲρ δοῦλον), thinks that here something more is asked, some further benefit to be granted to Onesimus with his liberty. Meyer and Wiesinger, who refuse to see even here a request for the emancipation of Onesimus, also regard these words as indicating some special benefaction to be added to the pardon granted him.

We can but hope that Philemon read the thought of Paul more truly than these interpreters. Paul had clearly asked him to give up Onesimus to him for the work of an evangelist. Now it is perfectly plain that such a gift must imply the liberation of Onesimus, and that this is what Paul means by the words, "knowing that thou wilt do even beyond what I say." The Apostle has been accused of sanctioning the institution of slavery by restoring to his master a slave who had escaped from the yoke. On the contrary, the way in which Paul sends him back, reminding his master that it is not a slave, but one better than a slave, a brother beloved, who returns to him, contains the moral premisses from which must follow, not only the immediate emancipation of that one slave, but the ultimate abrogation of slavery itself.

We have seen that the Epistles of Paul usually conclude with some personal references, greetings and commissions to the various brethren. It is so in this Epistle. There is something very touching in the request to Philemon in v. 22. Paul has just been asking him to receive Onesimus as himself; now he adds, as though with a smile, "Withal prepare me also a lodging; for I hope that through your prayers I shall be granted unto you." If there remained any doubt about this letter being written from Rome, these words would be conclusive. When Paul was imprisoned at Cæsarea, he had just taken leave, and as he believed for ever, of the Churches in Asia Minor (Acts xx. 22), and all his thoughts were turned towards Rome. How could he at that time have been cherishing the hope of again visiting Colosse? In order to do so, he would have had to cross by sea from Cæsarea to Ephesus, and travel thence inland to Colosse; or to traverse the whole of Asia Minor, passing through Phrygia. We know that nothing was farther from the Apostle's thoughts than such a journey. But the case was altogether different when, after his captivity in Cæsarea, he had already passed one or two years in Rome. Circumstances had materially changed in the East, and particularly in Asia Minor. Colosse itself was in danger through the introduction of false doctrine. The evil had come of which he had forewarned the Ephesian elders (Acts xx. 29): "I know that after my departing grievous wolves shall enter in among you, not sparing the flock." Before starting for Spain, the extreme limit of the then known world, and so cutting himself off finally from his old field of labour, the Apostle had a longing to go once more to the East to consolidate his work there. He expresses the same desire in writing from Rome to the Church at Philippi (Phil. ii. 24): "I trust in the Lord that I myself also shall come shortly." It may be said that the Apostle thus himself contradicts his farewell words to the elders of Ephesus (Acts xx. 25). "Now behold I know that ye all among whom I went about preaching the kingdom, shall see my face no more." But in any case the contradiction remains between these words and the passage in Philippians which we have just quoted, a passage which, as all critics agree, must have been written from Rome. At the time when the Apostle took leave of the elders of Asia, he was leaving for the West, to fulfil a mission which, as far as he could judge, would absorb all the rest of his life, and it was very natural that he should look upon his farewell as final. And even if this presentiment had not proved true, there would have been nothing contrary to apostolic inspiration, rightly understood; for that inspiration only extended to the great facts of salvation. (See the Pastoral Epistles.)

The salutations contained in vv. 23, 24 are the same as those in the Epistle to the Colossians, with the exception of those addressed to the Church at Colosse generally and to neighbouring Churches. These would have been inappropriate in a private letter.

After this detailed study of this short Epistle, which is at once so simple and so *naïf*, so full of heart and fine of wit; so appropriate to the particular circumstances, and, with all its playfulness, so earnest, we find it difficult to understand how any critic could ever have been found to call in question its genuineness.

This has been done, however, by Ferdinand Baur, who, to use his own expression, discerns in this Epistle "the embryo of a Christian novel, in which the author proposed to illustrate by a short narrative this great idea : that that which is lost in this world and for time, is found again in Christianity for all eternity. It was in order to work out the idea that the Gospel united for ever those who have been severed for a time by outward circumstances, that the unknown author conceived this fiction of the relation between Onesimus, Paul, and Philemon." Only a theologian very much preoccupied with erudite ideas, could have come to regard the simple fact which forms the basis of the Epistle to Philemon as only the fictitious illustration of a theory; or rather the author must have been very much driven into a corner by the consequences of his own system before he could have invented such a way of escape. Baur was forced by his own theory of primitive Christianity to deny the authenticity of the Epistle to the Colossians, because the Christology of that Epistle was inconsistent with the limitations which he had laid down for the Apostle Paul, and approached too nearly the theology of the Apostle John. Now the Epistles to the Colossians and to Philemon are so closely linked together that it would be impossible to accept the one and reject the other. Hence Baur was compelled to sacrifice this innocent little Epistle, and to perpetrate a sort of critical murder.

We are now in a position to estimate the full

importance of this short Scripture, and to pay our
tribute to the wisdom of those who were not afraid
to give it a place in the canon of the New Testament.
It brings out two points of inestimable value and
interest. First: It shows us what St. Paul was in
little things. We know what he was in the treatment
of great principles, and in carrying out the main work
of his life, his mission to the Gentiles. But there
are many great philanthropists who have undertaken
to reform the world, and yet in their private life have
shown themselves the proudest, most hard and self-
seeking of men. In theory they have been full of
the love of humanity; in fact, full of self-love. The
Divine charity which the love of God had enkindled
in the heart of Paul showed itself in little unnoticed
things no less than in the great overt acts of his public
life. We see him in this letter concerned (and with
what tender solicitude!) for the reception which a
poor guilty slave would meet with from his master.
He writes in his behalf a letter as carefully considered,
both in form and substance, as those which he addressed
to the Churches of Rome and of Corinth. He throws
as much heart into it as if the gravest interests of
his apostleship were involved. And in order to show
the importance he attached to it, instead of dictating
it, as was his custom, he writes it with his own hand.
Such is the difference between true Christian love and
that of mere humanitarian reformers.

This Epistle brings out secondly the marked difference between the Gospel method of action and the way in which men set to work to accomplish social revolutions. It was not by calling on the unhappy slaves to rise in armed rebellion against their masters that the Gospel struck off their fetters. It rather melted them by the fervour of Christian love, and so penetrated society with the principles of the Gospel that emancipation became a necessity.

The Epistle to Philemon was the first indication of the tendency in this direction, and may therefore be fairly called the first petition in favour of the abolition of slavery. In this respect Wilberforce was but a follower of St. Paul.

9

THE THANKS OF AN APOSTLE

(Philippians)

IN the Epistle to Philemon we saw the way in which an Apostle asks a favour; in the Epistle to the Philippians we see how the same Apostle returns thanks. We know that St. Paul refused to take any payment from the Churches which he founded, and over which he watched. It was not that he did not feel he had any right to this mark of gratitude, but he abstained from using this right from personal reasons, which he explains in 1 Cor. ix. Not having entered freely, like the Twelve, into the apostolic ministry, but having been, as it were, forced into it by Divine constraint, he was specially anxious to show that he freely fulfilled the mission thus laid upon him, so to speak, against his will. The idea of performing his apostolic functions like one sentenced to forced labour was insupportable to him; he had rather die than so preach. He felt that in the service of the Gospel he must breathe the pure air of liberty and love, and this he could only do by preaching it without

charge.   This disinterested conduct brought honour
to the Gospel among those to whom he carried it,
and distinguished the messenger of Christ from the
mercenary rhetors who itinerated among the cities of
Greece.   It was thus the practice of the Apostle to
support himself entirely with the work of his hands.
He even provided in the same way for the maintenance
and travelling expenses of his fellow-workers.   He
himself reminds the elders of the Church of Ephesus
of this, when taking leave of them with the pathetic
words, "Ye yourselves know how these hands have
ministered to my necessities, and to them that were
with me" (Acts xx. 34).

There was one Church, however, with regard to which
he made an exception, and from which he consented
to accept, from time to time, help in his missionary
work.   This was the Church at Philippi, the first
Church founded by him in Europe.   He had found
there, from the very first, such warm and devoted
hearts, that he felt free to accept gifts from them without fear of compromising the dignity of his ministry
or the honour of the gospel.   In the Epistle we are
about to study he says : "Ye yourselves also know,
ye Philippians, that in the beginning of the gospel,
when I departed from Macedonia, no Church had
fellowship with me in the matter of giving and receiving, but ye only ; for even in Thessalonica ye sent
once and again unto my need" (Phil. iv. 15-17).

This relation, so honourable to the Church at Philippi,

was kept up through the whole course of his ministry, so that he wrote many years later to the Church at Corinth : "I robbed other Churches, taking wages of them that I might minister unto you ; and when I was present with you, and was in want, I was not a burden on any man ; for the brethren, when they came from Macedonia, supplied the measure of my want" (2 Cor. xi. 8, 9).

It seems, however, that in the course of time the zeal of the Philippian Church for its Apostle had somewhat abated, and that it had neglected to testify its affection for him, at any rate in this form. We gather this from Philippians iv. 10, where Paul says : "I rejoice in the Lord greatly, that now at length ye have revived your thought for me; wherein ye did indeed take thought, but ye lacked opportunity."

Paul's captivity in Rome seems, however, to have revived their affectionate solicitude, and by one of themselves, Epaphroditus, they had again sent help to the Apostle ; and it is to acknowledge this kindness that he writes the Epistle now before us. This is properly therefore a letter of thanks, but the thanks are those of an Apostle. Just as the father of a family, absent for a time from home and children, on receiving from them some token of affection, does not simply write to thank them, but goes on to give them tidings of himself, of the state of his affairs, and his hope of coming back, and adds such instructions and warnings as he thinks needful for their good: so the Apostle, in writing to his spiritual children at Philippi, blends admonitions with tidings of himself, and closes with words of gratitude for the benefit received from them. Such is the simple outline of the Epistle to the Philippians.

We may notice first one or two points of interest in the opening verses. Paul associates Timothy with himself as the sender of this letter. He writes it indeed with his own hand, and speaks of Timothy in the third person; but he desires to give his young fellow-worker this place of honour, for he does not forget that Timothy worked with him in founding the Church at Philippi (Acts xvi.). In the same way, in writing the two letters to the Thessalonian Church, he associates with himself Silas and Timothy, who had assisted him in founding it, and who were with him at Corinth at the time when he wrote. The bearing of the Apostle towards his fellow-labourers in the Gospel is always marked by this gentle and courteous consideration. We have another proof of this in the opening verses. He does not describe himself by the name Apostle, in which Timothy could not have shared, but by the more general and humble title, "servant of Jesus Christ," in which they were both one.

Those to whom the Epistle is addressed are called "saints in Christ Jesus," which means those who are consecrated to God by the faith which joins them to Christ. The name of Christ is the bond which unites in one body the writers and those to whom they are writing. It is in the holy atmosphere of communion with Christ that this letter was written and is to be read.

Lastly, he adds a more special feature. In contemplating the Church he is addressing, the Apostle's thought rests on two classes of persons in it who bear a special seal of their office. These are the bishops and deacons;[1] the former entrusted with the administration of the Church and its direction, temporal and spiritual; the latter set apart to minister to the wants of the poor of the Church, the widows and orphans, the sick, Christian travellers passing through the city, etc. This is the first time that these two sets of officers are mentioned in the Apostle's addresses to the Churches; and we note with interest this reference to these simple and indispensable elements of ecclesiastical organisation, the foundations of the historical development of the Church in all ages. We may well suppose that the Church of Philippi was thus thoroughly equipped for service, because, as the oldest of the Churches in Europe, it had had more time to develop its institutions.

In St. Paul's Epistles, the opening words are generally followed by thanksgiving rendered to God for the work of salvation wrought by Him among the believers to whom the letter is addressed. The Epistle to the

---

[1] We shall discuss, when we come to the Pastoral Epistles, the question of the relation between the bishops and the elders or presbyters in the New Testament.

Philippians is not likely to be an exception in this respect. And as in the other thanksgivings special and characteristic points are brought out, so it is here. In vv. 3-11 the Apostle dwells with peculiar gladness on the interest which the Philippians have taken from the very first in the preaching of the Gospel,[1] being confident that the good work thus begun in them will be perfected until the day of Jesus Christ. This assurance has been strengthened by the love they have shown him during the severe imprisonment which he is enduring at the time for the gospel's sake. Thus his love prompts him to pray for them that their "love may abound yet more and more in knowledge and in all discernment, that they may approve things that are excellent, and be sincere and void of offence unto the day of Christ."

With v. 12 the letter properly begins. It may be divided into four parts—two of tidings, two of exhortations. And, first, he brings before them the state of things in Rome, that they may see what progress the Gospel has made since his coming to that city (chap. i. 12-26). His captivity, so far from having been a hindrance, has in many ways helped forward the work of evangelisation in the capital. In the first place, the

---

[1] It seems to me that the expression used by Paul in v. 5 implies something more than their own fellowship in the Gospel. The term εὐαγγέλιον is used by St. Paul sometimes for the Gospel objectively, but more usually for the act of preaching the Gospel. See especially 1 Thess. i. 5.

knowledge of Christ has spread throughout the whole prætorian guard, those vast barracks of the emperor's bodyguard. It was carried there no doubt by means of the soldiers who took it in turns to be the Apostle's keepers, and through the visitors who came to him in prison. Thus the very presence of the Apostle in Rome stimulated the missionary zeal of the Christians themselves. There were no doubt many who became propagandists from unworthy motives, and out of a spirit of hostility to Paul. These were the Judaisers, the fanatical adherents of the law, who preached Jesus rather in the interests of Judaism than of the gospel. But, as St. Paul nobly says, "What then? in every way, whether in pretence or in truth, Christ is proclaimed; and therein I rejoice, yea, and will rejoice" (vv. 12-18).

It has been objected that these words are opposed to the anathema which the Apostle pronounces (Gal. i. 6 *et seq.*) against Judaising preachers. But the two positions are altogether different. The Judaisers in Galatia came on purpose to overthrow Churches which had been founded by Paul and were doing well: the Judaisers in Rome preached Jesus among the heathen of the capital; and this preaching might have good results, in spite of the admixture of error.

From this point the Apostle passes on to more directly personal matters. He has a full assurance that all the events to which he has thus referred will turn to his salvation,—whether by death, if the Lord is pleased to call him to the honour of martyrdom, or by life, if He permits him still to labour on a little longer for the good of the Church on earth. He himself is perfectly content with either alternative. But he has a conviction that he shall live, and that it will yet be given him to stand once again in the midst of the Philippian Church, for their furtherance and joy of faith (vv. 19-22).

Such is the first section of the Epistle, by means of which the reader can easily realise the whole position of things in Rome. And now Paul transports himself in thought into the midst of the Church at Philippi, and addresses to it some exhortations which, from the report brought by Epaphroditus, he judges to be needful. This second section is comprised in chaps. i. 27-ii. 18.

He first charges them to be united in the defence of the faith and in resistance to their adversaries. If in this warfare they are called to suffer, let them look at these sufferings, endured for Christ's sake, as a privilege bringing them into yet more complete oneness with Him. He charges them by the love they bear him to fill him with joy by laying aside all the selfish and vainglorious considerations which so easily disturb the mind, and to be of the same mind which was in Christ Jesus, who, dwelling in the eternal glory before He stooped to earth, might have come to reign, to rule, to judge, to be worshipped in His Godhead, but chose rather to empty Himself, and to lay aside His glorious prerogative. Instead of claiming, as He might justly have done, to be equal with God, He despoiled Himself of His Divine attributes, and took the form of a servant, and was found in fashion as a man. And even as a man, He humbled Himself yet more, becoming obedient to the laws of God and man, and laying down of Himself that human life for which He had exchanged the Divine. And how has God testified His satisfaction in love like this? "He hath highly exalted Him, and given Him the name which is above every name, that at the name of Jesus every knee should bow, of things in heaven, and things on earth, and things under the earth, and that every tongue should confess that Jesus Christ is Lord, to the glory of God the Father" (chap. ii. 5-11). How could the Apostle have said more eloquently to the Philippians, "Fear not to humble and to empty yourselves: it is the way to fill up that which is behind of the sufferings of Christ" (chap. ii. 11)? To this exhortation to unity through humility, which bears on their common Church life, the Apostle adds another, which naturally follows, but has a more personal reference. He charges them to work out with diligence, nay, even with fear and trembling, their own salvation; by which he means their sanctification. Let them bear in mind that, separated from God, they have no power either to do or even to will that which is good, and that a very little thing suffices to break the union between the soul and God; murmurings, disputings, self-will,

—any or all of these alienate from the life of God. Hence even the most advanced have still ground for fear and trembling (vv. 12, 13). The Philippians have moreover duties towards the world, in the midst of which they are to shine like torches; and to this end they must be blameless and harmless, sons of God without rebuke among a crooked and perverse genera-tion (vv. 14-16). And if, as they walk along this way which St. Paul has marked out for them, they find that he himself has been offered upon the sacrifice and service of their faith, they must not give themselves up to bitter lamentations. Let them rather rejoice with him that such an honour has been put upon him (chap. ii. 17-28).

This is the second section of the Epistle, containing a series of exhortations relative to the duties of the Philippians to one another, to themselves, to the world in which they live, and to the Apostle himself. They all arise very naturally out of the position of the Church and his relation to it.

In the third section (chap. ii. 19-30) Paul proceeds to give the Philippians tidings of two brethren in whom they have a special interest. One of these is Timothy, who, with Silas, had helped Paul to found the Church at Philippi, and whom the Apostle is preparing to send shortly to them, that he may bring him back tidings of their welfare after a sojourn among them. He is worthy to be received by them with all respect, for while others are absorbed in their own affairs (perhaps

Paul is thinking of Demas, Col. iv. 14 and 2 Tim.
iv. 10), Timothy seeks the things that are Christ
Jesus'. The Apostle adds in passing that he himself
hopes soon to follow Timothy to Philippi.

But before sending to them his young fellow-worker,
he deems it needful at once to send back Epaphroditus,
one of themselves, their messenger, who had brought
to him their bounty, and had fallen sick after his
arrival. He had even been nigh unto death ; but God
had mercy on him, and on the Apostle also, that he
might not have sorrow upon sorrow. Paul commends
him to their most loving care, since it was "for the
work of Christ he had come nigh unto death, not
regarding his life to supply that which was lacking
in their service. From the expression in v. 28, "I
have sent him," we gather that Epaphroditus was
already returned at the time when the Philippian
Church was gathered to read Paul's letter, and consequently that he himself had been the bearer of it.

It has sometimes been thought that the Apostle
intended to end his letter here, but felt himself suddenly pressed to add the hortatory passage which
follows. It would have been impossible, however, that
he should close his letter without expressing the
thanks which were its special object. Hence it cannot
have been his intention to lay down his pen at this
point.

The fourth section, which is again one of exhortation,
and which includes chaps. iii. 1-iv. 1, forms a complete

and beautiful whole. It is an exhortation to Christian joy. The exhortation itself is contained in the first two verses of chap. iii. The joy to which Paul bids them is joy in the Lord. He has already charged them to be joyful (chap. ii. 18), and he comes back to the same point now to put them on their guard against anything that might rob them of their rejoicing and to encourage them by his own example. The adversaries against whom they are to guard this treasure are the same of whom he has so often warned them, whom he calls "dogs" because of their daring, "evil workers" because of their cupidity, the "concision" (mutilation) because of their zeal for circumcision. They are Jews and Judaisers. The Philippians must not forget that those are of the true circumcision in the sight of God whom the Spirit of God has consecrated and who serve Him in spirit and in truth.

Here Paul sets before them as an encouragement his own example. He, who possessed in a higher and fuller degree than any of these Judaisers the righteousness of the law, had not feared to cast away this self-righteousness as so much dung, that he might win Christ, in whom is the righteousness of God by faith (vv. 4-9). And now, possessing this righteousness before God, he is striving after holiness, and to this end he needs no other means but Christ Himself, the power of whose resurrection-life he seeks to know, and by the fellowship of His sufferings to become conformed unto His death. He has ever before him this great end—that he may attain to the resurrection of the faithful at the coming of Christ. But in order to this end, it is needful for him to act like the athlete in the arena ; he never stops to look back and to regret the things he has left behind, but gazes steadily before him, his soul bent on laying hold of that crown for which Christ has laid hold of him (vv. 10-14).

Paul next teaches the Philippians that those who are perfect will show it by striving, as he is striving, after perfection. It is evident that by the perfect Paul does not mean perfect saints. Those who are perfect are contrasted with those who are babes in Christ (1 Cor. xiv. 20). He thus designates men who have arrived at Christian maturity, the state of constant communion with the Lord. Such a state does not exclude the necessity of progress, as Paul himself proves. If they are as yet divided by some differences of view, let them seek the Divine illumination in which all such differences will vanish. But on this one point, at least, let them be agreed—that they are all striving after perfection, as imitators together of Paul and of those who with him are their ensample (vv. 15-17).

By this stedfast course they will break loose from those merely nominal Christians, against whom the Apostle has so often warned them, and of whom he cannot now speak without tears—men who dishonour the cross of Christ, who make a god of their belly, who mind earthly things, and whose end will be perdition (vv. 18, 19).

But, on the other hand, those who are stedfast and immovable have their pattern in the heavenlies, from whence they look for Him who shall glorify, by changing into His own likeness, the very body of their humiliation. In Him therefore let these Christians stand fast, who are now the joy of the Apostle and soon will be his crown.

This fourth section may be summed up in two words : joy in Christ arising out of the righteousness of faith ; and a constant striving after perfection in Him.

We have already observed, that after the treatment of the main subject there is generally a concluding passage in Paul's letters, containing personal communications, commissions, and greetings. It is so in this Epistle, only this concluding portion is longer than in the other letters, because the Apostle has to speak of two subjects in considerable detail.

The first is a rivalry between two women of influence in the Church, which was hindering its welfare. The Apostle invites his faithful colleague, probably the head of the episcopal college, to help these women in the struggle with themselves, for they had been valuable fellow-labourers with him in his work at Philippi, no less than Clement and the other brethren. As the names of these two women are *Euodias*, which means *the good way*, and *Syntyche, happy meeting*, some critics, whose one idea it is to discover everywhere traces of antagonism between the Pauline and Judæo-Christian party, have fancied that in the names of these two women there was the symbolic designation of the two parties. The one called *the good way* designates the Pauline party, which had always adhered to the good way ; the other, *happy meeting*, represents the Judæo-Christian party, which is ultimately to fall in with the other and pursue the same track. Such are the ingenious vagaries sometimes resorted to by a school which boasts its critical acumen. "Greatly astonished," says Reuss, "would these good deaconesses be, if they came back to life and found themselves thus transformed into theological puppets !"

At this point the Apostle returns to the hortatory tone, and again briefly charges the Church to delight itself in whatsoever things are true, honourable, just, pure, lovely, and of good report (vv. 4-9).

Then he passes to the second matter of a personal nature on which he wishes to speak. He had already twice alluded to the help in money which the Philippians had sent him (chaps. i. 5, 7 ; ii. 25, 30). But he had not yet distinctly thanked them. This grateful task he had reserved to the close of his letter. He performs it in the most graceful and noble manner. He gives the Philippians to understand that if this act on their part has given him lively joy, it is even more on their account than his own. He has indeed long learned in whatsoever state he is, even in abject poverty, therewith to be content. But none the less he has received with true gladness of heart the generous ministry of the Philippians to his needs, for he knows, not only how to be in want, but how to abound. Strange that the same critic to whom we just now referred, should call this a "thankless thanksgiving," so construing it in order to support his own view that the Epistle is not genuine! In conclusion, the Apostle declares that *his* God, to whom the Philippians have ministered in the person of His servant, will repay all his indebtedness, and will fulfil every need of theirs according to His riches in glory by Christ Jesus (iv. 10-20).

The Epistle closes with some greetings. Paul salutes every saint in Christ Jesus, in his own name and that of the brethren with him, without naming any of them; which is an argument that Luke, who was so well known to the Philippians, was not now with him. He sends a salutation from the saints in Rome, specially mentioning those of Cæsar's household. This has been interpreted as betraying some vanity on Paul's part, as if his whole life were not sufficient disproof of any such unworthy feeling. Let us rather say that in these first converts in the imperial palace he saw the earnest of the future conversion of the Roman world, and of the emperor himself, to the Gospel of Christ, now kept in bonds in Rome in his person.

The mention of the household of Cæsar, as well as of the prætorian guard (chap. i. 13), leaves no room to doubt that this letter was written from Rome; and the detailed description (chap. i.) of the influence of Paul's presence in the capital proves that it was written after the Epistles to the Colossians, to Philemon, and to the Ephesians, consequently towards the close of the year 63 or early in 64. Those who hold that it was written at Cæsarea are compelled to have recourse to very forced explanations of the expression, " Cæsar's household."

This has been called the most epistolary of all the Pauline epistles. It was not indeed intended to treat didactically any aspect of Scripture truth. The only doctrinal passage which it contains at all is that relating to the person of Christ (chap. ii. 5-11); and this is introduced for a directly practical purpose, namely, to show the Philippians, by this supreme example of self-abnegation, the sacrifices which they ought to be willing to make for one another's sake. His aim is to incite them to the practice of a Christ-like humility, not to teach them anything new in the way of abstract doctrine.

We are therefore at a loss to understand what motive could have induced any one to forge such a letter, which contains scarcely anything but practical exhortations and messages. Baur was the first who had the courage to cast doubt upon its authenticity; but he found many who differed from him even in

his own school, particularly Hilgenfeld, who calls this
Epistle " the swan-song of St. Paul." Holsten adopts,
but on different grounds, the same theory as Baur.
He regards this Epistle as the oldest canonical record
of the attempt to reconcile the Judaisers and the
Paulites. It is certainly a curious way of attempting
to conciliate the two parties, to speak in such terms
as Paul uses at the beginning of chap. iii. in reference
to the Judaisers. The same critic says again : " Paul
would never have represented the Christian doctrine
of justification as it is put in chap. iii. 2-14, where it
is made to consist in the progress of the knowledge
of Christ in the heart of the believer. The justification taught by Paul is based upon the objective
righteousness of Christ Himself." But is not this
precisely what St. Paul says in this passage, where
he contrasts the righteousness acquired by works,
which he counts but dung, with " that which is
through faith in Christ, the righteousness which is
of God by faith " (iii. 9) ? And if he goes on to say,
in v. 10, " that I may know Him, and the power of
His resurrection, and the fellowship of His sufferings,
becoming conformed to His death," this inward knowledge of Christ is not represented as the basis of
justification, but, on the contrary, as its end (" that
I may know Him "). These two verses, 9, 10, give
us, in fact, an epitome respectively of Rom. i.-iv. and
Rom. vi.-viii. 1.

Holsten thinks that he discovers a contradiction

between Paul's conception of the person of Christ and that of the writer of the Epistle to the Philippians. Both hold the pre-existence of the Lord : but, according to 1 Corinthians xv. 45, Paul seems to regard the pre-existent Christ only as a man endowed with a spiritual body, and serving as a type of the natural man ; while in the Epistle to the Philippians, the expression, " being in the form of God " (chap. ii. 6) implies the divinity of the pre-existing Christ. That Paul believed in the divinity of the pre-existent Christ is an unquestionable fact, though Holzmann has quite recently attempted to deny it ; but that he believed in the humanity of the pre-existent Christ is false, and derives no support from the passage quoted (1 Cor. xv.), for the simple reason that that Scripture is referring not to the pre-existent Christ at all, but to the Christ glorified in His spiritual body, the life of our glorified resurrection bodies.

Schürer, who shows a singular independence in his criticism, says : " It is generally recognised in our day that the rejection by Baur of the Epistle to the Philippians was a great mistake. He has had but few followers on this point; among them is Holsten, who has devoted much labour to the subject. But his arguments are so foolish that one is sometimes tempted to put them down as slips of the pen."[1] In an earlier article Schürer had said : " The researches of Holsten are full of sagacity ; but the reasons alleged

---

[1] *Literaturzeitung*, Nov. 5th, 1880.

by him for denying the genuineness of the Epistle
to the Philippians can have no weight, unless we take
the Apostle Paul (the most living and versatile character the world has ever seen) to be such a slave of
rigid routine that he cannot write one epistle that
shall not be exactly like all the others, that he can
only repeat in each what he has said in the preceding,
and in the very same words. If we are not prepared
to admit this, all the objections raised against the
authenticity of the Epistle to the Philippians fall to
the ground."

Let us only think for a moment of the passage in
this Epistle relating to Epaphroditus (chap. ii.). This
messenger of the Philippian Church had been ill, very
ill ; but, says Paul, " God had mercy on him, and not
on him only, but on me also, lest I should have
sorrow upon sorrow." What writer of the second
century would have put such words as these into
the mouth of Paul ? Here is nothing extraordinary,
nothing distinctively apostolic, one may be tempted
to say. Here is no miracle ; everything is simply
natural and human. Paul is in sorrow, like any one
of us ; he prays, as we might pray ; he is heard.
There is nothing here characteristic of the time when
the glorification of the Apostles had already begun.
What would have been the object of inventing such
details, which are of no value except as marking the
relation between Paul and his readers ? In the
absence of any reasonable object to be answered by

such a deception, Reuss is surely right in saying that "the apocryphal author could not have had any other aim but to prove, by a composition in Pauline style, that it was possible in the second century to write just as Paul wrote in the first."

The Epistle to the Philippians is a familiar letter, but it bears none the less the impress of an Apostle ; and though shorter and more colloquial than the rest, it has its own place, and that an important one, in the sacred canon. It serves as a commentary on the last two verses of the book of the Acts, which contain but a very cursory allusion to St. Paul's captivity in Rome. It is only by the help of this Epistle that we can form an exact idea of the religious movement in the capital, which followed on the arrival of the Apostle. As we read these lines we understand how exultant his soul became, as he witnessed the irresistible power of the Gospel in the midst of the heathen world.

This Epistle brings home to us the cheering conviction that among the Churches founded by the Apostle there was at least one which fitly responded to his care, and realised that which he fondly desired to see in all. Among the several letters to the Churches which have come down to us as written by Paul, this letter to the Church at Philippi occupies the same place as the letter to the Church at Philadelphia among the seven in the Revelation. There were some little rivalries in the Church, and a certain spirit of self-complacency, which hindered progress in sanctification, and, as a consequence, spiritual joy; but this was all the fault Paul had to find with a Church which he lovingly describes as his "joy and crown." At the same time he rejoices to see in it the first carrying out of the complete organisation which he desires for all the Churches. The Epistle to the Philippians thus becomes, as it were, the natural stepping-stone to the Pastoral Epistles, in which Paul institutes, distinctly and for all time, the two orders of ministry here mentioned—the bishops and deacons.

Lastly, the great Christological passage in chapter ii., written with a definite practical purpose, acquires a double value from this very circumstance, that it alludes, as an accepted and recognised fact in the Philippian Church, to a view of the person of Christ entirely in harmony with the teaching of the fourth Gospel. That fundamental saying of St. John, "*The Word was made flesh*," has nowhere so striking a parallel, or, so to speak, so exact a commentary, as in these words of St. Paul: "Who, being in the form of God, counted it not a prize to be on an equality with God, but emptied Himself, taking the form of a servant." If the Epistle to the Philippians is really genuine, as we can see no room to doubt, there can be no ground for relegating to the second century the origin of the formula of St. John. We have but to seek its roots in the teaching and therefore in the consciousness of Him who was the Master at once of Paul and of John.

10

THE LAST LABORS OF A SOLDIER OF CHRIST

(1 and 2 Timothy, Titus)

AS we read the Epistle to the Philippians, we feel that the Apostle in his Roman prison was looking for speedy martrydom. In many respects therefore he regarded his work as finished. At the same time he felt that his " abiding in the flesh " was a help to the Churches which he had founded, and which he would fain visit once again (Phil. i. 24). In this aspect there seemed still a work for him to do.

We are not told in the Book of the Acts which of the two possibilities was realised. In its closing verses it refers to the two years of Paul's captivity in Rome, but does not tell us to what issue they led. This abrupt conclusion of the narrative in the Acts is remarkable and difficult to explain ; but it appears to me more easy to account for it on the supposition that these two years of imprisonment were followed by a period of renewed activity, into the details of which the writer did not propose to enter, than on the supposition that they terminated in a violent death, to which he could so easily have referred in a single line.

We are inclined therefore to accept, as the more probable, the idea that the Apostle was set free, and was thus enabled to renew his labours for the good of the Church either in the East or West. We know that his plan, when in the year 59 he left Corinth to repair to Jerusalem and thence to Rome, was not to take up his abode in Rome, but simply to pass through it on his way into Spain, that he might fulfil the ministry which he had received of the Lord, to carry to the very end of the earth the testimony of the gospel of His grace. Was it given him to fulfil this purpose? Most modern writers think not. Even those critics who, like Weiss and Farrar, believe in the liberation of the Apostle after his two years of captivity in Rome, do not suppose him to have ever visited Spain. They cite the words used in the Epistle to the Philippians and in that to Philemon, in which Paul encourages his readers to look for a speedy visit from him in the East, and take them to imply that he had abandoned all thought of a mission to Spain. They note also that no Church in Spain pretends to the honour of having been founded by the Apostle. But none of these reasons are decisive. The Apostle might, during his captivity, have received tidings from the East, making him feel bound to return there as soon as possible, and to defer his visit to Spain till these more pressing claims had been met. And if there is no Church in Spain claiming the honour of having Paul for its founder, it is at least possible that, having reached Spain, his work may have been intercepted by a fresh arrest, before he had time to raise any lasting monument of his visit. Thirty years after the death of St. Paul, Clement, Bishop of Rome, writing to the Corinthians, says that "Paul, after preaching the Gospel from the rising to the setting sun, and teaching righteousness throughout the whole world, arrived at the extremity of the West; and after suffering martyrdom in the presence of the rulers, he was set free from this earth and reached the holy place prepared for him." Now it does not seem to me possible to suppose, as so many critics do, that by this expression, "the *extremity* of the West," Rome is meant; especially after the words going before, "from the rising to the setting sun," and "throughout the whole world." Rome, so far from being the "extremity" of the world, was rather regarded as its centre. It was not the seven hills of Rome, but the Pillars of Hercules, which Strabo, writing at this period, called "The Ends of the Earth," $\pi\acute{\epsilon}\rho\alpha\tau\alpha$ $\tau\hat{\eta}s$ $oi\kappa ov\mu\acute{\epsilon}v\eta s$, and Velleius Paterculus, *Extremus nostri orbis terminus*.[1] That an author writing at Jerusalem or at Ephesus might perchance have so designated Rome, would be conceivable, but that any one writing from Rome itself should use such an expression, seems to me

---

[1] See Schaff's *History of the Christian Church*, p. 332.

an altogether inadmissible supposition.[1] We are confirmed in the idea that this is not Clement's true meaning by another passage also written at Rome, and bearing testimony to the tradition then current in that Church. It occurs in the Fragment of Muratori, where the writer refers to the " passion of Peter and the departure of Paul from Rome for Spain." It is possible, of course, that this tradition, which is handed down also in the writings of the later Fathers, may have been only a conclusion drawn by them from Romans xv. 24. But this explanation does not seem to me probable in view of the two passages we have quoted, in which the circumstance of Paul's departure for Spain is mentioned quite incidentally, as a well-known and positive fact.

We are not so much concerned at present with the question whether Paul went into Spain, as whether, in the event of his liberation, he again visited the Churches of Macedonia, the Church at Philippi, and the Churches in Asia, according to the hope expressed by him in the Epistle to Philemon. This question is inseparable from that of the authenticity of the Pastoral Epistles. Some scholars have endeavoured to separate the two, assigning to these epistles, of which they acknowledge the genuineness, some date prior to Paul's imprisonment

---

[1] It is objected that in this expression, " having arrived at the extremity of the West, and having suffered martyrdom before the rulers," Clement clearly describes the well-known scene of Paul's martyrdom as " the extremity of the West." But this is not exact.

in Rome and during the course of his active ministry.[1]
But these suppositions are more and more untenable.
It is impossible to find, during Paul's active ministry
in Greece and in Asia Minor, or during the two years
of his first captivity in Rome, circumstances corresponding to the biographical details contained in the
three Pastoral Epistles. This has been demonstrated
so often and so decisively that we need not stay now
to adduce proof. Moreover, these three epistles are so
closely connected both in thought and in style, and
so distinctly marked out from all the other writings of
Paul, that it is impossible to intersperse them among
the rest. Lastly, the unsound teaching to which
reference is made in the Pastoral Epistles is clearly
the heresy of the false teachers at Colosse, which only
arose during the captivity of the Apostle in Rome.
If this false doctrine had already spread through the
Churches of Asia before Paul's arrest at Jerusalem, he
would certainly have alluded to it in his charge to the
pastors of the Churches of Ephesus and Miletus, to
watch against the " grievous wolves " which, after his

The expression used by Clement will bear the construction that Paul,
after reaching Spain, was arrested in that country, and afterwards
suffered martyrdom in Rome before the rulers.

[1] Thus an attempt has been made to fix the date of 1st Timothy
between the Epistles to the Galatians and Corinthians, during Paul's
sojourn at Ephesus. The same date, or a little later, is given to the
Epistle to Titus, it being placed between 1st and 2nd Corinthians.
The 2nd Timothy is supposed to have been written during Paul's
imprisonment in Cæsarea, or very early in the Roman captivity.

departing, would enter in among them to destroy the flock (Acts xx.).

We find ourselves then shut up to two alternatives. Either the Pastoral Epistles are genuine, and, in that case, they date from the time between the liberation of the Apostle and his martyrdom, and are the latest monument we have of his apostolic work; or they are spurious productions. On the latter supposition, criticism must find some explanation of the purpose of such a forgery.

The majority of the critics at the present day incline to the view last given, though the evidence of tradition is as strong in favour of the authenticity of the Pastoral as of any of the other Epistles. There is a correspondence scarcely to be mistaken between certain expressions in the Epistle to Titus and the First Epistle to Timothy, and the Epistle of Clement of Rome, while it is impossible to deny the allusions to the Pastoral Epistles in the letters of Ignatius and Polycarp. These are indeed recognised even by those who dispute the authenticity of those Epistles. The ancient Syriac Bible, as well as the Latin, in the second half of the second century, contained the Pastoral Epistles with all the others, and the Fragment of Muratori expressly records their admission into the canon, notwithstanding their originally private character. The Fathers at the close of the second century quote them as unanimously accepted. The two Gnostics, Basilides and Marcion, seem indeed to have rejected them, but this is not to be wondered at.

If then in modern times the majority of critics coincide in denying the authenticity of all three, or of one or other of them, it must be on account of their contents. Schleiermacher was the first to call in question the First Epistle to Timothy, mainly on the ground of the want of connection in the thoughts. Eichhorn and De Wette, feeling that the three letters bore too strong a resemblance not to proceed from the same writer rejected also the two others. Baur endeavoured to explain the purpose of these apocryphal writings, as being to combat the Gnostic heresies of the second century, particularly the heresy of Marcion, and to reconcile the two parties into which the Church was at that time divided. He thought that they were the work of three different writers. At the present day many critics are reverting to a modified view, and are prepared to admit that at least the Epistle to Titus and the Second to Timothy are in part genuine. Their theory is, that these were originally short letters addressed by St. Paul to his two colleagues, and receiving their present form from later hands. These critics endeavour to reproduce the short original letters, by a process of arbitrary selection, in which it is scarcely needful to say each of them is guided by his own particular bias.

One thing is clear : these Epistles do differ from all the rest in certain very marked particulars. The Apostle seems in them to be more occupied than was his wont with the future of the Church, and attaches greater importance to the various ecclesiastical offices on which that future might largely depend. He has before him dangerous teaching, which is spreading among the Churches, and which, if it became prevalent, would gravely undermine true piety. This teaching is of an altogether different character from the Pharisaic, Judaising doctrine, against which he had protested in his earlier epistles. Lastly, there is an evident want of cohesion in the ideas expressed and in the subjects treated, and a frequent repetition of certain forms of speech, which do not occur in the earlier epistles.

What conclusion must be drawn from these various indications ? Is it true that there never was a period in the life of the Apostle when new considerations, of which there is no trace in his earlier epistles, may have come to occupy his mind ? Is it true that there is no reason to suppose that towards the close of his life his teaching may have taken a new direction, and found expression in new modes of speech appropriate to the changed conditions ? Is it true that the unsound teaching, against which he charges his colleagues to contend earnestly, can be no other than the Gnostic heresies of the second century, which would necessarily imply that these epistles are the work of some forger assuming the name of St. Paul? Is it true, lastly, that the ecclesiastical organisation, to which the writer distinctly refers, belongs to a time long subsequent to the life of St. Paul ?

These are the main questions which present themselves at the present stage of the discussion, and which we now propose to examine as briefly as possible. Before doing so, however, let us give a short summary of the contents of the three epistles.

Summary of the Three Epistles

First Epistle to Timothy.—The title of *Apostle* which Paul applies to himself in the opening words of this Epistle, and which has been regarded as an indication of its spuriousness, only shows that Paul does not consider this a purely private letter, but rather addresses Timothy as a functionary of the Church under his direction.

The Epistle consists of two parts. In the first the Apostle treats of three subjects: 1st, The true gospel teaching, which must be preserved from any admixture, and especially from any legal element. It was with a view to this that, when Paul was departing into Macedonia, he desired Timothy to remain at Ephesus. There he would have to contend with persons who, while calling themselves doctors of the law, had no true comprehension of it, and applied to the faithful that which was really only for evil-doers. The Gospel which Paul teaches, and which he has himself been taught by deep experience, excludes any such admixture. It was to be Timothy's task to uphold in its purity this Gospel which others were thrusting from them (ch. i.). 2nd, The second subject treated is worship. It is the duty of the Church to pray for the pagan rulers of the land, and for all men without distinction. In the assemblies of the Church the women are to wear modest attire, and to keep silence. Their sphere is home (ch. ii.). 3rd, The third subject is the ministry. Reference is made to the bishopric and the diaconate—two offices indispensable to the life of the Church, and in regard to which Timothy is enjoined to use special vigilance. The Apostle describes the moral qualifications required in bishops and deacons, without which they could not command the respect of the Church (iii. 1-13).

In the second part of the Epistle (beginning ch. iii. 14), instructions are given to Timothy as to the way in which he ought to conduct himself towards the Church in general, and its various classes in particular. And first towards the Church as a whole. He must keep before him its high destiny. It is the pillar on which the mystery of salvation is inscribed that all the world may read. Timothy is charged to use the more watchfulness over it, because the spirit of prophecy foretells a time coming when there shall be a great falling away from the faith ; when a spirit of false asceticism will creep into the Church under the guise of superior sanctity, but based in truth upon the impious idea that the whole material part of the works of God is to be ascribed to the spirit of evil. Timothy is to put the Church specially on its guard against such teaching, and is himself sedulously to avoid any approach to this error. He is to command the respect of the Church in spite of his youth, and is not to allow anything to quench the gift which is in him, and which had been imparted " by prophecy with the laying on of the hands of the presbytery " (ch. iii. 14-iv. 16). Then follow counsels as to his behaviour towards the older members of both sexes, and towards the younger sisters and widows. The Apostle here adds some injunctions with regard to widows who may be called to a ministry of practical benevolence in the Church. He then gives rules as to the treatment of presbyters, or elders, who are evidently the same as the bishops spoken of in ch. iii. They were there designated bishops or overseers, with reference to their function in the Church ; here they are spoken of as presbyters or elders, in recognition of their dignity. Paul adds, on this subject, a little word of counsel to Timothy himself (ch. v.) ; and concludes with some further admonitions to slaves who have become " believers and beloved " (ch. vi. 1, 2) ; to those who have already been led away from the truth by false teachers ; and to the rich in this world's goods (ch. vi. 17-19). A brief salutation, and one final word of warning (ch. vi. 20-22), bring the Epistle to a close.

The Epistle to Titus.—The elaborate superscription of this letter shows that this is not in any way a private communication, but an official charge given by Paul to his deputy. The main body of the letter (ch. i. 5-iii. 11) treats of two subjects : 1st, *The presbytery.* Paul had left Titus in Crete for this express purpose—that he should appoint elders in every city to carry on the work commenced. He had there to contend with false Judaising teaching (ch. i.). 2nd, In the second part of the Epistle (ch. ii. 1-iii. 11) Paul goes on, as in the Epistle to Timothy, to give counsels to Titus as to his behaviour towards various classes in the Church—the old, the young, slaves, etc. The grace offered to all ought to sanctify all, and Titus is to conduct himself in such a manner as to commend this grace of God to all. Paul then adds directions as to the bearing to be maintained towards pagan magistrates, and pagans generally; lastly towards the Church as a whole, which must be carefully guarded against profane teaching.

The Epistle closes as usual, with commissions and salutations. When Titus is released from his responsibility by the arrival of his successor, he is to rejoin Paul at Nicopolis, where the Apostle will pass the winter.

Second Epistle to Timothy.—This letter is of a more private, personal, and intimate character; hence in the superscription Paul omits the title Apostle.

In the body of the letter (ch. i. 6-iv. 8) three subjects are dealt with: 1st, *Timothy's own deportment.* He is to stir up the gift which is in him, and not allow himself to be daunted by fear of the sufferings which the service of Christ may bring upon him. Paul encourages him by four considerations: the grandeur of the Gospel, his own example and that of the faithful Onesiphorus, and lastly by the sure hope of the

Christian (ch. i. 6-ii. 13). 2nd, *The Church.* This has been invaded by teaching to no profit, and tending only to barren disputations. Nevertheless there still remains a nucleus of true believers, bearing the Divine seal of holiness. Timothy must not be discouraged therefore, but contend firmly and patiently for the truth. There is even reason to expect that in the last times a moral corruption, like that of the heathen world, may find its way into the Church itself. Already some Christians have become perverted. In order to counteract their influence, the Apostle gives Timothy three counsels. He is to remember the example of constancy which he had witnessed in Paul himself (during his first sojourn in Lycaonia) ; he is to feed continually upon the Scriptures inspired of God; and to redouble his vigilance and activity in evangelistic work (ii. 14-iv. 5). 3rd, The third subject is the Apostle himself. He speaks first of his approaching martyrdom ; then he asks Timothy to come as soon as possible, because all his fellow-workers, except Luke, are absent. He urges that Mark should come with him, and desires him to bring also the cloak and the books which he (Paul) had left in Asia Minor. Lastly, he refers to his first appearance before the imperial judgment-seat, which gave him an opportunity of fully proclaiming the gospel message, and yet did not lead to his condemnation.

In the concluding sentences he refers to, or explains incidentally, the absence of two of his fellow-workers

(v. 20). Then come greetings to a few brethren, all of them bearing Roman names.

We must now turn to the main objections to which we have already alluded.

Objections

1. *The teaching of the Apostle*, both as to form and substance.

It is asserted that the conception of the Gospel presented in these letters differs notably from the well-known teaching of the Apostle Paul. The great fundamental doctrines of the Apostle of the Gentiles, justification by faith and regeneration by the Holy Spirit, are scarcely touched upon. The great theme in these Epistles is the application of the Gospel to outward conduct. Those who have believed in God are to be "careful to maintain good works, for these things are good and profitable to men" (Titus iii. 8). "The end of the commandment is love" (1 Tim. i. 5). For the most part the practical side of the Christian virtues is alone brought into prominence. We shall see presently what particular reasons the Apostle may have had for insisting on this aspect of Christian truth. But independently of such considerations, it is easy to understand that the Gospel teaching having been once clearly formulated, and thoroughly established by the earlier labours of the Apostle in the Churches founded by him, as well as in the minds of his colleagues, he might now feel it opportune to insist rather on the practical appli-

cation of the truths learned to daily life. Those who
have witnessed a great revival, such as took place half
a century ago in the Reformed Churches of the Conti-
nent, know with what somewhat excessive insistence
the doctrines were preached which Paul brought into
prominence in his earlier epistles. The almost ex-
clusive theme of the preaching was salvation by grace,
in opposition to works. Then when these doctrines
had laid hold of the minds of men, and had become, so
to speak, a bond of union for the whole religious public,
preachers began again, little by little, to insist on the
moral aspect of the Gospel. M. Vinet's famous sermon,
" Faith—a Work," clearly marked this new phase in
the life of our Churches. Not that this fresh departure
was really in an opposite direction ; but it was determined by new needs which had arisen, and was, in a
manner, supplementary to that which preceded it. The
present writer has personally known preachers, who,
after being foremost among their brethren in re-
discovering, so to speak, the foundation-truths of the
Gospel, took a no less prominent part when the preaching
again assumed a decidedly practical character. If such
a change as this has been traceable in our own day,
why may we not suppose a similar modification in the
apostolic teaching of St. Paul, especially if the circumstances of the time seemed to demand it ?

Criticism exacts, however, that the mode of speech
at any rate should not change, and that the style of the
Apostle in these Epistles should not differ markedly

from that of his other Epistles recognised as genuine. But we are told that such a strongly marked difference does exist. It is shown that a number of words are used in these three Epistles which do not occur in any of the earlier letters. In the First Epistle to Timothy there are 81 such words ; in the Second, 63 ; in Titus, 44. Several expressions also occur repeatedly, such as "faithful is the saying," "sound doctrine," "a life in all godliness," etc., which are not found in any of the earlier writings, and some entirely new terms descriptive of the unsound teaching leavening the Church at this time : "endless genealogies," "vain talking," "old wives' fables," etc.

To this we reply that diversity of verbiage is a marked feature throughout the literary career of the Apostle. It results partly no doubt from the wealth and creative fulness of his genius, partly from the ever-varying experiences through which he passed in his intercourse with the Churches. M. Reuss himself remarks that the two Epistles to the Corinthians contain as many words foreign to those to the Romans and Galatians, as the Pastoral Epistles contain of expressions foreign to all the other letters. In the Epistle to the Galatians there are 57 terms which occur nowhere else ; in the Philippians, 54 ; in the Colossians and Ephesians together, 143. To the causes already assigned for this constant variation, other indirect influences may be added ; as, for instance, the natural wealth of the Greek language and the fruitfulness of Christian thought.

Hence M. Reuss attaches no weight to the argument derived from style; and in order to show what an unsafe guide such criticism is, he mentions that, among those who follow it, Schleiermacher concludes that the Pastoral Epistles are the work of two authors, Baur of three, and De Wette of one writer only. We conclude then that the teaching of these letters furnishes no proof, either in form or in substance, that they are not from the pen of St. Paul. It only shows that they belong to a particular period—the closing period of his apostolic labours. This conclusion is confirmed by the analysis we are about to make of the teaching against which he contends, and which presented itself to his two fellow-labourers in the Churches where they were at work.

2. *The teaching protested against in the Pastoral Epistles.* It has been said that this heretical teaching cannot be of an earlier date than the second century; that the different Gnostic systems of that advanced period are clearly described, particularly those of Valentinus and Marcion. Other critics dispute this, and suppose the heresies referred to to be those of Cerinthus and the Ophites, at the beginning of the second or the close of the first century. This theory is equally opposed to the authorship of St. Paul.

But two features of the heresies indicated by the Apostle are incompatible with either of these suppositions. The first is that they do not appear to contain elements directly opposed to the Gospel, as do the systems of Marcion and Valentinus. The Gnostic system taught that the God who created the world was not the same God whom Jesus Christ called His Father; they maintained that the Jewish law was also the work of this other God, who was inferior to the Father of Jesus Christ. They did not hold that the Saviour appeared in a true human body, etc. Such doctrines as these are wholly subversive of the Gospel preached by Paul. But the errors referred to in the Pastoral Epistles are characterised merely as "profane and old wives' fables," "vain babblings," "oppositions of science falsely so called." Those who formulate them are spoken of as "vain talkers," tickling the fancy of men without real piety, who look upon religion rather as a harmless amusement than as a serious means of sanctification. The danger here is of substituting intellectualism in religion for piety of heart and life. Had the writer been a Christian of the second century trying, under the name of Paul, to stigmatise the Gnostic systems, he would certainly have used much stronger expressions to describe their character and influence. He would have found in the first chapter of the Epistle to the Galatians a model of the Pauline polemics with regard to teachings subversive of the Gospel. The second characteristic of the heresies referred to in the Pastoral Epistles is their Jewish origin. The doctors who propagate them are called "teachers of the law, though they understand neither what they say nor whereof they confidently affirm."

They are Judaising Christians ("they of the circumcision," Titus i. 10), raising foolish contentions about the law (ch. iii. 9), and teaching "Jewish fables" (ch. i. 14), to which they add "endless genealogies," evidently also Jewish, for they are classed by the writer with "fightings about the law" (Titus iii. 9; 1 Tim. i. 4), and form part of the teaching of those who call themselves "teachers of the law" (v. 7). It has sometimes been asserted that this term "genealogies" refers to the successive emanations of æons, taught by Valentinus. But this Gnostic was the sworn foe of everything Jewish. A much more natural reference is to the genealogies in Genesis, which these teachers were in the habit of allegorising, and in which they contrived to discover all sorts of mysteries, with which they entertained their followers. But the epithet "*endless*" which the Apostle gives to these genealogies excludes this reference, for each of the genealogies in Genesis is composed of a fixed and easily calculable number of terms—the number *ten*. It seems therefore more probable that the reference here is to a sphere in which imagination might have full play, namely, the genealogies of angels. We know to what an extent the Judaism of later times delighted to amplify the sober references to the angels made in Scripture. The Book of Enoch, which was widely circulated at this time, even in the Church (as is evident from the use made of it in Jude), is an illustration in point. The Essenes had in their teaching a special chapter on the *names of angels*, which the initiate swore not to divulge. There were then probably teachers who traded in these so-called revelations, and who, as we read in Titus i. 11, "taught them for filthy lucre's sake." The First Epistle to Timothy and the Epistle to Titus teach us, further, that these doctors made legal distinctions between meats pure and impure, which is obviously Jewish, and contrary to the Gnostic systems of the second century. Cerinthus, who lived at the close of the first century, was indeed a Jew, and introduced Judaising elements into his teaching. For example, he recognised circumcision. But there is not a word in the Epistles before us pointing to this error. In fact, two men of such different schools of thought as Weiss and Holzmann agree in the acknowledgment that no recognised heresy corresponds to the picture drawn in the Pastoral Epistles. This would be indeed strange if the writer had intended to combat forms of error so well known as those of the close of the first, and of the second century.

The natural solution presents itself, if we accept the Pastoral Epistles as closely connected with the Epistle to the Colossians. There we read of teachers who were trying to bring the Church into legal bondage, advocating the law as a higher means of sanctification and illumination; making distinctions between days and meats, like the weak Christians spoken of in Rom. xiv., and taking up the worship of angels, in order to obtain from them revelations as to the celestial world (Col. ii. 16-18). One step further in the same direction will put us in touch with the false teachers of the Pastoral Epistles, who only represent a further stage of degeneracy in the direction of Judaism. They are the precursors of the Cabbala, which is a natural outgrowth of their doctrine.

De Wette lays much stress on this difficulty—that the heretics referred to in the Pastoral Epistles are sometimes spoken of as actually present in the Church, while in other passages (such as 1 Tim. iv. 1 *et seq.;* 2 Tim. iii. 1 *et seq.*) they are referred to as threatening the Church of the future. By this, we are told, the forger betrays himself. In the former passages he forgets himself, and makes the mistake of representing as actually existing forms of error which in the times of the Apostle were still in the future. But in that case, as Weiss justly observes, these moments of forgetfulness, in which heresy is spoken of as a present fact, ought to be the exception, not the rule. But the very opposite is the case. And if we look into it more closely, we find that all this supposed confusion of present and future vanishes away. The adversaries to be combated—those foolish and profane teachers who lead away superficial believers by their vain imaginings—are actually present in the Churches under the care of Titus and Timothy. But in one passage (1 Tim. iv. 1 *et seq.*) the reference is to an entirely different form of error—a doctrine of asceticism, based upon a dualist theory, by which certain meats and natural acts are forbidden as immoral. The history of the Church contains many fulfilments of this prophecy. In another passage (2 Tim. iii. 1 *et seq.*) the reference is to a growing corruption of the Church itself, of which there are already indications. There is no allusion to any of the great heresies. It is a prophecy of that general corruption which Christ Himself predicted as coming at the end of the age. Paul has already referred to this prophetic picture in one of his earlier letters (2 Thess. ii. 7), adding: "For the mystery of lawlessness does already work."

There is then no confusion in this respect in the Epistles before us, and we are afresh led to this result: That the false teachings referred to by Paul are, for the most part, those of his own lifetime, but that they belong to a period rather more advanced than the Epistles written from his Roman prison, especially that to the Colossians.

Church Organization in the Epistles

Church Organisation.—Several modern critics, following Baur, have assumed that the ecclesiastical offices referred to in the Pastoral Epistles indicate a much later date than the apostolic age. The functions of presbyter and deacon seem much more strictly defined than is likely to have been the case in the first century. The position of Titus and of Timothy, in relation to the elders or presbyters, seems suggestive rather of the monarchical episcopate of the second century. The ministry of widows, as described (1 Tim. v.), can hardly be anything else than the office of deaconess-sisters, spoken of in ecclesiastical writings of a later date; as, for instance, when Ignatius says to the Christians at Smyrna, "I salute the virgins, called widows."

But there are two insuperable difficulties in the way of this theory: (1) the plurality of presbyters in each Church (Titus i. 5; 1 Tim. iv. 14), and (2) their complete equality of position. These are the distinctive marks of the presbytery or episcopate of apostolic times, in opposition to that of a later period, when the bishopric was entrusted to one man, who was set over the college of presbyters.[1] Undoubtedly reference is made in 1 Tim. iv. 14 to a council of presbyters as an organised body, which had concurred with Paul in setting Timothy apart for his office, by the laying on

---

[1] I do not propose to enter here in detail into the question so much under discussion at the present time, of the relation between the presbyter and the bishop in the apostolic Church. It seems to me, from the latest evidence, that the *bishop* referred to in Titus i. 7 must be the same person with regard to whom Paul has just said (v. 5) that Titus should "appoint *elders* in every city." It is clear also that the *bishop* of whom Paul speaks (1 Tim. iii. 1) is one of those presbyters or elders referred to in ch. v. 17-22. For, as Paul passes directly in ch. iii. from the bishop to the deacon, no place is left for the presbyters, as holding a separate office from the bishop. Compare again Acts xx. 17 and 28, where Paul says to the presbyters of the Ephesian Church, "That the Holy Ghost has made them bishops to feed the Church of God." Perhaps I may find another opportunity to take up this question with reference to recent discussions on the subject.

of hands.   But, in the first place, that which was thus
conferred on Timothy was not the office of bishop, but
simply a call to evangelistic work (2 Tim. iv. 5).   And
this rite of the laying on of hands to set apart to some
work of ministry was practised in the Church from the
earliest times, as, for example, at Antioch, where the
prophets and teachers laid hands on Barnabas and
Saul to designate them for their missionary journey
among the Gentiles.   Even earlier than this the same
practice is referred to in the Church at Jerusalem,
when the Apostles laid hands on the "seven men of
good report" chosen to administer the alms of the
Church to the poor.   It is, indeed, an Old Testament
usage, for Moses laid his hands on Joshua to transmit
to him his office ; and the same practice was observed
when the heads of an Israelite household transferred
to the Levites the duty properly devolving on their eldest
sons, to serve in the sanctuary.   It is then perfectly
natural, that when Timothy departed from Lycaonia
with Paul and Silas for a new mission among the
Gentiles, the elders of the Church should have united
with Paul in imploring for him the unction of the Holy
One to qualify him for his evangelistic work, to which
he was thus set apart.

It is no matter of surprise then if, in 1 Tim. iii.,
Paul speaks of the diaconate as a recognised office,
especially in a large Church like that of Ephesus.   The
opening words of the Epistle to the Philippians show
that in another and probably much smaller Church

this office was already existing side by side with that of the bishop. If the Epistles before us had been written in the second century, by some one assuming the name of Paul, why should he have omitted the deacons in the Epistle to Titus ? On the other hand, it is quite natural that if the Church of Crete had been only recently founded, this second office should not yet have been required.

In the passage referring to *widows* in I Tim. v., careful attention should be paid to the transition in v. 9 from those who are widows in the ordinary sense to those who may be enrolled as such for the service of the Church, in the care of orphans, strangers, and the poor. Whatever Weizsäcker may say on this point, it seems to us perfectly clear that it is in this sense, of a recognised servant of the Church, that the title of deaconess is given to Phœbe, in Rom. xii. 1, 2.

All the references then in the Pastoral Epistles to offices in the Church seem to be closely connected with the elements of Church organisation which we find mentioned in the earlier Epistles. The Apostle is indeed more occupied than formerly with the duties and responsibilities of these servants of the Church. This arises no doubt partly from the ever-increasing gravity of the danger to the Churches from these unsound doctrines, and from the yet more deadly errors which he forecasts in the future. Then the Apostle has a prevision of his own approaching end ;

and to these two causes of anxiety on the Church's
account, a third is to be added, of which we must now
speak more at length.

In the early days of the Church at Jerusalem, reference is made to presbyters or elders, in whose hands
Barnabas and Paul placed the moneys collected at
Antioch for the poor of the flock at Jerusalem (Acts xi.
30). These same elders are spoken of again as taking
part in the assembly which decided the conditions of
the admission of the Gentiles into the Church (Acts
xv. 2, 6, 22). But it does not appear that these elders,
as such, were preachers. Their office seems rather to
have been administrative. Paul and Barnabas, in their
first mission into Asia Minor, before leaving the
Churches which they had founded there, appointed
elders whom they set apart with fasting and prayer.
It is probable that the ministry of these elders was of
a spiritual as well as administrative character. For
the Apostles not being themselves present in the
Churches, the oversight and spiritual guidance of them
would naturally devolve on these elders. This could
not be the case to the same degree in Jerusalem, where
the Apostles themselves still resided.

Somewhat later, at Thessalonica, there were in the
Church leaders or overseers, who carried on the work
among the faithful. The reference here is clearly to
a ministry of a spiritual nature, but only under the
form of the cure of souls (ch. v. 12-14), not under
that of preaching. This is spoken of as the gift of

prophecy, and was doubtless bestowed on those who filled the post of teachers in the Church (ch. v. 19, 20).

At Corinth, the spontaneous manifestation of the Spirit under the three forms of prophecy, the gift of tongues, and teaching, seems exceptionally abundant. Yet the regular offices could not be dispensed with. Why should not Paul have instituted them here as well as in Lycaonia and at Thessalonica? They are indeed mentioned in the long enumeration of the various gifts, under the name of "helps" and "governments," ἀντιλήψεις, κυβερνήσεις (1 Cor. xii. 28). Both are spoken of in the plural, because these two functions had their various spheres of duty; but both offices were certainly recognised. For if they had no existence, why does the Apostle say at the commencement of this passage, "Now there are diversities of gifts, but the same spirit; and there are diversities of ministrations, but the same Lord" (xii. 4, 5)? Certain gifts then were to be freely exercised: those, namely, which the Apostle describes by the special name of "*gifts*" (χαρίσματα). But there were others which were to be exercised by regular functionaries appointed by the Church itself, as in the case of the gifts of "helps and governments," which belonged to the presbyters and deacons.

In the Epistle to the Romans, instead of the twelve gifts which flourished at Corinth, we find only seven (Rom. xii. 8); prophecy, ministry (διακονία)—which includes no doubt the two offices of which we have just spoken—teaching, and a series of other gifts appertaining to the individual life. We feel that the extraordinary outpouring of gifts at Corinth was a local and temporary fact. The tongues disappeared, and teaching took their place ; the gift of prophecy was directly perpetuated in the offices of the Church. Everything indicates a calmer and more settled state.

Strong confirmation is given to this view by the Epistle to the Ephesians. Here Paul embraces the ministry in all its breadth, as concerning not only the particular Church, but the Church universal. He sees the gifts bestowed by the risen and glorified Lord, and the functions arising out of them, taking three forms. First, there is the *foundation* ministry, represented by the apostles and prophets. Secondly, a ministry of *extension*, carried on by the evangelists or missionaries. Thirdly, a ministry of *edification*, entrusted to the pastors and teachers (iv. 11).

And this is all. The rich abundance of gifts enumerated in the Epistle to the Corinthians seems to have vanished ; or at any rate their place in the Church is a subordinate one. Of all the gifts and offices belonging to the Corinthian Church, there remain only two— those of pastors and teachers—the pastorate as an office, the teaching as a free gift. The first of these terms clearly includes presbyters and deacons ; the second refers to public teaching. But it must be observed that the way in which the Apostle expresses himself (using a singular article for the two names) implies a very close connexion between the functions of pastor and teacher.

Very much the same state of things is suggested by the superscription of the Epistle to the Philippians, "To all the saints which are at Philippi, with the bishops and deacons." Doubtless it is natural that, in addressing a letter, only the offices should be mentioned, the gifts being too uncertain an element to be enumerated. But the absence of any allusion to these gifts in the course of the Epistle shows how far we are receding from the early Corinthian phase of Church life.

If now we turn again to the Pastoral Epistles, we shall naturally expect to find a continuance of the same tendency to blend the gift of teaching with the office of elder. And so it is. According to Titus i. 9, the choice of a presbyter or bishop must only fall on a man who "is able both to exhort in the sound doctrine and to convict the gainsayers." According to 1 Tim. iii. 2, the bishop must be a man "apt to teach" (see also 2 Tim. ii. 24). Lastly, according to 1 Tim. v. 17, there are two classes of elders—those who confine themselves to administering the affairs of the Church, and those who in addition to this, "labour in word and in teaching." The latter are to be "counted worthy of double honour." We see that in proportion as the extraordinary gifts of primitive times cease, the offices in the Church increase in importance and in influence, and that the principal gift—that of teaching—which survived all the rest, came to be more and more closely identified with the office of the regular ministry.

The monarchical episcopate of later times is the natural result in part of this progressive fusion of teaching with the primitive episcopate, and in part of the natural tendency of all administrative work to become concentrated in one hand. This change has been realised, at least in Asia Minor, at the time brought before us in the Revelation. The free exercise of the gifts, especially that of prophecy, even by women, still exists, only it is placed under the control of a personage called the Angel of the particular Church, who is charged with the oversight of the flock.[1]

This personage can neither be a celestial being nor a purely ideal and poetic personification of the Church. He is a living, responsible, human being, whose mission it is to watch over the progress of the Church, and who is worthy of praise or blame, reward or punishment. This personage can be no other than the head of the presbyterial council, and therefore the representative of the flock, seated, as Ignatius

---

[1] It will one day be seen that it is an utter mistake to place the date of the Apocalypse before the fall of Jerusalem. M. Harnack himself, who holds that the book is in substance Jewish with Christian interpolations, now places the date of the Christian interpolator under Domitian, that is, at the close of the first century. Now the idea of the Angel of the Church belongs to the Christian portion. The German Professor is therefore completely in accord with my view of the composition of the whole book.

says, surrounded by the circle of elders as by a spiritual crown, with the deacons as helpers.[1] This development of Church organisation, which was realised in Asia Minor towards the close of the first century, was adopted more gradually in other countries. Just as the current in the middle of a stream is more rapid than that near the banks, so, as Dr. Lightfoot has beautifully demonstrated, Asia Minor appears in this respect to have been in advance of the West on the one side (see Clement and Hermes), and of the East on the other, at least with regard to the Judæo-Christian Churches of those countries (see the *Didaché*). Both in Hermes and the *Didaché*, the free gifts are still in exercise, but it is easy to see that they are already degenerating, and that among them also there is a tendency to unite the teaching with the episcopate (*Didaché* c. 11 and 15). In the time of Justin, the union appears to have been consummated in Rome itself.

The Pastoral Epistles represent one particular point in this movement, the intermediate stage between the Epistles to the Ephesians and Philippians on the one hand, and the Revelation on the other. They do not go beyond the horizon of the life of Paul, but they mark its extreme limit. The Apostle, like a dying father, provides with anxious care, in these the last documents from his pen, for the right guidance of

---

[1] *Ad Magnes*, c. 13.

the family he leaves behind. He does, with regard to the Church, but on a lower plane, what Jesus did when He instituted the apostolate.

These then are the main questions throwing doubt on the authenticity of the Pastoral Epistles, and we have seen that, impartially investigated, they resolve themselves rather into proofs of their genuineness. Objections have been also drawn from some details in the letters. It has been asked whether, after the year 64, Paul could have spoken of the youth of Timothy (1 Tim. iv. 12). But if Timothy was eighteen years old when Paul took him with him in the year 52, he would have been rather more than thirty in 65, which, from the standpoint of the ancients was still young. We may add that the expression used is called forth by the contrast between the comparative youth of Timothy and the gravity of the charge entrusted to him. Again, it is said that in 1 Tim. v. 18, the term *Scripture* is applied to the Gospel of Luke, which would clearly imply a time subsequent to the life of Paul. Undoubtedly, but then it would also imply a date later than that which the same critics assign to the Pastoral Epistles. This objection also falls to the ground, if the term Scripture be referred only to the first of the two books quoted —the Book of Deuteronomy. (See also 1 Cor. ix. 9, 10, 14.) A much more weighty objection is raised by M. Reuss. Why does the Apostle give himself the trouble to write to his colleagues of things which he might have said to them a hundred times while he was with them, or which he could talk over with them when they met again? We reply: with regard to the question of doctrine, it is possible that the errors against which Paul urges them both to contend, may have been of quite recent growth; and as to the establishment of the proper offices in the Church, it was natural that he should be greatly concerned about it, as he saw his end drawing near.

In the critical position of the Church, he might feel very keenly the need of giving his colleagues, who were, in a measure, to bear the burden after him, the most precise and urgent and weighty counsels. Events have shown how great was the need for such instructions; for upon these two offices—the episcopate and the diaconate—which Paul, in a manner, institutes in these letters, has depended, and will depend to the end, the normal progress of the Church. The Pastoral Epistles are, in this respect, the Apostle's testament. It is in this sense that the Church has carefully preserved them in the Canon.[1]

Against these difficulties of detail, advanced by those who dispute the authenticity of the Pastoral Epistles, we may set others, which we submit to those who attribute these letters to a forger, writing half or three-quarters of a century after the death of St. Paul. Would the supposed forger put into the mouth of Paul the advice he gives to Timothy to take " a little

---

[1] See the Fragment of Muratori.

wine for his stomach's sake " ? or again the entreaty
that he would come to see him in Rome before winter,
and bring him from Troas the cloak and the parchments
which he had left with Carpus ? Would he mention
a sojourn of Paul and Titus in Crete, of which not a
word is said in the Acts of the Apostles ? Would he
ask him to join him in Nicopolis—a town which has
no connexion with any known journey of St. Paul ?
Would he speak of the speedy coming of Artemas
and Tychicus, as his representatives ? Would he
remind Timothy of the prophecies which accompanied
his calling to the work of an evangelist ? Would he
speak to him of his mother and grandmother by name ?
If all this is not natural and real, then it is the very
height of charlatanism. But such an idea is in manifest
moral contradiction with the deeply serious tone of the
whole Epistles. The most incongruous thing of all is
that Paul, wishing, as we are told, to make Titus and
Timothy the representatives of the episcopate of the
second century, should have represented Timothy first
as a simple evangelist, then as in danger of neglecting
his gift and of being ashamed of the Gospel testimony,
as shrinking back from suffering and scorn, and of
allowing himself to be hindered in this way from
coming back to his master and friend. Lastly, instead
of speaking of them as fixed at their post, as were the
bishops, Timothy and Titus are only sojourning for a
while with their Churches, and are very shortly to
rejoin Paul.

Historical Facts of the Epistles

It remains for us to inquire whether the historical allusions which occur repeatedly in these letters can be brought together in one period, with any semblance of probability or even possibility. Here we are clearly in the domain of hypothesis. The following explanation seems to me best to reconcile all the data.

Set free from his captivity in the spring of the year 64, Paul departed for the East, as he had said to Philemon and to the Philippian Church. Embarking at Brindisi, the most frequented port of Italy on the eastern side, he arrived at Crete. There he found Titus, who had already preached the gospel there and founded Churches. Here Paul remained some time with Titus. Then, desiring to fulfil his promise to the Philippians, he left there his faithful servant, who was still to carry on the work, and departed into Macedonia. Trophimus, who accompanied him, fell sick as the ship coasted along the shores of Asia Minor, and was left at Miletus. Paul had only a glimpse in passing of Timothy, who was at this time stationed at Ephesus. Paul exhorted him to remain at his difficult post, instead of becoming his companion, as Timothy would doubtless have preferred. As it was Paul's intention in any case to visit Asia Minor, before leaving for the West, he promised Timothy to come back shortly, and continued his voyage. He disembarked at Troas, where he left his cloak and books with Carpus, meaning to take them up again on his return. Arrived in Macedonia, his mind full of anxious thoughts about the grave duties devolving on his two young companions in labour, he wrote to them both—to Timothy with a view to encourage him, to give him fresh counsel, and assure him again of his speedy return ; and to Titus to tell him that some one was being sent to take his place, and to beg him to come without delay to join Paul at Nicopolis, probably the town in Thrace, where he proposed to pass the winter, before starting again in the spring for Asia Minor. As far as we can gather, St. Paul seems to have been prevented by some unforeseen circumstance from carrying out this plan. He was not able either to go back to Troas to fetch the things he had left there, or to rejoin Timothy at Ephesus, or to avail himself of Philemon's hospitality at Colosse. He was compelled suddenly to return west. Either he was carried there as a prisoner, having been arrested in Macedonia, or he went of his own accord into Italy in response to some urgent demand upon him. This sudden call may have been the dispersion and comparative destruction of the Church of Rome under the persecution by Nero. It needed a hand like Paul's to raise again the building from its ruins. It is possible that after performing this duty, he may, at length, in the course of the year 65, have left for Spain, as says the Fragment of Muratori (perfectionem Pauli ab urbe ad Spaniam proficiscentis). There he must soon have been again taken prisoner and brought back to Rome.   From his prison he wrote the Second Epistle to Timothy, in which he describes his almost utter loneliness, and begs him to come to him before the winter of 65-66.   Notwithstanding the favourable issue of his first appearance at the imperial tribunal, when he was enabled to bear his full testimony before the heads of the State, he was soon condemned and executed (probably beheaded) on the Appian Way, near which his tomb was still shown in the second century.

We do not see what valid objection there can be to this hypothetical explanation, which bears out all the allusions contained in the three Epistles before us. Even the prophetic words spoken to the Ephesian elders at Miletus (Acts xx. 25) thus find their fulfilment: "Behold, I know that ye also, among whom I went about preaching the kingdom, shall see my face no more"; for he was never able to carry out his purpose of again visiting Asia Minor.   His presentiment of his coming end (to which, as we see from his words to Philemon, he did not attach the certainty of prophecy) proved truer than at one time he himself supposed.

11

THE MESSAGE TO THE JUDEO-CHRISTIANS

(Hebrews)

THE Epistle to the Hebrews is one of the New Testament writings which bring the new economy before us as a transfiguration of the old. In the Epistle of James the moral law delivered to Israel is translated into the "law of liberty," the "royal law." In the First Epistle of Peter, the theocratic prerogatives of ancient Israel are handed down to the Church in a higher and abiding form. In the Revelation, we have the completed history of the kingdom of God, which was begun under the old covenant. In the Epistle to the Hebrews, the whole system of ceremonial worship is transferred to the heavenlies, and invested with a spiritual and truly life-giving significance.

In treating this Scripture, which is unique in its kind, we shall ask three questions, the answer to which will embrace all minor points demanding attention.

I. To what Churches was this letter addressed ?

II. What was the object which the writer proposed to himself ?

III. Who was the writer, who, unlike the authors of the other New Testament epistles, never gives his name?

I. The superscription of the letter describes those to whom it was sent as *Hebrews*. Is this superscription from the pen of the writer himself ? or was it added by those who were the first to enrol this Scripture among the other apostolic writings, out of which they were compiling the sacred library of their Church ? Obviously when we read such a heading as First Epistle to the Corinthians, we may be sure that it was not written by Paul himself. When he penned the First Epistle, he did not know that he should afterwards write a Second ; and indeed in that letter, such a heading was unnecessary, since the opening words described those to whom it was addressed. It is otherwise with the Epistle to the Hebrews. The writer enters at once upon his subject without any mention of names. Hence I am disposed to think that the superscription of the Epistle to the Hebrews is from the author's own pen. Weiss objects, that it was enough that the bearer of the letter knew its destination. This is true ; but it might fall into other hands, or in some way go astray.

Who then are these whom the writer describes as "the Hebrews" ? The word properly designates the

members of the Jewish nation at large. It is so used
in Philippians iii. 5. But it may have a more restricted
meaning, as in Acts vi. 1, where, as used by the
Christians of Jerusalem, it distinguishes the Hebrew-
speaking Jews from the Hellenists, or Greek-speaking
Jews of the same city. Neither of these meanings
is admissible in the heading of the Epistle to the
Hebrews, for the readers of this Epistle were certainly
Christians and Greek-speaking Christians. It would
be absurd to suppose such a letter addressed to Jews
who were not Christians, or to Hebrew-speaking
Jewish converts only. We must have recourse then to
a third meaning. The reference here is to the Judeo-
Christian Churches generally. This is the sense in
which the name occurs in the title " Gospel to the
Hebrews," given in the second century to the Gospel
used by preference in the Judeo-Christian Churches.
The heading of this Epistle therefore indicates that
the writer is addressing himself to certain Churches
of Jewish origin.

But it may be asked whether, in thus expressing
himself, he has reference to Judeo-Christians at large,
or to one or more Churches in particular, coming
within this category ? The former supposition has
been supported by many theologians, ancient and
modern. M. Reuss maintains that in this Epistle we
have a theological treatise intended for the whole
Church. Hofmann describes it as a sermon in the
form of a letter. This theory however fails to explain

a number of passages in the course of the Epistle, which clearly indicate that the writer had in view one particular Church, or more than one. For instance, in chap. v. 11, 12, he reproaches his readers with being slow to apprehend Christian truth, though they had been so long converted. Again, in chap. x. 34, he praises them for their sympathy with the sufferings of those who were in bonds (the true reading τοῖς δεσμίοις), that is, certain prisoners known to them and to him, and for the readiness of their self-sacrifice on their behalf. Again, in chap. xiii. 7, he speaks of the death of their leaders, whose faith they should imitate. These passages are quite in harmony with the conclusion of the Epistle, which is of an epistolary character, and the genuineness of which has been gratuitously called in question. The writer is so evidently addressing himself to particular readers, that he speaks of coming shortly with Timothy to visit them.

Where then are we to look for these Christians of Jewish origin to whom this Epistle is addressed? For the last century, criticism has been making exhaustive attempts to answer this question. The whole world has been scoured to find the readers of this Epistle. Some say they are to be found in Cyprus; others, in Asia Minor (Lycaonia, Galatia, Phrygia, Ephesus); others, again, in Greece (Thessalonica, Corinth); yet others, in Spain. The hypotheses in support of which reasons more or less solid have

been advanced, are the following : Antioch (Hofmann) ;
Alexandria (Schleiermacher, Ritschl, Bunsen, and
more particularly Wieseler) ; Rome, according to the
theory now most commonly received (Holtzmann,
Kurtz, Renan, Harnack, Von Soden) ; lastly, the
traditional view, strongly vindicated by Weiss, regards
the Churches of Palestine as those referred to by the
writer.

The *primâ facie* argument in favour of this opinion
is that there is not the slightest allusion in the whole
course of the Epistle to the presence of any section of
Christians of Gentile origin among the readers. Now
there were no purely Judeo-Christian Churches except
in Palestine and in those regions of the East where
dwelt those " myriads of Jews who had believed," as
James says (Acts xxi. 20). It was to these same
Churches, it would appear, that James himself
addressed his Epistle (James i. 1). It is further manifest, from the tenor of the whole Epistle, that it appeals
to men who were hindered in their spiritual progress,
by such an obstinate attachment to the worship of the
visible sanctuary, as was in danger of leading them
to renounce the gospel. Such an attitude of mind is
conceivable only among persons living in proximity
to the Temple of Jerusalem, where the old worship
was still celebrated. This hypothesis is supported by
chap. v. 12, where the readers are spoken of as
converts of long standing ; and by chap. ii. 3, where
we see that they had been brought into the faith by

those who had themselves heard the Lord. Lastly, the reference in chap. xiii. 7 to the glorious death of the leaders of the flock agrees perfectly with that which Josephus tells us (*Ant.* xx. 9, § 1) of the judicial murder of James and other chief men of the Church in Jerusalem, which took place in the year 62, under the high priest Ananus. Thus the position taken up on this question by the early Church, which is stated by Clement of Alexandria, and upheld among critics by Hug, Bleek, De Wette, Tholuck, Thiersch, Delitzsch, Riehm, and Weiss, appears to us, after all that has been advanced to the contrary, unassailable. It is also, as we have seen, the only explanation which bears out the meaning of the title, " Epistle to the Hebrews."

What considerations then, we ask, have led so many writers to seek another solution ? In the Epistle itself there is, as it seems to me, only one passage which presents any difficulty from the traditional point of view. This occurs in chap. vi. 10, where the writer commends his readers for the love they have shown and are still showing in ministering to the saints. If these words refer to collections made on behalf of suffering Christians, they would seem to have no application to the Church of Jerusalem, which was itself in deep poverty, and on behalf of which other Churches made contributions. But the writer may have in view the many Churches scattered over Judea, rather than the Church in the capital. Even in that

Church there certainly were some rich persons who could, if it were needful, minister to their poor brethren. The expression which Paul uses (Rom. xv. 26), that the "contribution is for the poor *among* the saints that are at Jerusalem," clearly distinguishes the poor from the whole body of the faithful. According to 2 Cor. viii. 2, the Christians of Macedonia were in deep poverty, and yet, as the Apostle says, "the abundance of their joy abounded unto the riches of their liberality." Why might it not have been the same in the Church of Jerusalem, even the poor contributing to the help of those who were yet poorer and suffering persecution, like those of whom James speaks in his Epistle?

In favour of the hypothesis that the Epistle was addressed to the Church in Egypt, stress is laid on the Alexandrine style of the writer, a certain correspondence of ideas with Philo, and, lastly, the many quotations from the Septuagint. This, if well founded at all, is an argument for the Alexandrine origin, not of the readers, but of the writer. As however he says, in chap. xiii. 19, "that I may be *restored* to you the sooner," there seems reason to suppose that he belonged originally to the Church to which he was writing. In weighing these arguments in favour of Alexandria, however, we must bear in mind that Alexandrine culture was diffused more or less among all Oriental Jews. In Acts vi. 9 we read of a synagogue of the Alexandrines at Jerusalem. There can be no doubt that in the worship of this synagogue, the Septuagint version of the Old Testament would be read ; and Alexandrine ideas, and even those of Philo, may easily have found their way into the Judaism of Palestine. The objections which occur to me to the theory that this Epistle was addressed to Alexandria are, first, that that Church was far from being purely Judeo-Christian ; and, second, that the Alexandrine teachers (Clement and Origen) never hint that their Church had any such claim.[1]

The opinion that the Epistle to the Hebrews was addressed to the Judeo-Christian portion of the Church in Rome found at one time great acceptance. This was at the time when critics were inclined to think that the Roman Church contained a large preponderating Judeo-Christian element. That time is past, and the only pretext for the idea just referred to is found in the words (chap. xiii. 24), " They of Italy salute you." At one time great importance was attached to these words, as showing that the Epistle was written from Italy. Now, those who advocate the theory that the letter was addressed to the Church of Rome, adduce the same words in support of their hypothesis. How can this be ? Those whose salutation the Apostle

---

[1] Wieseler, in his zealous advocacy of this view, brings forward the fact that a temple was built at Leontopolis in Egypt, to serve as a visible sanctuary for the Israelites of that region. This temple however never attained any importance, and the writer could not compare it to the Temple of Jerusalem, as on this theory he would be doing throughout the Epistle. This idea is now abandoned.

conveys are supposed to be Christians from Italy, who had taken refuge in the place from which the Epistle was written. They make the writer the medium of their greetings to their fellow-countrymen. But if this were the case, why does he not add a salutation from the Church in the midst of which he finds himself with these Italian refugees ? Again, does it seem probable that any Church of Italy (whether of Rome, according to Holtzmann, or of Ravenna, according to Ewald)— should have been so strongly tempted to fall back into Judaism, as those seem to have been for whom this Epistle was intended ? The argument drawn from the passage quoted has nothing solid to rest upon. It has not been observed that the preposition ἀπό (of) stands in connexion here, as in many other places, both with the pronoun οἱ (they) and the verb ἀσπάζεσθαι (salute you). " They of Italy salute you from Italy " ; as in Acts x. 23, where the ἀπό ("*from* Joppa ") refers both to the subject, the brethren, and to the verb, " went with him " ; or again, in Acts xvii. 13, where the same preposition ἀπό stands in connexion both with the pronoun *they* and the verb "should come." This construction occurs also in classic Greek, as in the *Anabasis* (v. 2, 24) : " When that house fell, those from the houses fled also (from those houses),"[1] where the ἀπό refers undoubtedly both to the verb *fled* and the subject *they*.

---

[1] ἔφευγον καὶ οἱ ἀπὸ τούτων τῶν οἰκιῶν.

It follows then that this letter was certainly written from Italy, from one of the Churches associated with those of Judæa. I do not say from Rome, though this supposition would naturally suggest itself; but as, according to chap. xiii. 23, Timothy, who had just been released from prison, probably in Rome, was coming to join the author in the place from which he was writing, it is presumable that he was not in Rome.

II. What was the religious state of those to whom the Epistle was written? and what was the purpose of the writer? These questions can only be answered by a rapid review of the contents of the letter.

The Epistle to the Hebrews is properly a treatise consisting of two parts—one didactic (chap. i.-x.), the other practical (xi.-xiii.). It concludes with a short epistolary appendix (xiii. 22-25). In this respect it resembles the Epistle to the Romans, with this difference, that there we have an epistolary preamble, which is altogether wanting in the Epistle before us. It has been conjectured that there may have been such a preamble originally, but that it was suppressed when the Epistle was placed among the canonical Scriptures. But such a liberty would scarcely have been taken with a writing which was to have the honour of being enrolled among the apostolic Scriptures preserved by the Church.

The Didactic Part of the Epistle

The first two chapters are seen at a glance to form a section by themselves in this grand argument. They

contain a comparison of Jesus, the Messiah, with the
angels. He is first shown to be higher than they by
His Divine nature ; and, next, to be made a little lower
than the angels by His incarnation and death. This
very humiliation however gives him a higher fitness for
His work as a Saviour.

The superiority of Messiah to the angels is demonstrated in chap. i. by a series of passages from the Old
Testament, some of which are applied in the original
context to Jehovah Himself. Hence it is evident that
the writer regarded the person of Messiah as nothing
less than the supreme manifestation of Jehovah. This
didactic statement is immediately followed by a short
practical application (chap. ii. 1-4). If every act of
disobedience to the law of Moses, which was given by
angels, had been severely punished, how much heavier
must be the guilt of neglecting the salvation brought by
the Son of God !

With chap. ii. 5 commences the second section,
showing forth the state of humiliation by which Messiah
had been made a little lower than the angels. The
perfect world for which we are looking had been made
subject by prophecy, not to an angel, but to One who
for a little while was made lower than the angels
(Psalm viii. 5). Jesus was such an One. He stooped
below the angels, and made Himself one with us for
the suffering of death. But He did this, that He might
bring many sons unto glory, and might become the
faithful Intercessor for all those who were subject

to temptations such as He Himself had known by experience.

A short exhortation (chap. iii. 1) gives the practical application of this second section. " Let us consider this Apostle and High Priest of our confession, even Jesus." Happily the truth here brought out is quite independent of the application made by the writer of the passage from Psalm viii. ; for that application rests, not upon the real sense of the Hebrew text, but upon the Septuagint version, which is now known to be inexact.

It may be asked, What led the writer to open his argument with this comparison between Jesus and the angels ? It must be remembered that, from a Jewish point of view (chap. ii. 2, Gal. iii. 20), the law, the distinguishing privilege of Israel, had been given through the medium of angels. This then was the highest theocratic authority, next to God Himself ; and the writer would now show the inferiority even of the angelic hierarchy to Jesus.

This is made clear by the section which follows (chaps. iii., iv.). The writer compares Jesus to the two greatest personages in Jewish history—Moses and Joshua. This section also is divided into two parts : in the first (chap. iii.) we have the comparison between Jesus and Moses ; in the second (chap. iv.), that between Jesus and Joshua. Each of these divisions, like the foregoing, consists first of a didactic statement, and then of a solemn warning.

Just as the master-builder is greater than the man who builds the house, so Jesus is greater than Moses (vv. 2-6). The long practical application which follows may be thus summed up. If the Jews in the wilderness were punished for their unbelief of Moses by not being allowed to enter Canaan, how much more certainly will those who let go their faith in Jesus be shut out from the rest of God !

This introduces the second section, the comparison with Joshua (chap. iv. 1-10). How can the writer speak of the shutting out of the Jews of his time from the promised rest, when from the time of Joshua they had been in actual possession of the land of Canaan ? The answer is given in the words of Psalm xcv. 11, which show that the Canaan into which Joshua led the tribes was not the true rest of God. Jesus alone leads His people into this true rest. Hence a solemn charge to hold fast their profession of faith in Jesus the Son of God, who is passed into the heavens (chap. iv. 11-16).

After comparing Jesus with the angels, and with Moses and Joshua, the lawgiver and leader of Israel, there remained yet a third comparison to be drawn. This occupies the third section, in which the writer establishes a parallel between Jesus and Aaron the high priest. The priesthood constituted, with the law and the possession of Canaan, the third great theocratic privilege of the chosen people (chaps. v.-x.).

This third section, like the others, consists of two parts. The first is a comparison of the ministry of

Jesus with that of Aaron in its nature and origin (chaps. v.-vii.) ; the second, a comparison of the two priesthoods as to their efficacy (chaps. viii.-x.).

In comparing the nature of the two priesthoods, the writer treats first of their equality (chap. v.), and next of the superiority of the priesthood of Jesus (chaps. vi., vii.).

Their equality is demonstrated by four characteristics which they have in common. These are as follows : 1st, Aaron was taken from among men to be their representative before God. 2nd, He was compassed with infirmity, that he might feel for the infirmities of his brethren. 3rd, He offered a sacrifice for himself, and not for the people only. 4th, He was directly called of God to his office.

We can but wonder at the boldness with which the writer applies these four characteristics to Jesus, especially the third. He is here alluding to the scene in Gethsemane, in which he sees the sacrifice offered by Jesus for Himself, before bearing our sins on the cross. In the agony in the garden, He consummated the voluntary offering up of His own human nature, that by this perfect obedience He might become the sacrifice for all mankind. Jesus is equal to Aaron on these four points, hence He is truly a high priest. But the writer is leading up to a far higher point. He will show that Jesus is the perfect High Priest, and in order to this, he must show that His priesthood is higher in its nature than that of Aaron.

Before entering on this subject, however, he gives a long preamble (chap. v. 10-vi. 20), in which he complains of the want of spiritual insight in his readers. He reminds them of the awful truth that if any one fall away after receiving the grace of regeneration and spiritual enlightenment, no further renovation is possible. He does indeed afterwards express the hope that such may not be the sad lot of any of his readers, but that they will hold fast even to the end, knowing that their hope of salvation rests, not only upon the promise, but upon the very oath of God.

After this introduction he takes up again the argument commenced in chap. v. 10, and proceeds to show how the priesthood of Jesus is higher than that of Aaron. He finds in the history of the patriarchs a point of comparison which, read in the light of some words of David, supplies the elements he needs for his argument. The point thus taken up is the history of Melchisedec (Gen. xiii.) in connexion with Psalm cx. 4, in which David, addressing the future Messiah, hails Him as the " priest after the order of Melchisedec."

The outline of the argument is this : Christ is equal to Melchisedec ; Melchisedec is higher than Aaron ; hence Christ is higher than Aaron (vii. 1-23).

The first of these propositions is proved by the fact that Abraham paid the tenth of the spoil which he had taken in war to " Melchisedec, king of Salem and priest of God Most High." Now the payment of tithe is a tribute from the lower to the higher. Hence

Abraham, and in him Levi and Aaron himself, were declared to be of a lower order than Melchisedec (vii. 1-10).

The second proposition is proved by the fact that Jesus does not come of the tribe of Levi, which was the priestly tribe, according to Moses, but that, like Melchisedec *king of Salem*, he was descended from the royal tribe of Judah, deriving, like Melchisedec, his priestly right not from human descent, but from the power of an endless life within Him (vii. 11-16).

From this fundamental analogy, which shows the identity of nature between Christ and Melchisedec, a third proposition follows. The priesthood of Christ, being equal to that of Melchisedec, which is higher than that of Aaron, is itself higher than that of Aaron.

This the writer proceeds to confirm by a few particular points of superiority. 1st, The oath of God, which, according to Psalm cx. 4, inaugurated the Messianic priesthood—an honour not conferred on the priesthood of Aaron. 2nd, The permanence of the priesthood of Christ (noticed also in Psalm cx.), while the sons of Aaron die one after another. 3rd, The one completed sacrifice of Christ for Himself and for the people, while in the Jewish temple fresh victims needed to be offered day by day. Lastly (4th), The spotless character of Christ, "The Son perfected for evermore," in contrast to the human infirmity of the descendants of Aaron (vv. 17-23).

But of what avail to us would be this superiority of the priesthood of Christ, in its nature and origin, to that of Aaron, unless it were also more efficacious in our behalf? This forms the theme of the third section of the Epistle, and is the key-note to the whole didactic portion (chaps. viii.-x.).

Its treatment is introduced by the analysis of a passage in the prophecies of Jeremiah (xxx. 31 and following), which foretells the substitution of a new covenant for the covenant of Sinai, which could bring nothing to perfection. The writer proceeds to set forth the superiority of this new covenant, showing how the sacrifice on which it is based is more efficacious than that of Aaron, on which the old covenant rested.

1. As to the place where the sacrifice is offered—the first, an earthly sanctuary; the second, heaven itself (chap. ix. 1-5).

2. As to the manner of the priest's entrance into the holy place—under the old covenant, once in the year; under the new, once for all (vv. 6-11).

3. As to the victims offered—under the old covenant, "the blood of goats and of calves"; under the new, Christ "offered Himself without blemish unto God" (vv. 12-24).

4. As to the offering of sacrifices—under the old covenant, the constant repetition of the same sacrifices proved their inadequacy; under the new, "the sacrifice once offered perfects for ever them that are sanctified" (v. 25-x. 11).

This central passage closes, like the rest, with a practical application. It is an invitation to enter at

once, through the blood of Jesus, into the holiest of all
(intimate communion with God), access to which was
closed under the old covenant, but is now open to the
followers of Christ by a new and living way. Then
follows another solemn warning. "Beware of forsaking
the assembling of yourselves together, lest you forsake
also your faith itself; for there would remain no more
sacrifice for the expiation of such a sin" (vv. 16-20).
Thus repeatedly does the writer hold up before his
readers the danger of falling away, with its awful
consequences.

The Practical Part of the Epistle

The general application, contained in chaps. xi.-xiii.,
is to the didactic portion, as a whole, what each particular parenesis was to its didactic premisses.

If we remember the tenacity with which the Churches
addressed appear to have clung to the visible sanctuary
at Jerusalem, and the value which they attached to the
maintenance of their oneness with the chosen nation
settled in the land of Canaan, we shall easily understand the scope of the writer's observations in chap. xi.,
in which he held before them the picture of the life of
faith and endurance led by the patriarchs and prophets.
All these, each in his own manner, let go the seen that
they might grasp the unseen. This is the very essence
of faith according to v. 1, which is, as it were, the text
of the whole chapter.

In chap. xii. the writer adds to the duty of faith the

duty of patience. Keeping the eye fixed upon Jesus, who was the first to mark out clearly the track of faith, and the first to reach its goal, the believers are to accept without dismay the sufferings by which God is educating them as His children, and are to strive after holiness ; for they are already citizens of the heavenly Jerusalem, and are already realising the efficacy of the blood which speaketh better things than that of Abel. Let them fear then to turn away from Him who speaketh to them from heaven, "for our God is a consuming fire." Lastly, to the two duties of faith and steadfast patience he adds, in chap. xiii., that of utter self-renunciation. He had long been leading up to this. It is indeed the gist of the whole Epistle. At length (chap. xiii. 13) he speaks out, and demands the supreme act of sacrifice. "Let us therefore go forth unto Him without the camp, bearing His reproach." As Jesus was led forth in ignominy outside the walls of Jerusalem, bearing His cross, so the time is come for those believing Jews, who have cherished till now the bond of oneness with the Jewish nation and religion, to make the great surrender, and break with a bond which threatens to lead them to their ruin. "Break loose from Judaism. Be wholly His who is better to you than the angels, better than Moses or Joshua, better than Aaron and his priesthood. Be all for Jesus, in whom you possess the eternal reality of all the good things of which Judaism offers you only the shadow."

Such, as it seems to me, is the thought brought out

in the Epistle to the Hebrews. The writer only adds
in conclusion a sort of epistolary postscript. He
excuses himself for having written such a letter of
exhortation to such readers. He speaks of his approaching visit with Timothy, who has lately been set
at liberty. Then he greets the heads of the flock in
his own name and that of the Christians of Italy, and
desires that grace may be with them all.

What was the spiritual need which this Epistle
was intended to meet ? There can be but one answer.
These Christians of Jewish origin were on the point of
reverting to Judaism, from which they had never more
than half broken loose. It is this falling back to the
things behind, against which the writer of the Epistle
would fain put them on their guard. It is at this he is
aiming in all the practical exhortations to which each
separate didactic period leads up. A critical time had
come for the Churches in Judæa, especially for the
Church in Jerusalem. The general cause of the danger
is easy to define. It was the overweening attachment
of these Judeo-Christians to outward rites and ceremonial worship. This ceremonialism had been a real
hindrance to the development of spiritual life in these
Christians, the firstfruits of the Gospel ; and, as the
writer of the Epistle points out reproachfully, they had
become spiritually " dull of hearing." And when, " by
reason of the time, they ought to be teachers, had need
to be taught again the rudiments of the first principles
of the oracles of God" (chap. v. 11, 12).

Beside this general cause of a stunted Christian life, there were also particular circumstances which added to the gravity of the position. There was the impending war with the Roman power, which placed the Christians in a strait between their faith and their patriotism. There was also the rapidly advancing work of Paul among the Gentile nations, which, tending as it did to minimise the obligations of the ceremonial law, was a constant source of irritation to those who still clung to the Mosaic institutions (see Acts xxi. 19-25).

Thiersch argues that after Paul's last visit to Jerusalem (Acts xx.), the believing Jews were excluded from the temple, into which James alone was still permitted to enter (according to Hegesippus), and that this deprivation of the worship to which they had been accustomed from childhood, greatly discouraged them and inclined them to go back to Judaism. It must be borne in mind, also, that this was about the time of the departure of the Apostles, and of the death of James and other leaders of the flock, who had succeeded to the apostolic charge. There is also one other circumstance to be taken into account, on which De Wette rightly lays stress : namely, the twofold disappointment caused, first, by the persistent refusal of the Jewish people to accept Jesus as the Messiah (whereas the Christians had always been looking for their conversion) : and, second, by the prolonged delay of the return of Christ, for which they had looked as immediate. If we put all these things together, we shall easily comprehend the distress of mind that took possession of the Judeo-Christians in the year 65-66, at which time it seems to us probable this Epistle was written.

This date is confirmed by the passage in which the writer speaks of the liberation of Timothy, and of his approaching arrival with himself. Timothy had no doubt repaired to Rome at the summons of Paul in his second captivity (2 Tim. iv. 19). He had then been imprisoned with Paul, and after Paul's martyrdom had been set at liberty. This seems the natural explanation of chap. xiii. 23, and fixes the date of the Epistle as approximately A.D. 66. Some critics assign to it a date after the fall of Jerusalem. Zahn gives the year 80 ; Holtzmann, Harnack, Von Soden date it under Domitian, between 80 and 96 ; others about the year 100, or a little later. It is no argument against these opinions to say that the present tense of the verb is used in speaking of the worship of the sanctuary, for we still use to-day, in referring to the Mosaic institutions, such expressions as "the sacrifice is offered morning and evening." But Hilgenfeld rightly asks, How could the writer have said, "Now if Jesus were on earth, He would not be a priest at all, seeing there are those who offer the gifts according to the law," if he had been writing at a time when no sacrifice could any longer be offered ? Or how could he have said, " In that He saith, A new covenant, He hath made the first old : but that which is becoming old and waxeth aged is nigh unto vanishing away" (chap. viii. 13), if the worship of the old covenant had already ceased ? Or how could he have expressed himself thus, " Else would they not have ceased to be offered," if they had actually already ceased to be offered ? Hilgenfeld concludes from these considerations that the Epistle was written between the years 64 and 66. The writer would certainly not have taken so much trouble to prove the insufficiency of that which no longer existed. If God had already sealed the doom of the old worship, no argument was needed on the part of man ; he had only to appeal to this decisive judgment.

The deep earnestness of this Epistle, its solemn warnings, threats, and exhortations, are only to be explained by the presence of a very real danger ; namely, that tendency to falling away from the faith which we have described above.

III. Who was the writer ?

The opinion which has become traditional and general in the Church since the close of the fourth century, and which assigns the authorship of this Epistle to St. Paul, had been accepted in the East long before that time. It was promulgated by the Alexandrine doctors, Pantenus, Clement, Origen. But until the close of the fourth century it had not been received in the West by Irenæus, or by the author of the *Fragment of Muratori*, or by Tertullian, Hippolytus, or Cyprian. Jerome testifies to this difference of opinion between the two great sections of the Church, up to the time when the question was resolved in the Synod of Carthage, in

397, in favour of the apostolic authorship. This decision was arrived at under the influence of Augustine, who had himself yielded on this point to the Eastern tradition.

The Alexandrine doctors did not however disguise from themselves the difficulties which stood in the way of their view. Pantenus admitted that the Apostle acted in a way quite contrary to his custom, in not mentioning his own name at the beginning of the letter. He explained this omission as arising from the modesty of Paul, who was unwilling to style himself an Apostle to the Hebrews, inasmuch as Jesus Himself was their Apostle (chap. iii. 1). Clement recognises that there is a great difference between the style of this Epistle and the other Epistles of Paul; but he explains it on the theory that Paul wrote the original in Aramaic, and that it was translated into Greek by Luke. Origen says that any one competent to judge of differences of style will observe that this Epistle is far more Greek in its form than the other writings of the Apostle; but, on the other hand, the thoughts are admirable and on a par with those which abound in the Epistles of Paul. The substance of the Epistle then is of Paul; as to the writer of it in its present form, God only knows who he is. Tradition, he says, points either to Clement, who became Bishop of Rome, or to Luke, the writer of the Gospel and of the Acts.

Criticism, after being long repressed by the decisions of the Council of Carthage, reasserted itself at the time of the Reformation. Erasmus attributed the Epistle to the Roman Clement ; Luther conceived the idea that Apollos was its author. Calvin pronounced in favour of Luke. The Council of Trent confirmed the old traditional opinion, which was accepted in the Lutheran Church till the middle of the eighteenth century, when rationalism lifted up its voice. From the time of Semler appeared a succession of writings for and against the authorship of Paul, until between 1826 and 1840 Bleek published his great work, which decisively turned the scale against the old received opinion. At the present day Hofmann is the only theologian of any weight who maintains the Pauline origin of the Epistle to the Hebrews.

Ebrard and Döllinger are in favour of Luke ; Riethmaier and Bisping, two Catholic divines, support Clement of Rome ; Semler, De Wette, Tholuck, Bunsen, Kurtz, Farrar, De Pressensé, Hilgenfeld, hold that the author is Apollos (following in this Tertullian, whose testimony we shall presently quote) ; Ullmann, Wieseler, Ritschl, Grau, Thiersch, Weiss, Renan, Zahn, Keil, conclude in favour of Barnabas ; Mynster and Böhme support Silas ; lastly, Ewald, Grimm, Lipsius, Von Soden, attribute the Epistle to some Alexandrine Christian of name unknown. Reuss hesitates between Apollos and Barnabas.

In favour of the authorship of Paul, Origen insists on the beauty of the thoughts ; but surely there were many men in the primitive Church whose thoughts were admirable. Another point urged is the exact agreement of the quotation given in chap. x. 30 with that of Paul (Rom. xii. 19), which does not tally verbally with Deuteronomy xxxii. 35, 36, either in the Hebrew or Septuagint version. This is no doubt a point difficult to explain. But if the letter was written from Italy, the writer might have read in Rome the Epistle to the Romans, and quoted from memory the words as given by Paul. In any case, such a point of detail is not sufficient to outweigh the much graver arguments against the apostolic authorship.

In the first place, we note the *order* of the Epistle— the absence of any heading or introductory thanksgiving, and the recurrence of short pareneses at the close of each didactic portion. All this is quite foreign to the manner of Paul. The style also is markedly different from that of Paul. Here we have rounded, oratorical periods, while Paul's phraseology is unstudied, broken, abrupt. Hofmann explains this difference by saying that Paul, released from prison, and awaiting at Brindisi the arrival of Timothy, had ample leisure to give attention to style in a way he had never done before. It is strange indeed that he should have written in polished Greek to the Hebrews, while all his life he had been writing to the Hellenes in a style abounding with rugged and barbarous Hebraisms. With regard to the vocabulary of this Epistle, as compared with that of Paul's letters, we commend to our readers' study Prof. Gardiner's work, *The Language of the Epistle to the Hebrews as Bearing upon its Authorship*. We know while in the teaching of Paul it centers in the cross. This is not a contradiction, for that which the Redeemer presents in the most holy place in the heavens is the blood shed upon the cross ; and in the teaching of Paul himself, the cross of Christ only saves us as it leads on to His resurrection and intercession in the heavens. Still the same truth is regarded from two very distinct points of view.[1]

We draw attention, in conclusion, to one passage, which could never have been written by St. Paul, the passage, namely, in which he says that he was taught the Gospel by those who had heard it from the mouth of the Lord (chap. ii. 3). Paul, when speaking of himself, categorically denies any such attitude of dependence on the other apostles of the Lord (Gal. i. 11-17).

Dr. Biesenthal[2] has reproduced in our day the theory first invented by Clement of Alexandria, that the Epistle to the Hebrews was written by Paul in Aramaic, and translated by Luke into Greek. In the translation however he is supposed to have fallen into a number of errors, as Dr. Biesenthal proves by himself re-translating the Epistle from Greek into Hebrew. But how many times has it been shown that the Epistle to the Hebrews cannot be a translation ? It abounds in compound words which are essentially Greek, and have

---

[1] The difference in the conception of faith, which has often been remarked, seems to me easily resolved if we look at Rom. iv. 20, 2 Cor. v. 7.

[2] *Das Trost-schreiben des Ap. Paulus an die Hebräer.* 1878.

no other work on the subject to compare with this, either for solidity or for the delicacy with which points of comparison are treated.   Prof. Gardiner himself was constrained to change his opinion as to the origin of the Epistle, so cogent and unexpected were the results of his researches (p. 19).   In the citations from the Old Testament, the writer of the Epistle to the Hebrews servilely copies the Septuagint, even when the translation is inexact.   Paul, on the contrary, often corrects the Septuagint by the Hebrew.   Again, the writer cites from the text of Codex Alexandrinus, Paul from the Codex Vaticanus.   The writer further reproduces long passages, which must have been copied ; Paul uses only short quotations, generally made, as far as we can judge, from memory.   The writer of this Epistle quotes with such introductory formulas as " God saith," " the Holy Spirit thus testifying," etc.   Paul either mentions the sacred writer from whom he quotes, or makes no allusion to his authority.

The difference is very marked, further, from a *religious point of view*.   We cannot here go into the question whether the author was writing on the basis of Pauline teaching, modified by Alexandrine influence, or whether he was simply working out the primitive apostolic teaching under Pauline influence.   But one point seems to us perfectly clear.   According to the writer of the Epistle to the Hebrews, the redemptive work of Christ is carried on rather in the heavenly sanctuary, as the outcome of the resurrection and ascension of the Lord ;

no analogues in Aramaic or in Hebrew, and it contains plays upon words such as could only occur in a composition originally Greek.[1] Can the writer of this original composition be St. Luke? The Christology of the third Gospel presents indeed some analogy with that of the Epistle to the Hebrews (as, for instance, the growth of Jesus in knowledge and obedience); and that which is said (chap. xiii. 23) of the personal relations of the author with Timothy might well apply to Luke. But could a Gentile Christian, a disciple of Paul, ask the Churches of Judea to pray for him " that he might be restored to them the sooner" (chap. xiii. 19)? The style of Luke's writing moreover is clear and flowing, but not at all oratorical.

Can the writer be Clement of Rome? But he has no originality of thought or brilliancy of style. It is enough to read a few lines of his Epistle to the Corinthians, to be struck with the difference between that and the Epistle before us. Clement imitates the Epistle to the Hebrews, but he is only a copyist.

Can the writer be Apollos? But how could this young Christian, a catechumen of Priscilla and Aquila, two disciples of Paul, say that he learned the Gospel from those who had themselves heard the Lord? How could such a one have the boldness to write such a letter to the Churches of Judea, the oldest and most venerable Churches of Christendom? How, lastly, could

---

[1] Ἔμαθεν—ἔπαθεν ; μένουσαν—μέλλουσαν ; διαθήκη (covenant and testament). Comp. v. 8; xiii. 14; ix. 15-26.

he speak of being restored to them, from whom he had never come out, and to whom he had never belonged ? [1]

We come now to the man who commands to-day the majority of votes—Barnabas. He was certainly one of the members of the primitive Church of Jerusalem, and one of its most eminent members, a disciple of the apostles, and almost their equal (Acts iv. 36, 37). He was moreover by birth a Levite, and consequently familiar from childhood with all the traditions of the temple worship. He was a Hellenist Jew from Cyprus, and competent as such to write in excellent Greek. We seem almost to read his very signature in the epilogue of the Epistle when he says (chap. xiii. 22), "Bear with the word of exhortation" (τοῦ λόγου τῆς παρακλήσεως), reminding us of the name which the Apostles had given him (Acts iv. 36), "son of exhortation" (τοῦ λόγου τῆς παρακλήσεως). The fact moreover that in the East an epistle was ascribed to him, of which he was certainly not the author, seems to prove that some genuine letter from his pen had existed. Lastly (and this is important), Barnabas is the only one of all the reputed authors in favour of whom a positive tradition can be shown ; for it is of the Epistle to the Hebrews Tertullian is speaking when he says : "There exists also a writing entitled *To the Hebrews*, by Barnabas, a man sufficiently authorised of God."

---

[1] As to the Alexandrinisms of the Epistle to the Hebrews, see Prof Gardiner, p. 21.

[2] *De Pudicitiâ*, c. 20.

One grave difficulty seems to me however to counter-
balance all the arguments just brought forward. How
is it possible that a well-known and all but apostolic
name, like that of Barnabas, should have been almost
completely lost? And is not the fact that another
writing was falsely assigned to Barnabas an added
argument against the suppression of his name in an
Epistle really written by him?

We cannot help asking if a less illustrious name
would not solve the problem more easily? May not
the writer have been Silas—himself also an eminent
member of the primitive Church of Jerusalem, and even
a prophet in that Church (Acts xv. 32); who was also
honoured by being made a delegate from the Apostles
to the Churches of Syria, who succeeded Barnabas as
fellow-labourer with Paul on his missionary journey,
and assisted him in forming the Churches of Greece;
who was subsequently associated with the work of
Peter (1 Peter v. 12), and, as one of the founders of the
Churches in Greece, must have come much into contact
with Timothy (1 Thess. i. 1; 2 Thess. i. 1; 2 Cor. i.
19)? This gives the key to the relations between the
writer and Timothy implied in Hebrews xiii. 23, "with
whom, if he come shortly, I will see you." Silas was
with Paul during nearly two years of his ministry in
Corinth, and this accounts for the apostolic character of
the teaching which many modern critics have observed
in the Epistle to the Hebrews. The writer had come
largely under the influence of Paul. If we compare

I Cor. iii. 2, "I fed you with milk, not with meat," with Heb. v. 12-14, "Ye are become such as have need of milk, not of strong meat . . . "; or again, I Cor. x. 1-11 with Heb. iii. 12-19—can we not clearly catch the echo of the teachings to which the writer had listened from the lips of Paul at Corinth ? Lastly, as the companion of the Apostle Peter towards the close of his career, Silas may have gone with him to Rome ; which would explain how he was able to tell the Judean Christians of the liberation of Timothy and of his approaching departure from Italy, adding the promise that he would visit them with him.

Whatever conclusion may be arrived at from a consideration of all these various theories, we are glad to close this study of the Epistle with the words of Thiersch : " If it should be found that a noble picture, which had been attributed to Raphael, was not by that artist, there would not be one masterpiece the less, but one great master the more."

To us it seems certain that the admirable Epistle we have been studying is not from the pen of Paul ; but this very fact only serves to reveal to us the abundance and excellence of the spiritual gifts possessed by men who occupied only the second rank in the apostolic Church. Whether they were named Barnabas or Apollos, Aquila or Silas, these stars of the second magnitude were able to send forth far-reaching rays of light ; and we recognise the fitness of the title *prophets* applied to some of them, " first apostles, then prophets" (1 Cor. xii. 28). Though the Epistle to the Hebrews is not of apostolic origin, it is none the less a prophetic scripture, a true document of revelation.[1]

---

[1] Different opinions prevail as to the epistolary supplement (chap. xiii. 22-25) and its relation to the rest of the letter. Delitzsch attributes these four verses to Paul himself, while he supposes the rest of the letter to have been written for Paul by a friend—probably Luke. Ebrard also thinks the letter was written at Paul's instance, but he holds that these four verses were added by the compiler. Zeller attributes the whole letter to a writer of later date, who added this supplement in order to make it pass as a Pauline Epistle. But surely, in such a case, the forger would have mentioned Paul in a more distinct and positive manner. The first two hypotheses have, critically, no ground to rest upon, and seem to have had no other design than to maintain a close connexion between the Epistle and Paul himself, since even the critics dare not go so far as to attribute the letter directly to the Apostle.

12

GENERAL REVIEW OF PAUL'S EPISTLES

THE Epistles of Paul were the completion and confirmation of his missionary work. It sometimes happened that his stay in a place where he had founded a Church was brought to an abrupt end before he had been able to complete the whole course of teaching which he proposed to give. Hence, when any difficulty arose, and was referred to him by such a Church, he endeavoured to supply the need of further teaching by a letter. In this way the two Epistles to the Thessalonians came to be written. Or it might be that his doctrine or his personal character was impugned in one of the Churches that he had founded, and he was constrained to take up his pen in defence of the truth, lest its very foundations should be shaken. This is the key to the Epistle to the Galatians and the two Epistles to the Corinthians. At other times some personal matter led him to write either to a particular Church or to a particular member, as when he sent his thanks to the Philippians for their loving ministrations to his need, or when he desired to com-

mend Onesimus to the kindness of Philemon. Sometimes, at the request of a third person, the Apostle
addressed letters to Churches which he had neither
founded nor visited; such were the Epistles to the
Colossians and Ephesians, and that to the Romans.

Do we possess all the Epistles written by St. Paul ?
It has been argued that it must be so, since God would
never have permitted any writings inspired by His
Spirit to be lost.   But why may not an inspired writing
have had a purely temporary and local value, so that
those who compiled the canon may not have thought
it necessary to perpetuate it ?   It appears to us clear
that in 1 Cor. v. 9-11 there is a reference to a letter
which has not come down to us, and that such is the
case also with that other epistle of which Paul speaks
in detail in 2 Cor. ii. 1-4 ; vii. 8-12. If we are not
prepared to refer the words in 2 Thess. iii. 17, " The
salutation of me Paul with mine own hand, which is
the token in every epistle, so I write," to some
unknown letters yet to be written (which would seem
a rather forced interpretation), we must conclude that
he had already written some which have not been
preserved.

As to other Epistles of Paul's still extant, and not
included in the New Testament canon, such as an
Epistle to the Corinthians discovered in Aramaic,
another addressed to the Laodiceans (which has even
crept into some Bibles of the Middle Ages); or the
supposed correspondence between Paul and Seneca,

of which Jerome and St. Augustine speak, and the genuineness of which has recently found advocates,— all these are only poor compilations of words taken from the authentic Epistles of St. Paul, and altogether destitute of that impress of originality which marks all the true writings of the Apostle. The first of these spurious writings is based upon 1 Cor. v. 9 ; the second on Col. iv. 16, which really refers to what we call the Epistle to the Ephesians. The correspondence with Seneca was suggested by the mention (Acts xviii. 12) of the arrival in Corinth, during Paul's sojourn there, of the Proconsul Gallio, brother of Seneca, and by the account of the Apostle's citation to appear before him.

Of the fourteen Epistles contained in our canonical collection, one only,—that to the Hebrews—appears to us not to bear either in form or substance the marks of Pauline authorship. This is also the only Epistle with regard to which the tradition of the primitive Church is doubtful. The genuineness of the other thirteen Epistles seems to us assured on the ground both of internal evidence and of concurrent tradition.

In studying each of these Epistles separately, we have tried to determine the time and place of their writing. Under this head we divide them into four groups : the first group comprising the two Epistles to the Thessalonians written during the journey on which Paul founded the Churches of Greece (A.D. 52-54) ; the second, comprising the Epistles to the

Galatians, the two Epistles to the Corinthians, and that to the Romans, which were written during Paul's stay at Ephesus, and his visit to the Churches of Greece (A.D. 54-59); the third, comprising the Epistles to the Colossians, to Philemon, and to the Ephesians, and lastly, that to the Philippians, which dates from Paul's Roman captivity (A.D. 62-64); the fourth group, consisting of what are called the three Pastoral Epistles, and belonging to the period which followed the Apostle's liberation and immediately preceded his death (A.D. 64-66).

We have arrived at this chronological arrangement by the particular study of each letter on its own merits. It remains for us to see whether this grouping is borne out by a review of all the Epistles collectively. Let us first inquire : What is the nature of the subjects treated in each of these groups?

We all know what was the engrossing subject of thought in the primitive Church, what was the object of supreme desire, the source of the liveliest joy, and the most powerful stimulus to Christian faithfulness. It was the promise made by Christ to the Apostles of His glorious return. He had always refused to fix the date of that event; He had said, "Of that day and of that hour knoweth no man; no, not the Son"; but He had charged His followers to live in the attitude of continual expectation. This charge, as it fell from His lips, had a purely moral significance; but, prompted by a very natural impatience, the early Christians took it to mean that the end was at hand, and that the temporal kingdom of Christ would immediately be set up. The Apostles themselves had no exact idea of the interval between the Ascension and the second coming of the Lord, as we gather from Matt. xxiv. and Mark xiii., where the Evangelists closely connect the destruction of Jerusalem, as the first act of judgment, with the return of Christ. The revelation which they had received as to the coming of the Lord related in truth wholly to the fact, not to the date.

Under these circumstances nothing could be more natural than that the principal subject treated in the first group of Pauline letters should have been that of the return of the Lord at the close of the existing economy. Some misconceptions had thus arisen, and the difficulties were referred to the Apostle. He reminded the Thessalonians of the teachings they had forgotten, and added new and valuable suggestions. In the First Epistle, he takes up the bright, glorious aspect of the end of all things—the coming of Christ; in the second, he looks at the dark, terrible side of the same event—the era of Antichrist, which is to precede the full manifestation of the Lord.

But soon this eager expectation of the early Church, while it does not wholly die away, gives place to more urgent questions of a spiritual nature. What are the essentials of Christianity? what is the Gospel as opposed to the existing religions—Judaism and paganism? These are questions which become of vital moment to the Church as it expands and develops. They form therefore the theme of the second group of letters. The great fact of salvation is treated in the Epistles to the Galatians and Romans ; the nature of the Church and the order which ought to prevail in it is the subject of the First Epistle to the Corinthians ; the Christian ministry is the theme of the Second Epistle. These three Epistles—the two to the Corinthians and that to the Romans—form a sort of trilogy, exhibiting in logical sequence the salvation offered by the Gospel, the Church which is entrusted with the Gospel, the ministry which is to build up the Church.

In proportion as the Church appropriates salvation, and seeks to realise it, as the gift of God in Jesus Christ, is it necessarily led to ask, Who is this through whom God has been pleased to accomplish so great a work ? Questions bearing on the personality of Christ naturally arise in the hearts of believers who are saved by Him. This then is the leading subject of the third group. St. Paul abandons himself to a kind of Christian speculation which he calls *wisdom*. If, as he has shown in an earlier group, the gospel is folly in the eyes of those who perish, it is none the less the wisdom of God, the revelation of the Divine plan, in the eyes of those who are saved. In the fact of the redemption wrought by Christ and interpreted by the Divine Spirit, the believer apprehends something of the thought present in the mind of the Creator of the universe, and of the sublime destiny of man. He by whom all things were created is also the Reconciler of all, the One who gathers together all things in Himself, that He may deliver them again to the Father in perfect subjection, so that God may be all in all. Christ then is at once Creator and Redeemer, the Alpha—the originating principle of the universe—and the Omega, its end. These are deep things which, as Chrysostom points out, Paul never preached, but they are unfolded in the third group of epistles.

After having thus explained all that had been revealed to him as to the fact of salvation and the person of Him by whom it was wrought out, the Apostle, seeing that his end was at hand, naturally turned his attention to the future of the Church on earth. He asks how it is to be maintained, as a society, when deprived of those who called it into being and who guided its infant life. The letters of the third and fourth group consist mainly of the answer to this question. Paul lays down as a condition of the continued life and growth of the Church that it should be sustained by the ministry of pastors and deacons. He institutes therefore a primary office for maintaining the preaching of gospel truth, and its application to the needs of individuals ; and a secondary office for attending to temporal necessities either in the Church or in the world. These two ministries thus represent faith and charity, the two essential elements of the life of the Church and the conditions of its influence in the world. The Apostles live on indeed in their writings, but personally they pass away. The prophets have bequeathed their message to the Church, but they too are no more. The simple preaching of the gospel by evangelists or missionaries outside the Church, and by pastors and teachers within it,—this is the ministry that is to be perpetuated till the Lord's return.

If we needed any confirmation of the results at which we have already arrived from a study of the particular Epistles, surely we have it in this perfect harmony between the successive requirements of the apostolic Church in the course of its development, and this series of four groups of epistles which respond so naturally to these needs as they arise.

We shall observe the same natural gradation among these groups, if we study more closely the manner in which particular subjects are treated in them.

Let us look first at the relation of the Church to Judaism.

In the first group, Judaism is entirely outside the Church, and avowedly hostile to it, obstructing, as far as it can, the preaching of the gospel among the Gentiles. In this way it "fills up its sins alway," as the Apostle says (1 Thess. ii. 16), "and brings wrath upon itself to the uttermost."

In the second group, a new phase presents itself. A Jewish faction, which has found its way into the Church, makes a great effort to bring in Mosaism. In the mother Church at Jerusalem there arises a party, which seeks to avail itself of the expansive power of the gospel among the Gentiles, in order to make Judaism also a world-wide religion. Missions among the Gentiles are recognised, but on this condition—that the newly baptized shall be circumcised, and incorporated with Israel by accepting the Jewish law, which would thus become cosmopolitan. Judaism lays down its hostility and becomes Christian, but only on condition that Christianity shall become Jewish. This is the wolf in the sheep's clothing, the Pharisaic principle of justification by works claiming to be the gospel. In the Epistle to the Galatians the conflict is declared. In the First Epistle to the Corinthians it seems that one of the leading Churches founded by Paul is on the verge of apostasy, but in the end it is won back by the Apostle. The Epistle to the Romans is like the song of victory after this sharp contest.

The third group shows us Judaism still seeking to make itself master of the Gospel, but under a new guise. It is no longer the mode of justification which is challenged. The question is no longer asked, faith or works? grace or merit? Judaism presents the Mosaic law to believers as a principle of sanctification and illumination far superior to the methods offered by Paul's Gospel. The ordinances of Moses are a ladder by which the Church can more speedily climb to a height at which the flesh shall be brought unto subjection and the spirit set free. More than this, the believers will thus be brought into direct relation with the heavenly spirits, and will attain through them more excellent revelations than those of the simple Gospel. This manner of looking at the law naturally derogated from the dignity of Christ as the one Mediator between God and the believing soul, and relegated Him to the second rank, below the angels, His creatures. Paul is constrained, especially in the Epistles to the Ephesians and Colossians, to vindicate the supremacy of Christ, and to show that in fellowship with Him was the source of all perfection and spiritual illumination, of all true holiness and wisdom worthy of the name.

The attitude of Judaism in the first group of epistles was, as we have shown, purely Jewish. The form of Judaising heresy which we trace in the second group was Pharisaic in character. In the third group it assumed the form of Essenism. The fourth group brings before us the same errors under a more complicated, subtle, and artificial form. There is a tendency to frivolity, almost to profanity, such as characterises the Judaism of the Kabbala. Judaising heresy sinks into charlatanism. Pretended revelations are given as to the names and genealogy of angels ; absurd ascetic rules are laid down as " counsels of perfection," while daring immorality defaces the actual life. Paul would not condescend to discuss or to refute heresies like these. He simply appeals to the moral sense of the Christians, and charges them to be faithful to it.

Such, in brief review, are the various phases of the relations of Judaism with the Church in the transition time which preceded the fall of Jerusalem. They fully

confirm the view taken by us of the scope and sequence
of the various Epistles. We are led to the same conclusion, if we examine the development of ecclesiastical
functions during the period covered by these thirteen
Epistles.

In the Epistles to the Thessalonians "spiritual gifts"
are first spoken of. See 1 Thess. v. 19, where we read
of manifestations of the Spirit, and specially of prophesyings. Side by side with this, allusion is made
to the existence of certain offices in the Church. In
the same chapter (v. 12) we read of "those who labour
among you, and are over you in the Lord and admonish
you." But such expressions as these show that Church
organisation was still very elementary.

In the Epistles to the Galatians, Corinthians, and
Romans, the offices in the Church seem of quite
secondary importance ; the free gifts, the spontaneous
manifestations of the Spirit, are the prevailing power
in the life of the Church. The expression in Gal. iii. 5
is remarkable. But it is chiefly at Corinth (1 Cor. xii.-
xiv.) that the manifestation of spiritual gifts reaches
its highest development. The words used in Rom.
xii. 3-8 show that in Rome also there was a preponderance of gifts, but in a far less degree than at
Corinth.

In the third group the official functions are clearly
in the ascendant. In Eph. iv. 11, 12, after speaking
of the Apostles, in whom the gift and the office were
united and of the prophets whose gift alone seems

to have been perpetuated, the Apostle only mentions evangelists (missionaries) and pastors, who are both office-bearers in the Church. The title of teachers, however, applied to the pastors, seems to point to the gift of teaching mentioned at Corinth. In the Colossians we find no mention of gifts. Paul only speaks of pastors such as Epaphras and Archippus his successor, and of Nymphas at Laodicea. The Epistle to the Philippians is addressed to the pastors and deacons; there is not the slightest allusion from beginning to end to "spiritual gifts."

Lastly, in the Pastoral Epistles we find mention only of the gift of teaching, which tends more and more to be merged in the office of elder or pastor, as in Eph. iv. 11. It is to the pastoral office thus endowed that Paul entrusts the future of the Church until the day of Christ.

What more simple and rational, if we reflect on it, than this gradual development of Church life, harmonising exactly, as we have seen it does, with the tenor of the thirteen Epistles?

There remains one point more for us to enquire into, How does Paul speak of the coming of Christ?

In the earlier Epistles, whilst disavowing any attempt to fix beforehand the time of that event, he yet expresses himself in such a way as to make us think that he expects to live to witness the second coming. "We that are alive, that are left unto the coming of the Lord." It must be observed, however, that this ex-

pression is not so positive in Greek as the translation
would lead us to suppose. The exact meaning is,
" We the living, *i.e.*, those who are left unto the coming
of the Lord." He does not include all the Christians
then living among those who will remain. How,
indeed, could Paul have supposed that of all the
Christians living at the time when he wrote, not a
single one would die before the second coming ? And
if he could not affirm this of others, neither could he
of himself. It must then be admitted that the clause,
"those who are left," is restrictive of the foregoing
words, "we that are alive," and implies those, at least,
who remain. But in any case, the expression used
implies the possibility that Paul might himself live to
see the event. So also in 1 Cor. xv. 32. "The dead
shall be raised, and we shall be changed." Yet in
the same Epistle, ch. vi. 14, Paul speaks of himself
not among the living who shall be "changed," but
among the dead who shall be raised. "God both raised
the Lord and will raise up us through His power
($\dot{\eta}\mu\hat{a}\varsigma$ $\dot{\epsilon}\xi\epsilon\gamma\epsilon\rho\hat{\epsilon}\hat{\imath}$). In Philippians Paul seems divided
between the expectation of martyrdom and that of
a speedy deliverance ; and he asks the Philippians to
rejoice if he is permitted to sprinkle with his blood
the sacrifice and service of their faith. Lastly, in the
Pastoral Epistles, he anticipates a long continuance of
the Church upon earth after the death of the Apostles.
For this reason he urges the settlement of pastors
over the Churches generally, and of himself he says,

"The Lord will save me unto His heavenly kingdom"
(2 Tim. iv. 18); which shows that he no longer
expected to live to see the second coming. In this
respect also, therefore, we see a marked gradation
confirming the chronological order of the four groups
of epistles.

We shall not attempt to go into any detailed criticism
of St. Paul's style of writing. This would involve
an analysis of Paul's own character, for no man ever
threw himself so completely into his writings as this
Apostle. I shall only allude here to two points : the
deep unity underlying the whole of this correspondence,
and at the same time the contrasts which abound
in it.

The one theme of all the Epistles is that which Paul
calls *my gospel*. It is the setting forth of the salvation
wrought by Christ, with its two distinctive characters
—freeness and universality, and its three essential
elements—justification, sanctification, and glory. Every
word Paul has written tends to commend this perfect
salvation, the gift of grace without human merit,
offered, therefore, to all alike, without regard to their
antecedents. Paul, the former persecutor of the
Church, felt truly that he was the normal example of
this free salvation ; and his life and his letters were
alike consecrated to its defence and proclamation.
However much the style of Paul may vary in other
respects, it has one uniform characteristic—that it

is always and everywhere the exact expression and
fitting garb of his thought. If the style is laboured,
it is only through the desire to faithfully convey the
thought of the writer to the readers. There is never
any self-seeking or any attempt at self-glorification in
the writings of Paul. " The love of Christ constraineth
me," describes the inspiration of his letters no less
than of his life.

May I say a word in passing on the influence of
Rabbinism which has often been supposed to be traceable in the writings of Paul? As to the form of his
argument, I do not pretend to deny the influence of the
teaching under which he had been brought up. The
questions, abruptly addressed to the reader, recall the
form of teaching in use between Rabbis and their
disciples. The short series of sentences logically
following one another, like the terms of a syllogism,
remind one of those short explanations called by the
Jews *Midrasch*, which give in a few words the epitome
of a subject, as in 1 Cor. xv. 56, Rom. x. 14, 15.
The quotations of Scripture, which bring the very
marrow of the text to bear upon the matter in hand,
are unquestionably after the Rabbinical method. But
St. Paul does not allow himself to be so carried away
by his argument as to put into the words that which
they do not really contain. This charge has been
brought against Gal. iii. 16; iv. 24, *et seq*. I have
already endeavoured to show that a careful exegesis
vindicates Paul from this accusation brought against

him by those who only study his writings literally and
superficially. The disciple of Gamaliel had undergone
too radical a change to retain more of the teaching
of his old master than certain modes of thought and
expression. I may add that such passages as Gal. iii.
17, 2 Tim. iii. 8, which are simply borrowed from
Jewish tradition, cannot be regarded as really characteristic of Paul's own style.

On the other hand, while we trace this unity of
subject, form, and intention, what a variety do we find
in the products of the Apostle's literary labours! If
it is true that a man is great in proportion to the
multiplicity and diversity of his gifts, it must be difficult,
even from a purely human standpoint, to find in history
a writer superior or even equal to St. Paul. With
what depth of view and breadth of feeling, with what
aptness, fulness and variety of application, does he
treat the one great theme! It is difficult to conceive
how there could be united in one person so much
intellectual vigour and penetration, with such warmth
of feeling, power of imagination, quickness of intuition,
and sound practical judgment. By these manifold
endowments Paul is fitted to be all things to all men,
and to exercise a many-sided apostleship. He appears
as a prophet in the Epistles to the Thessalonians, to
whom he unveils the final issues of the present economy.
In his Epistle to the Galatians he is the skilful dialec-
tician, disentangling the webs of error in which they had
been craftily caught. To the Corinthians he writes in

his First Epistle as a pastor, resolving with admirable wisdom the practical problems which arose out of the first impact of Christianity with paganism. In the Second Epistle to the same Church he vindicates the authority of his ministry as an Apostle of Christ. In the Epistles to the Romans, Ephesians, and Colossians, he is the consummate teacher setting forth his Gospel to the Churches in which he had not been able to preach himself. In the Pastoral Epistles he appears as the far-seeing organiser of the Church of the future. To the Philippians he writes, as a tender father to dear children, words of exhortation and loving gratitude. To Philemon he writes as to a brother from whom he has a brotherly service to ask.

It would be hard to say whether the Paul, whom we learn to know from these thirteen letters, is more remarkable for the unity or the variety of his life-work. In him we see brought out, in full relief, all the perfections latent in Him who was Paul's model, or more truly his very life, and of whom he said to his disciples, " Be ye imitators of me, even as I am of Christ."

BIBLE STUDY AIDS by Frederic L. Godet

The works of Frederic L. Godet (1812-1900) are classics in the field of Old and New Testament studies. With the blend of the scholar's mind, the pastor's heart and the reformer's courage, this author refutes the stance of rational and mythical interpreters to staunchly defend the historic Christian faith, using principles as valid today as when they were first recorded. Scholarship, thoroughness and reverence characterize Godet's writings.

STUDIES IN THE OLD TESTAMENT. In this in-depth study of the Old Testament, the author masterfully handles the higher-critic's objections and arguments while discussing in a scholarly manner these subjects: Angels, God's Plan to Develop Life on Earth, The Six Days of Creation, The Four Greater Prophets, The Book of Job, and Song of Songs. 350 pp.

STUDIES IN THE NEW TESTAMENT. In a most interesting and instructive manner, this work covers the key elements of the entire New Testament. Godet's insight is profound and his teaching is weighty and suggestive as he deals with: The Origin of the Four Gospels, The Person and Work of Jesus Christ, The Four Principal Apostles and The Book of Revelation. 408 pp.

STUDIES IN PAUL'S EPISTLES. The author maintains a level of careful scholarship, critical sagacity and practical piety. Godet ably discusses these themes: The Excitement of Christians of Thessalonica, The Lord's Second Coming, The Conflict Between the Law and the Gospel in Galatia, The First Indication of Gnosticism in Asia Minor, The First Anti-Slavery Petition and The Message to the Gentile Church. 352 pp.

COMMENTARY ON LUKE. In this exhaustive commentary, the author defends the cardinal doctrines of the Christian faith while expounding the text from the original language. Godet uniquely gives a critical analysis and a spiritual application of the text. 584 pp.

COMMENTARY ON JOHN'S GOSPEL. Of this monumental, scholarly and exegetical commentary, Wilbur M. Smith said, "From a theological standpoint and for going to the uttermost depths of the profound teachings of the fourth Gospel, Godet is *THE supreme* work, containing some of the finest pages of christology to be found anywhere." 1130 pp.

COMMENTARY ON ROMANS. This verse-by-verse critical commentary on the Greek text brings a clarity of doctrinal instruction to the student of God's Word, even the beginning Bible scholar will see Scriptural concepts made practical by looking into Godet's clear stream of explanation and exegesis. 544 pp.

COMMENTARY ON FIRST CORINTHIANS. In this commentary of enduring quality, Godet presents a veritable garden of beautiful truth. In addition to the seed thoughts concisely given to inspire further study, the reader reaps a harvest of nourishing spiritual food, for Christian maturity from the Greek roots of the text. 928 pp.